# 52 WEEKEND MAKEOVERS

# 52 WEEKEND MAKEOVERS

The Taunton Press

**The Taunton Press**
Inspiration for hands-on living®

The Taunton Press, Inc., 63 South Main Street, PO Box 5506, Newtown, CT 06470-5506

e-mail: tp@taunton.com


JACKET/COVER DESIGN: Howard Grossman

COVER PHOTOGRAPHERS: (front cover, clockwise from top left) Carl Weese, ©The Taunton Press, Inc.; ©Belgard/APG Oldcastle; ©Randy O'Rourke; ©Randy O'Rourke; The Container Store; ©Randy O'Rourke; (back cover, top left) Carl Weese, ©The Taunton Press, Inc.; (middle, left to right) ©Belgard/APG Oldcastle; ©Randy O'Rourke; Schulte Graphics Library; (bottom) John Rickard, ©The Taunton Press.


LIBRARY OF CONGRESS CATALOGING-IN-PUBLICATION DATA
52 weekend makeovers : easy projects to transform your home inside and out.
      p. cm.
  Includes bibliographical references and index.
  ISBN-13: 978-1-56158-863-3 (alk. paper)
  ISBN-10: 1-56158-863-6 (alk. paper)
 1. Dwellings--Remodeling--Amateurs' manuals. 2. Dwellings--Maintenance and repair--Amateurs' manuals. 3. Interior decoration--Amateurs' manuals. 4. Garden construction--Amateurs' manuals. I. Title: Fifty two weekend makeovers.

TH4817.A155 2007
643'.7--dc22

                                    2006021544


Printed in China
10 9 8 7 6 5 4 3 2 1


The following manufacturers/names appearing in *52 Weekend Makeovers* are trademarks:
Alligator®; Dewey®; Hardibacker®; Kevlar®; Romex®; Phillips®; Tapcon®; Teflon®;
Toggler® Snaptoggle®; Wagner®.

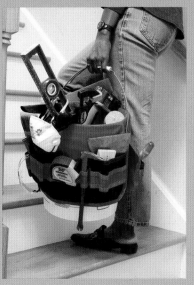

# Contents

## PROJECTS

### Painting a Room  44

A fresh **COAT OF COLOR** gives any room a new personality

### Strie & Chambray  56

Dragging a glaze using **DRY BRUSH TECHNIQUES** opens a world of painting possibilities

### Painting Trim  64

To make a good room look great, transform **MOLDINGS, WINDOWS & DOORS** with fresh coats of paint

### Colonial Casing  76

Passageways are important! Use some **CLASSIC CASING** to dress up the transition between rooms

### Wainscot  86

Thin **TONGUE-AND-GROOVE BOARDS** make a durable, great-looking wall that's easy to install

18

86

106

126

138

150

162

# Get Set

**With the right TOOLS, GEAR & MATERIALS,** you can tackle any home improvement project with confidence and ease

**E**MBARKING on a home improvement project is an exciting adventure that will yield dramatic results and useful solutions. With the right supplies, a few tools, and a little know-how, you can add character and detail to any

room of your house, as well as outdoor living areas. You'll find that the tools needed for these projects are all available at your local home center, and the step-by-step instructions will help make your project a success.

◑ NEED A HAND?

**Save your back** by following proper lifting techniques: face the object squarely, center your shoulders over it, crouch down until you can grasp it as you keep your back straight, and lift with your legs, not with your arms or back. If the load is too heavy for you to lift alone—more than about 40 lbs.— get help.

### PROPER LIFTING

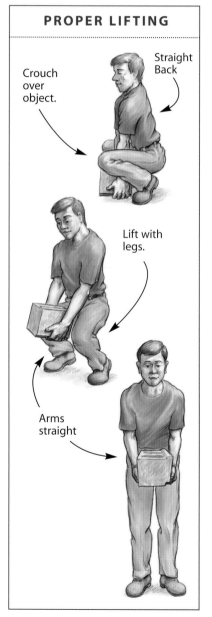

Crouch over object.

Straight Back

Lift with legs.

Arms straight

# Safety First

A key measure of success for any project is walking away unscathed from a variety of hazards. Gear up for safety with the following items:

**EYE PROTECTION.** Get a good pair of ventilated wrap-around safety goggles that fit snugly and comfortably while providing clear view. Keep them free of dust, smudges, and scratches. If you wear eyeglasses, choose a pair of goggles that fits over your prescription lenses.

**EARPLUGS OR PROTECTORS.** Keep these handy to protect your hearing if you rent any mechanical or gas-powered tools. Disposable foam earplugs are one option; headphones with muffling insulation are another.

**DUST MASK OR RESPIRATOR.** Disposable dust masks keep your mouth and nose clear of fine dust and debris; buy them by the box. For heavy dust conditions and when working with powdered cement containing silica, rent a respirator and change or clean its filters frequently.

**KNEE PADS.** Protect your knees without hindering circulation with a pair of cushioned knee pads.

**WORK GLOVES.** Tough leather or Kevlar® gloves protect your hands and fingers from blisters and cuts as you work. In fact, you should never take them off until the job's finished.

**WORK BOOTS.** Steel-toed work boots are ideal, but the overall goal is to avoid open-toed shoes or sandals when working around heavy objects such as paving stones.

**FIRST-AID KIT.** Every house and every garage should have its own kit, complete with compression and adhesive bandages, gauze, antiseptic wipes, small tubes of antibacterial and burn creams, small but sharp scissors, waterproof tape, and tweezers. A book of matches or a disposable lighter also comes in handy for sterilizing tools. Use hydrogen peroxide, applied with a cotton swab, to clean small wounds before you bandage them.

# Know the Codes

Although plumbing and electrical codes may seem to be a nuisance, they're written and enforced to protect you. It's important that you make sure your project adheres to the local codes, so check them before you start. The codes are often available for free or for a small fee from the local building department.

*Examples of a fixture shutoff (above) and a main shutoff (below).*

## KNOW THE PLUMBING SYSTEM

**WATER LINES.** Hot and cold water lines need to be shut off before removing or replacing a fixture. Sinks and toilets usually have valves under or next to them for easy shut off. When working on the tub or shower, you may have to find a valve (behind an access panel or in the basement) that shuts off water to the whole bathroom. If you can't shut off water at the valve, shut off all water to the house at the main valve where the water line comes in from the street or well. Remember, there will still be water in the lines that will drain when a connection is opened, so have a bucket or towel handy.

**DRAIN LINES.** Drain lines carry wastewater from a fixture to a sewer or septic system. To prevent sewer gasses from entering the house, each fixture drain has a U-shaped bend in the pipe called a trap. As long as the trap is filled with water, gasses cannot enter the home. If you must remove a trap, tightly stuff the opening with a rag.

**TRAP REPLACEMENT.** There are two main types of sink traps: P-traps and S-traps. A P-trap is designed for drain lines coming out of a wall. S-traps are common when drain lines come up through the floor. S-traps are prone to self-siphoning, which can cause the seal to fail and allow sewer gas into the home. They are prohibited by most codes in new construction. If you have an S-trap and install a new sink, you'll likely need to replace it with a P-trap.

# The Right Tools for the Job

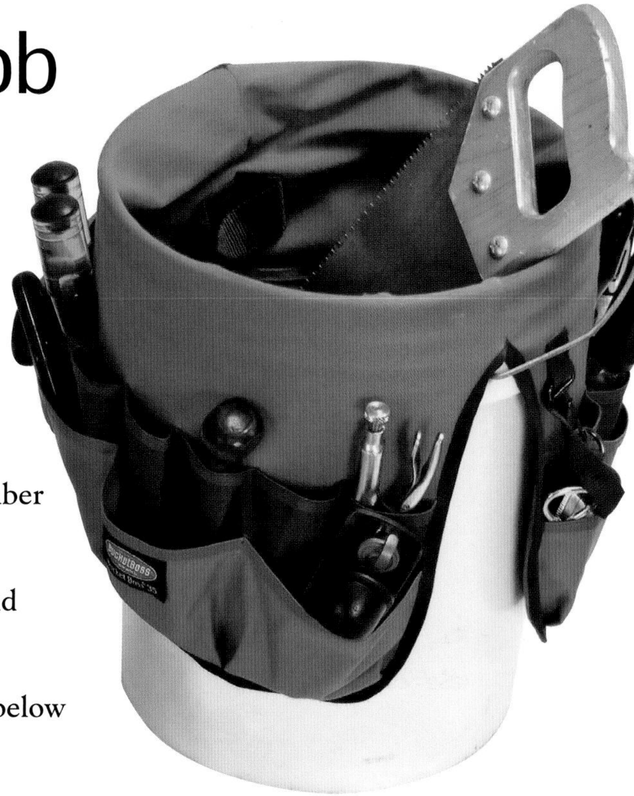

OK, so you've decided on a project and you've obtained a permit, if needed. You're ready to go, right? Not quite. Before you get started it's a good idea to look over the project, make a list of the tools you own, and determine what you'll need. Creating tool "kits" is a helpful way to get organized.

The kit that you'll reach for most often consists of tools commonly used for general carpentry. The bucket organizer shown here slips into an ordinary 5-gallon bucket and holds a surprisingly large number of tools.

**CLAW HAMMER.** This old standby is needed for general assembly and demolition.

**NAIL SETS.** You'll need these in a variety of sizes to sink nailheads below the worksurface.

**COPING SAW.** This saw is used for cutting curved parts, and it's also the tool of choice for making a coped cut for trim.

**TAPE MEASURE.** Most homeowners find it useful to have both a 12-ft. and a 25-ft. tape on hand.

**CORDLESS DRILL/DRIVER.** This portable power tool makes drilling holes and driving screws a snap.

**LEVELS.** A 4-ft. bubble level is best used on large surfaces—the smaller torpedo level works nicely in confined spaces.

**COMBINATION SQUARE.** This square is used to position parts such as hinges on doors and to check 90-degree and 45-degree angles.

**CARPENTER'S PENCIL.** There's still nothing better for marking and laying out parts. The pencil's flat design keeps it from rolling off a worksurface.

**UTILITY KNIFE & PUTTY KNIFE.** A utility knife will handle most cutting and trimming jobs. You'll need a putty knife for filling holes and general patching.

**MITER BOX.** Use this with a handsaw to cut accurate 45-degree and 90-degree angles. The miter box is most often used for cutting trim and molding to length.

**SCREWDRIVERS.** Make sure you have a couple of different sizes in both Phillips and flathead. Better yet, consider the newer 4-in-1 screwdriver that holds four bits—two standard and two Phillips—to handle most jobs.

**SAFETY GEAR.** See p. 6 for a list of everything you'll need.

# SCREWS

Screws have loads more holding power than nails, and they're easier than ever to use, thanks to all of the quick-change "drill-and-drive" accessories available.

**THREADS & HEADS.** It's smart to have a selection of "drywall" screws in lengths ranging from ¾ in. to 3 in. This type of screw has a "bugle" head, with a cross-shaped Phillips recess. "Coarse-thread" screws are usually better than "fine-thread" versions when you're joining wood parts together. Black-colored drywall screws are what to use for interior projects.

**PILOT HOLES.** In most cases, you'll need to drill a pilot hole before driving a screw. The hole should be about the same diameter as the diameter of the screw, excluding its threads. The best way to drill pilot holes for screws is with a combination countersink/counterbore bit (see photo at right).

# MEASURING & LAYOUT TOOLS

In carpentry language, "layout" can be used as a noun or as a verb. Either way, it refers to the precise work of marking where wood needs to be cut, where fasteners need to be driven, and how parts need to fit.

**TAPES, LEVELS, SQUARES & LINES.** The most versatile tape to have is a 25-ft. model. A level does more than its name suggests. It also helps you test for vertical or plumb. It's good to have a 2-ft. or 4-ft. level as well as a smaller "torpedo" level. Squares are also important layout tools, and it's good to have three of these: a framing square, a triangle-shaped rafter or speed square, and a combination square.

When you need to mark a long, straight line between two points, a chalkline (aka chalkbox) will get the job done quickly. There's a spool of string and a supply of powdered chalk inside the chalkbox. Stretching the line tight and then "snapping" the string leaves a colored layout line.

The only electronic tool in your layout kit is a stud finder. When you move this device along the wall surface, it lights up or beeps when a stud is detected.

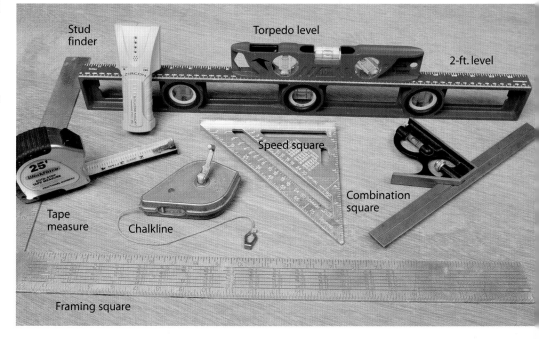

Stud finder

Torpedo level

2-ft. level

Speed square

Combination square

Tape measure

Chalkline

Framing square

*⚙* **WHAT'S DIFFERENT?**

**Both plumber's putty** and Teflon® tape create a seal. But putty works best under sink lips, faucets, and strainers. Teflon tape works best for sealing threaded parts, such as connections between shut-off valves and flexible supply lines.

**◑ NEED A HAND?**

**Quick-action-style clamps** allow you to position the clamp and close the jaws with one hand—any other style clamp requires both hands.

**∷ LINGO**

In level language the terms carpenter's, torpedo, and bubble all generally refer to the same type of tool—one that uses a straight-edge and series of bubbles in water-filled glass tubes to determine the relative level or slope of a given surface, such as a path or patio.

# Basic Plumbing Kit

It's always good to have a basic plumbing kit on hand for a project, but it really shines in an emergency. When water starts leaking out of a cabinet, the last thing you want to do is search through a toolbox for an adjustable wrench. The following tools will make a good start for a plumbing kit.

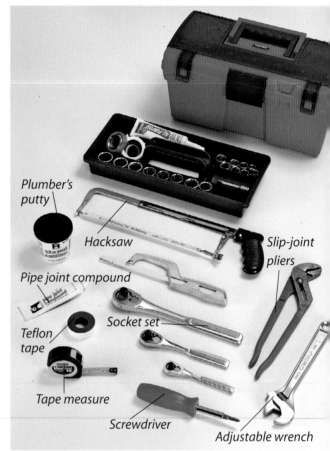

Plumber's putty

Hacksaw

Slip-joint pliers

Pipe joint compound

Teflon tape

Socket set

Tape measure

Screwdriver

Adjustable wrench

**ADJUSTABLE WRENCH.** The 4-in. and 8-in. sizes can handle nuts and bolts of nearly any size.

**SCREWDRIVERS.** A Phillips and flathead or a 4-in-1 screwdriver will handle general assembly/disassembly.

**SLIP-JOINT PLIERS.** These pliers ratchet open to loosen or tighten larger nuts and slip-joint fittings.

**SOCKET SET.** The standard set with various-size ratchets can handle many assembly/disassembly jobs.

**PLUMBER'S PUTTY.** You'll need putty for sealing fixtures such as sinks and faucets.

**HACKSAW.** You'll need a hacksaw to cut metal and plastic pipe to length.

**PIPE JOINT COMPOUND.** This seals threaded parts and compression fittings. It's useful for tight spaces where using Teflon tape isn't possible.

**TEFLON TAPE.** Use Teflon tape for sealing threaded parts without the mess of pipe joint compound.

**TAPE MEASURE.** Use this for measuring when cutting pipe to length and for identifying part sizes for replacement.

# Outdoor Projects Tool Kit

Every home should have a basic set of tools that serves a variety of needs, from day-to-day maintenance to one-time projects. In a few instances, you'll want to rent rather than buy a particular tool for a specific task. Consider the following tools and equipment to help make your patio and path dreams a reality:

**SHOVELS.** One flat-edged and one pointed-edged (or spade) shovel address almost any light digging needs and help transfer loose materials from cart to site.

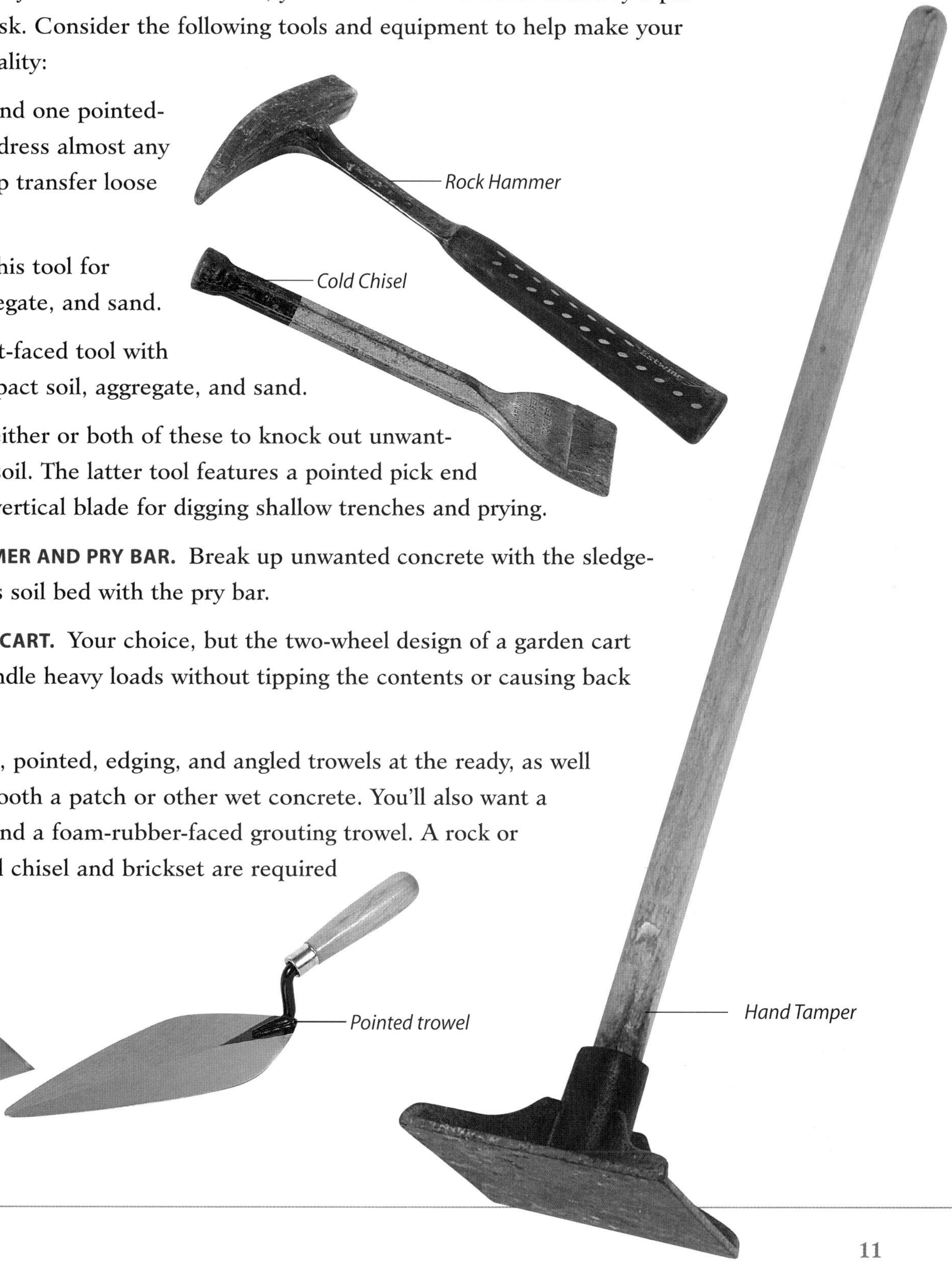

**STEEL GARDEN RAKE.** Use this tool for spreading soil, gravel, aggregate, and sand.

**HAND TAMPER.** Use this flat-faced tool with or without padding to compact soil, aggregate, and sand.

**PICKAX OR MATTOCK.** Get either or both of these to knock out unwanted concrete and to trench soil. The latter tool features a pointed pick end for penetrating and a flat, vertical blade for digging shallow trenches and prying.

**8-LB. TO 12-LB. SLEDGEHAMMER AND PRY BAR.** Break up unwanted concrete with the sledgehammer and pull it from its soil bed with the pry bar.

**WHEELBARROW OR GARDEN CART.** Your choice, but the two-wheel design of a garden cart often makes it easier to handle heavy loads without tipping the contents or causing back strain.

**MASONRY TOOLS.** Have flat, pointed, edging, and angled trowels at the ready, as well as a float to spread and smooth a patch or other wet concrete. You'll also want a notched mortaring trowel and a foam-rubber-faced grouting trowel. A rock or mason's hammer and a cold chisel and brickset are required for manual paver cuts.

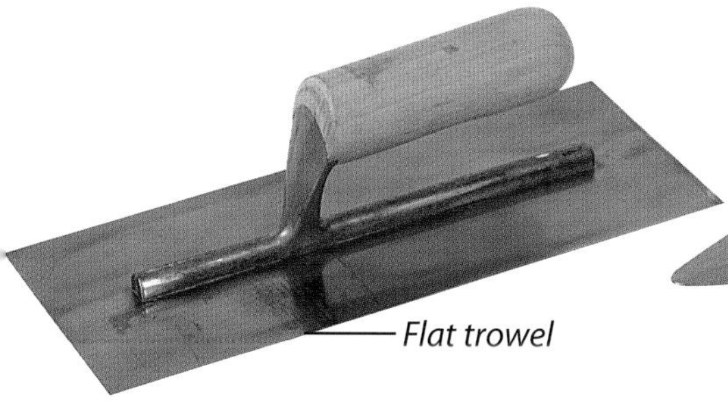

Rock Hammer

Cold Chisel

Hand Tamper

Pointed trowel

Flat trowel

**Getting set to paint** usually involves more than basic gear like brushes, rollers, and drop cloths. With a few extra items, you'll have what it takes to complete common repairs and prep projects. Consider adding these tools and materials to your toolbox:

### TOOLS
- Multitip screwdriver
- Caulking gun
- Putty knife
- 5-in-1 tool
- Utility knife

### MATERIALS
- Disposable gloves
- Joint tape (paper & fiberglass mesh)
- Joint compound
- Sandpaper (120 grit)
- White acrylic caulk

**Stepladders are essential** for many painting projects, but you may be tempted to buy more ladder than you need. If your house has standard 8-ft. ceilings, a small stepladder will usually give you the elevation you need, and it's much easier to move around and store than larger models.

# Ready, Set, Paint!

**PAINTING IS EASIER** and more fun when you've got a place to keep your gear. Try setting up a work area along a garage, basement, or utility room wall. Paint cans, roller trays, drop cloths, and other large items can fit on a countertop or on some wide shelves. Brushes, rollers, putty knives, and other tools are all hang-up items. Attach some wood strips or pegboard to the wall and buy a supply of hooks, hangers, and long finish nails so you can keep these tools in order.

## 10 TIPS FOR CONTROLLING THE MESS

**1 | MASK WITH PAINTER'S TAPE.** This tape comes in different widths and different levels of tack, or stickiness. Have a good selection of tape on hand, and use it to mask areas adjacent to those that will be painted. Painter's tape can also cover electrical switches and outlets.

**2 | PROTECT FLOORS WITH CANVAS DROP CLOTHS.** Canvas is best on the floor because (unlike plastic) it absorbs paint drips so they don't get transferred to your shoes. Protect carpet with a double layer of canvas.

**3 | MOVE WHAT YOU CAN, COVER WHAT YOU CAN'T.** Remove everything you can from the room. As for the big stuff that needs to stay, move it to the center of the room and cover it with painter's plastic—thin, inexpensive sheeting that comes on a roll. You can also use painter's plastic to cover chandeliers and other fixtures.

**4 | DRESS FOR A MESS.** Old clothes that fit comfortably are best. You'll also want to wear a painter's hat (ask for one where you buy your paint)

and protective eyewear when painting overhead.

**5 | ISOLATE THE ROOM.** Control traffic into and out of the room where you're painting. Only one doorway or opening needs to be used.

**6 | USE A BOX FAN TO EXHAUST SANDING DUST AND PAINT FUMES.** If you have to sand trim or wallboard surfaces, use a box fan to blow dust-laden air outdoors (see the drawing below). By increasing air circulation, a fan also helps to get paint fumes out of the house.

**7 | USE PLASTIC PAINT BUCKETS.** When brushing, don't apply paint straight from the paint can, especially if the can is full. Instead, pour a manageable amount of paint into a plastic paint bucket. These inexpensive containers are easier to handle and very easy to clean and reuse.

**8 | AVOID OVERLOADING.** Trying to carry too much paint on your roller or brush can lead to dripping disasters. Get a feel for how much finish you can get on your roller or brush without causing big drips or roller spray and stick with this amount.

**9 | KEEP A RAG IN YOUR BACK POCKET.** It's important to wipe up spills right away.

**10 | HAVE A CLEANUP PLAN.** Before you begin to paint, clear the sink of dirty dishes and know where your rags and paper towels are. Set up a paint work station to keep your supplies and gear organized. Finally, always leave enough time for cleaning brushes and your work area.

*Mix and pour paints in an out-of-the-way area where accidents don't become disasters.*

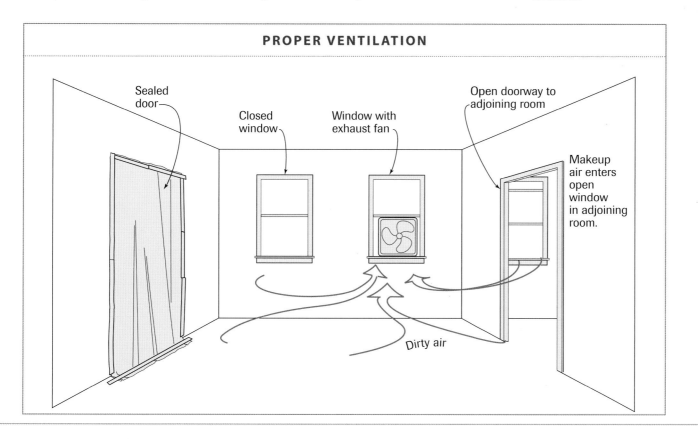

**PROPER VENTILATION**

Sealed door

Open doorway to adjoining room

Closed window

Window with exhaust fan

Makeup air enters open window in adjoining room.

Dirty air

▶ DO IT RIGHT

**It's a good idea** to buy your molding at least two days in advance and store it in the room you will be working in. Unwrap your molding if it comes wrapped in plastic. This will give the material a chance to acclimate to the room's normal temperature and humidity. Don't store trim by leaning it against the wall. Instead, stack your pieces flat on the floor.

# Molding 101

**WHAT SHOULD MY MOLDING BE MADE OF?** Once upon a time, there was really only one answer to that question—solid wood—but today there are many more choices.

**SOLID WOOD.** Pine is the most common softwood used to make solid-wood molding. It's normally painted but can also be stained or varnished. The same goes for poplar, a common hardwood used to make molding. Oak molding, also common, typically is stained and varnished or just varnished.

**FINGER-JOINTED WOOD.** Less expensive than solid-wood molding, finger-jointed versions look just as good when they're painted, and this type of wood trim is more resistant to warping and twisting than solid wood.

**FIBERBOARD.** Medium-density fiberboard (MDF) is made from wood fiber. MDF is used to make a limited selection of molding profiles. It costs less than solid wood and looks great when painted. Because MDF is denser than wood, you'll want to predrill nail holes to prevent the material from puckering up around the nail.

**FOAM.** It may seem strange, but urethane foam is a great material for making moldings. It's lighter than wood and just as easy to cut. It won't warp, bow, or split. And it can be manufactured in a wide variety of sizes and shapes, including some of the most detailed profiles you'll find.

## JOINERY DETAILS

**BUTT JOINTS** are the simplest. The joining parts butt together, so it just takes a couple of square cuts to make a butt joint.

**MITER JOINTS** are used to join picture frames together and to run trim around an outside corner.

**COPE JOINTS** are tricky to cut, but fortunately they're only required where trim has to extend around inside corners. In a cope joint, the first piece simply butts into the corner. Then the second piece is cut (coped) to follow the profile of the installed piece.

**SCARF JOINTS** are used where identical molding pieces have to join each other in a straight run. You create the overlapping scarf joint by making complementary angle cuts in joining pieces.

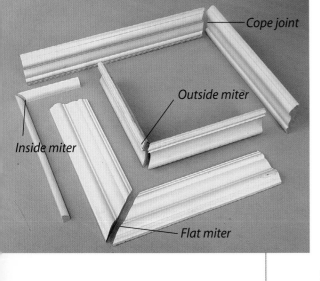

Cope joint

Outside miter

Inside miter

Flat miter

# Trim Terminology

Knowing what to look for makes all the difference when you arrive at the molding section of your local lumberyard or home center. Don't spend too much time worrying about the difference between trim and molding. These terms have been used interchangeably for years. What's more important is to decide what type of molding you need for your project, what profile looks best, and what material you want your trim to be made of. Molding and trim pieces are named based on how and where they will be installed. A 1x6 board, for example, can become a door jamb or a baseboard. The drawing below illustrates the lingo you should familiarize yourself with.

## TRIM LINGO

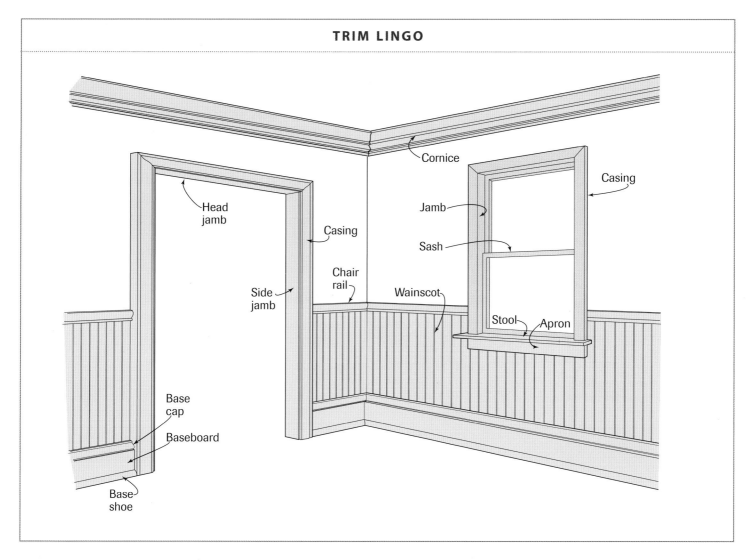

**A straightedge** is a handy tool for many projects. When tiling, lay it across the top and against the edges of set tiles to see if they are flat and in line. Make adjustments before moving on to the next section.

**Virtually any project you take on** will require a worksurface. To make a simple workstation, use a pair of sawhorses to form a foundation and lay a ¾-in.-thick piece of plywood on top. A 2-ft. by 4-ft. piece works well for most jobs. For a larger surface, consider using a hollow-core door. Secure the top to the sawhorses with clamps.

# Tiling Basics

## THE RIGHT START

A tile floor requires a solid foundation that consists of sturdy wood framing (joists), and subflooring and underlayment with a combined thickness of 1 in. To silence squeaks, drive 2-in. coarse-threaded screws through the underlayment and into

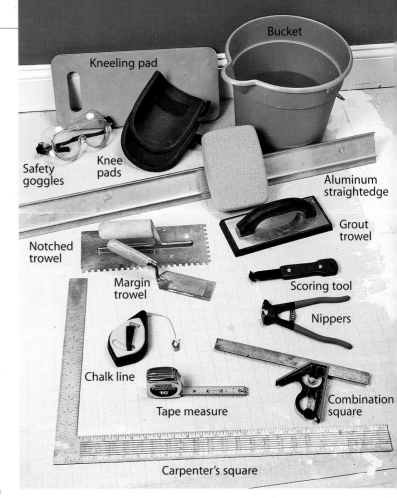

the joists. An optimal tile floor system includes a sandwich of backer board, "thin-set" adhesive (to bond the backer board to the floor and the tile to the backer board), tiles, grout to fill the joints, and sealer.

## BUYING AND MIXING ADHESIVE

The most common and recommended adhesive used on tile floors is a cement-like material called thin-set. Buy one with powdered acrylic additive incorporated into the mix to make mixing foolproof. Determine the approximate quantity needed for the area to be covered and fill a bucket with about three-quarters of the water specified. Then add the powder and mix. Add additional water until the mix is just stiff enough to hold a peak. Then allow the mix to rest (called slake) for about 10 minutes and mix again. If more water is required, add it and let it rest again before mixing and using it. Follow the same procedure when mixing grout.

# TILER'S TOOL KIT

Preparing for and installing tile requires a few specialized tools.

**BACKERBOARD BASICS.** To "cut" backerboard, you'll need a carbide scoring tool. Score the surface of the backerboard and then break it along the scored line. A drill/driver, corded or cordless, is ideal for securing backerboard to the subfloor with screws. Or simply use a hammer to drive in galvanized roofing nails.

**MIXING AND SPREADING.** The best tool for mixing small quantities of adhesive is a margin trowel. If you own a heavy-duty drill, buy a mixing paddle for faster and better results with large batches. You'll need a notched trowel to evenly spread adhesive. Use the straight edge of a notched trowel to spread adhesive over a 3-ft.- or 4-ft.-square area. Then use the notched edge, held at a 45-degree angle, to comb the adhesive and to ensure an even distribution.

**TILE CUTTING.** Two tools will handle your tile-cutting chores. Use a rented tile saw for making straight cuts. Use tile nippers to nibble away bits of tile at a time to make curved cuts.

**GROUTING TOOLS.** Work grout into the joints with a grout trowel (also called a rubber float), working back and forth diagonally. Then strike off the excess with the trowel held nearly perpendicular to the surface. Use a grout sponge to clean the grout off the surface before it dries.

Bucket

Sealer

Sponge

Grout mix

Grout trowel

# Prep Projects

You'll **WORK FASTER AND BETTER** if you **PREPARE THE JOB SITE** before tackling a project.

THE AMOUNT OF PREP WORK that you need to do depends on what projects you're tackling. Preparation is the key to the success of any job, so be sure you have all tools and materials handy and have allocated the time to get the job done. And don't forget to call in help when you need it, either from a friend if you simply need an extra hand or a pro if you need more experience than you have. The information on the following pages will help you complete every project right the first time.

**REMOVE WALLPAPER**    **INSULATE**    **ADD AN OUTLET**    **LAY A BASE**

### ▸ LINGO

A hawk is a flat piece of metal or wood with a handle on the underside. It's used to hold a working supply of joint compound. You can also use a commercially available mud pan or bread pan.

### ● WHAT'S DIFFERENT?

**Aside from its lighter weight**, lightweight joint compound has the advantage that it dries much faster than standard compound. On the downside, the finished product is not as hard, making it somewhat more vulnerable to damage.

# Patch Holes

**1** **PREPARE TO PATCH.** Use a utility knife to cut a patch piece of drywall. Score along the cut line, then fold and cut all the way through from the opposite side. Hold the patch over the damaged wall area and trace its perimeter. Cut along your marks using a drywall saw.

**2** **INSTALL THE PATCH.** Cut two pieces of scrap lumber, such as plywood or a strip of wood, so they are at least 6 in. longer than the opening height. Attach these pieces with two 1¼-in. drywall screws at each end. Then secure the drywall to the nailers with screws at each corner.

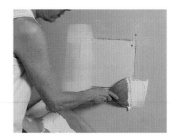

**3** **TAPE & MUD.** Apply self-adhering, fiberglass-mesh joint tape over the joints, smoothing it with a taping knife. Working from a supply of joint compound on a hawk (shown) or in a bread pan, use a taping knife to apply the "mud" and then smooth the compound over the tape. Scrape the compound off the knife on the edge of the hawk (or pan) after each smoothing pass. Allow the compound to dry completely between coats (it turns bright white).

**4** **APPLY TWO ADDITIONAL COATS OF COMPOUND.** Extend each application past the previous coat. If available, use a wider knife for the third coat. Although sanding is typically done only after the final coat, sand the second coat lightly if it dries rough or uneven. If you do sand, brush off the dust before applying the next coat.

**5** **SAND & PRIME.** Use a rubber sanding block and 120-grit sandpaper to smooth the repair. Sand until you can no longer see or feel any ridges at the outer edges, but avoid sanding into the paper facing, as it will become fuzzy. If necessary apply another very thin coat to fill pinholes, scratches, or fuzz. Vacuum off the dust and apply your primer.

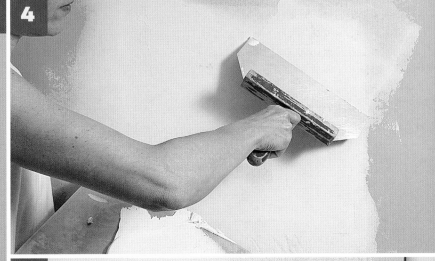

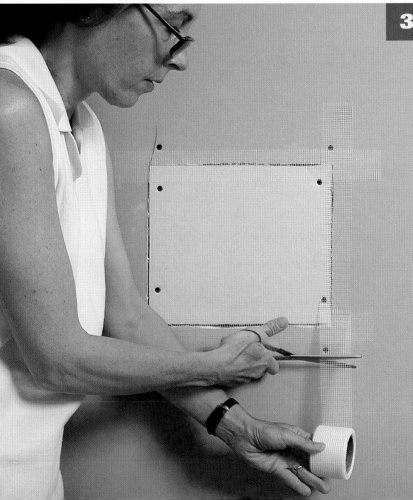

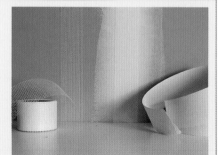

# Fix Nail Pops & Loose Corner Beads

**1** **SECURE DRYWALL AT THE NAIL POP.** Use two 1⅝-in. drywall screws. Press firmly to hold the drywall tight as you drive the screws until the heads are just below the surface but not through the paper facing. Then hammer the popped fastener below the surface. Cut away any damaged or delaminated paper facing and apply three coats of compound.

**2** **SECURE LOOSE CORNER BEAD.** Drive one or more screws, making sure each screw head is just below the surface. (Tip: To make sure it's below the surface, draw a taping knife across the surface—you should not hear a metallic "click" as the blade passes over the screw.) Cut away any loose material, apply joint tape, and finish as described below.

# Repair Cracks

**1** **FILL FINE CRACKS.** Apply painter's caulk with a caulking gun, then smooth the caulk with a wet finger. Repair larger cracks (such as those over doorways) with tape and drywall compound.

**2** **TAPE LARGER CRACKS.** Scrape the crack with a 5-in-1 tool or screwdriver to make sure nothing sticks up above the surface and that there are no loose fragments. Apply a bedding coat of fast-drying lightweight compound and press on a piece of paper joint tape. (If you use fiberglass-mesh tape, smooth it in place over the crack before applying any compound.) Apply second and third coats as necessary.

# Remove Wallpaper

**1** **PEEL OFF THE DECORATIVE LAYER.** Get under the top corner with a taping or putty knife and peel it off across the top. Then roll the paper onto a dowel or cardboard tube and roll the tube down the wall. For vinyl-coated paper, use a special perforating tool (see COOL TOOL, left) or scrape a saw down the wall to penetrate the surface so the wallpaper remover can soak in.

**2** **SPRAY ON SOME WALLPAPER REMOVER.** This solution needs to soak through the paper to dissolve the wallpaper adhesive. Wipe the surface with a latex-gloved hand to distribute the remover evenly and then wait.

**3** **SCRAPE OFF THE WET PAPER.** Use a wallpaper scraper to remove the paper. Regular wallpaper should scrape off after a few minutes. Vinyl-coated paper can take an hour or more and require repeated applications of remover. Work carefully and patiently to avoid damaging the wall.

**4** **USE A WALLPAPER STEAMER.** If wallpaper remover isn't working well, try steaming stubborn paper off with a wallpaper steamer. To protect wood floors, adhere a 2-ft.-wide strip of plastic to the baseboard trim and cover it with absorbent toweling or other material to absorb the water that drips down the wall.

**5** **WASH OFF RESIDUE.** When all the paper is removed, wash the walls with a detergent and warm water solution. Rinse and wring out your sponge, and change the water often. You want to remove the paste, not just move it around. Use clean water for a final wipe-down.

# Remove Old Trim

**1** **BREAK THE SEAL.** In most cases, the edges of your old trim will be sealed to the drywall with a bead of caulk and layers of paint that have been applied over the years. If you try to remove the trim without breaking the seal first, you will most likely rip the top layer of paper off

the drywall surface. To break the seal, put a new blade in your utility knife. Insert the knife between the trim and wall, and carefully cut through the paint and caulk. It might take three or four passes, depending on how many layers of paint you have to cut through.

**2** **PULL THE TRIM AWAY FROM THE WALL.** Grab a 6-in. drywall-finishing knife, and tap it with your hammer to wedge it between the trim and the wall. Do this in several places along the trim. The idea is to create just enough space to get your flatbar started.

**3** **PRY OFF THE TRIM.** Place the blade of your flatbar between the wall and the trim, then protect the wall with a piece of ¼-in.- thick plywood. Gently pry the molding away at several spots until you can see where the nails are. Now position the bar and plywood near each nail, and pry the molding farther away from the wall until you can easily pull it off.

**4** **REMOVE THE NAILS.** Whether or not you intend to save the old trim, get in the habit of removing the nails before you put down each piece—trim with nails sticking out is very dangerous. The easiest way to remove nails is to use end nips to pry them out through the back of the molding. This also prevents damage to the face of the molding in case you intend to reuse it.

1

2

3

4

# Prefinish the Trim

**1** **APPLY A COAT OF PRIMER.** Lay your trim pieces across two sawhorses to work at a convenient height. To protect the floor from drips, put newspaper or a dropcloth under the horses. Give the trim a coat of latex primer, working the primer into the wood by brushing back and forth. If any drips get on the back of the trim, wipe them off—it's annoying to have to scrape off dried drips so that the trim can lay flat against the wall.

**2** **APPLY THE FIRST COAT OF PAINT.** The job will be easier and neater if you pour a few inches of paint into a separate bucket instead of working out of the paint can. Dip your brush about one-third of the way into your paint bucket, and lightly tap it twice against the sides to prevent drips. Apply the paint in long, smooth strokes.

# Caulk, Fill & Paint Trim

**1** **CAULK & FILL.** Even if you manage to install trim without gaps, it's still a good idea to run a bead of paintable latex caulk at joints and where trim meets the wall. The trim may shrink, and caulk is flexible enough to prevent future gaps. Work the caulk in with a wet finger, then smooth with a wet sponge or paper towel. Fill nail holes with wood putty and sand.

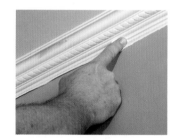

**2** **APPLY THE LAST PAINT COAT.** For top coats, 100% acrylic trim paint in a semigloss sheen is a good choice. Use a quality brush to apply the final coats of paint to the molding. If you plan to paint the wall, you can let your trim coat extend onto the wall surface. You'll paint over this extra finish when applying wall paint.

# Insulate with Rolls

**1** **ROLL IT OUT.** Choose insulation with the same widths and thicknesses as are found in your wall cavities between studs (typically 3½ in. deep for a 2 × 4 wall). Wear gloves and a dust mask. Start at the top of the wall, unrolling the insulation with its Kraft-paper side facing out, and filling the cavity completely without compressing the insulation. Unfold the Kraft-paper flaps as you go, stapling them to the studs every 12 in. Cut the roll to length at the bottom with a utility knife.

**2** **CUT AROUND INTRUSIONS.** Use a utility knife to cut the insulation to fit it around and sandwich any pipes or electrical wires running through the wall studs. To preserve the insulation's R-value (see LINGO, left), avoid compressing or forcing it around intrusions or junction boxes. To work around particularly complex intrusions, cut the roll into smaller sections and overlap the paper backing when you hang it.

# Insulate with Foam Panels

**1** **FRAME THE WALL.** To create a stud wall cavity on a concrete wall, first measure the wall's height and use a circular saw to cut 2 × 4 studs that length. Space studs 16 in. apart, measuring between the centers of each pair of studs. Fasten each stud's wide face to the the concrete wall with fluted masonry nails or Tapcon® screws, making a 1½-in.-deep cavity.

**2** **FASTEN THE PANELS.** Measure the height and width of each cavity. Cut 1½-in.-thick rigid foam insulation panels with a utility knife and a straightedge to fit each cavity. Cut or notch the panels to fit around obstructions or to fill areas with odd dimensions. Apply construction adhesive  to the concrete wall, press the panel firmly into the cavity, and hold it in place for a few minutes until the adhesive bonds the panel to the wall surface.

**1**

**2**

**1**

**2**

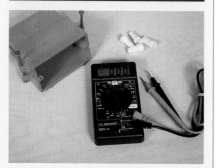
# Add an Electrical Outlet

**1** **FIND THE SOURCE.** Find the wall stud you want to mount your new outlet on, and locate the nearest existing outlet from which you'll extend the power. Ideally, use the last outlet in the chain (or "run") from the service panel so you don't have to connect two sets of wires; it'll be the one farthest away from the panel. Shut off the power to that run at the panel—confirm it with a voltage tester—and remove the outlet's faceplate. Next, unscrew and remove the outlet from the box to gain access to its wires and the terminal clamps behind it. Measure the distance to the new outlet and cut Romex® cable to that length *plus* an extra 12 in. for slack.

**2** **DRILL THE STUDS.** Use a carpenter's level and pencil to mark a straight line from the existing outlet to the new outlet location on the exposed wall studs. On those marks, bore a ¾-in. hole through the center of each stud along the line. Fasten steel guard plates on the outside narrow face of the studs, over the holes, to protect the wires running through the studs from wallboard nails or screws.

**3** **CONNECT THE WIRES.** Fasten the outlet box flush with the wall studs plus the thickness of the wallboard. Run the end of the cable from any keyhole in the box, clamping the cable with box clamps and stapling it to the studs along vertical runs. Insert the cable into the existing outlet, leaving some slack, and clamp it in place. At each end, strip back 6 in. of the sheathing to reveal the cable wires; separate the wires, and strip their insulation ⅜ in. from their ends. Connect the black-sheathed wire to a brass outlet clamp and the white-sheathed wire to a silver clamp. Wrap the green grounding wire around the screws in the back of each outlet box.

**4** **TEST AND FINISH.** Turn on power to the circuit and use a voltage tester to check that both outlets are receiving power (typically 115 volts). Turn off the power, fasten the receptacles to their respective outlet boxes, then attach their faceplates with screws.

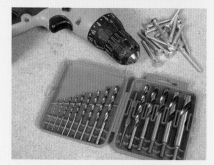
# Fasten Items to a Wall

**1** **FIND THE FRAMING.** If wallboard or paneling covers the frame members, use a stud finder to locate them. Mark the location of each stud with a pencil, then use a level to draw a line along its vertical length.

**2** **FASTEN WITH LAG SCREWS.** Whatever you're fastening to a framing member, such as a wall stud, a lag screw is the best choice to hold it in place and to support its weight. Position the unit on the wall—a cabinet, shelf, or rack—and mark each screw's location on the unit's back panel by transferring the line from step 1, above. Drill a pilot hole through the unit into the center of the frame member behind it, "grease" the screw's threads with soap or graphite to reduce friction, then use a socket wrench to tighten the lag screw.

**3** **USE HOLLOW-WALL ANCHORS.** While you should always attach at least one fastener to a frame member, it may be necessary to secure the other end of a long, lightweight storage unit through the wallboard between framing members and still give it adequate support. Drill a hole in the wallboard just large enough to accept a hollow-wall anchor, unscrew the bolt from the anchor's sleeve, thread it onto the storage unit, and rethread the bolt into the sleeve. Insert the hollow-wall anchor into the hole in the wallboard, then tighten its bolt. The anchor's outer sleeve will compress behind the wallboard as you tighten it, grasping the wallboard.

**4** **ATTACH TO CONCRETE.** Concrete walls are structural and they can carry the added weight of shelves, cabinets, or racks. To ensure a secure hold, mark and drill pilot holes for Tapcon® screws that are at least ¼ in. deeper than the length of the screws, using  the bit provided with the fasteners or one that fits the screwhead. Screw-fasten your storage unit, cleat, or ledger board to the wall, taking care not to over-tighten the fasteners in the pilot holes—it can cause their heads to snap off.

1

2

3

4

**Shallow subsurface utility lines** may cross beneath your work area. Excavate them carefully, then reroute the pipes or electrical lines at greater depth before you build a walk or patio over them. They should be buried at least 6 in. beneath your base aggregate or paving.

**+ WHAT CAN GO WRONG**

**Make sure you have a clear path** to easily navigate your wheelbarrow or garden cart when carrying materials, and make sure you can safely manage the load. Not only is an overloaded wheelbarrow apt to tip over and dump its cargo, but trying to control it can cause injury.

# Demolish & Remove Concrete

**1** **CUT IT OUT.** To get rid of a weed-ridden patch of concrete, use a rented walk-behind concrete saw equipped with a water-cooled blade to cut along the existing expansion joints to 1 in. or so below the depth of the concrete. If necessary, make a second, deeper cut. Take it slow, making sure you're staying on line and not lifting the blade as you go.

**2** **BREAK IT UP.** Use a 8-lb. to 12-lb. sledgehammer with a 36-in. handle to break up the sections you've cut with the saw. Wear eye protection, leather or fabric gloves, a dust mask, and closed-toed shoes or boots to avoid injury from flying debris and blisters from the sledgehammer, and to protect yourself from a misguided swing. Take a full swing each time and break the sections into pieces you can easily lift and carry to a wheelbarrow or garden cart.

**3** **PRY THE PIECES.** Though your work with the sledgehammer will likely loosen most of the pieces, a few stubborn ones will cling to the soil. Use a 3-ft.-long pry bar to lift and separate pieces of concrete from their soil bed. Keep your feet and hands a safe distance away as you pry the pieces loose—they can fall, crushing fingers and toes.

**4** **HAUL THEM AWAY.** Even though the concrete pieces are small, use proper lifting techniques (using your back and legs) to remove and carry the broken concrete to a nearby wheelbarrow or garden cart and their disposal location. Once the big pieces are gone, use a rake to gather up the small (and often sharp!) leftover bits and carefully haul them away to be disposed of. Many waste disposers now recycle concrete, so check with your recycling center before adding to the load on your landfill.

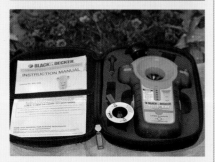
# Lay Out

**1** **CREATE THE CORNERS.** For layouts with square corners, use 2-ft. sections of 1×4 lumber to create corner, or batter, boards at each outside corner, at least 8 in. beyond the actual finished area. Nail two stakes to the inside face of one board, with one stake flush to the outside edge of the board, and pound the assembly in place. Next, nail a second board to the corner stake at right angles to the first board. Pound a stake on this board's inside face, then nail the board to the stake. Level the top of the corner boards. For circular or curved layouts, use a garden hose to mark the area.

**2** **SET THE STRING LINES.** Use a laser sight to line up and pound nails in the corner boards at points marking the dimensions of your finished area. Tie strings stretched tautly between the boards to the nails on the tops of the corner boards.

# Excavate

**1** **START DIGGING.** Once you've had your utility providers—or their outside service company— mark the depth and location of any utility lines in the area to be excavated, use a flat shovel to start digging at one corner and work your way across and lengthwise (as if in rows). Try to maintain a consistent depth; pile your excavated soil and debris nearby to haul it away later (and possibly reuse it elsewhere).

**2** **FINISH THE EXCAVATION.** Excavate about 6 in. *past* your string line. A carpenter's level is handy to make sure your excavated area is flat or maintains a slight slope away from the house, if desired for drainage; use a 4-ft. level to check your work as you progress. Remove any rocks, weeds, and other debris to leave a clean, smooth area for the next layer.

# Lay a Base and Tamp

**1** **ROLL OUT THE WEED SCREEN.** Working lengthwise to minimize the number of pieces to cover the area, roll out the weed screen (or landscape fabric) and secure each section every 12 in. to 15 in. with 6-in., U-shaped stakes hammered into the ground. Take care not to tear the fabric as you go. Overlap sections at least 8 in. and stake the edge of the overlapping section to secure it and the fabric underneath.

**2** **ADD THE AGGREGATE.** Fill a wheelbarrow or garden cart to a manageable level and dump each load of aggregate in a different location within the excavated area, which makes spreading it out with a rake easier and faster. Avoid snagging the landscape fabric, but if you do, repair any damage before covering it with aggregate.

**3** **SMOOTH IT OUT.** To keep from snagging the landscape fabric layer below, use the backside of your rake to spread the aggregate over the excavated area, eyeballing it to an even level and consistent depth. Then use your carpen-

ter's level to check level (or slope) and a tape measure to check depth more precisely. Adjust as necessary.

**4** **TAMP THE BASE.** Rent a power tamper to quickly and easily compact the aggregate base in preparation for the next layer. Start at one corner and work across and lengthwise. Don't rush, but make sure the tamper is moving evenly and consistently across the aggregate to avoid high and low spots. Check level (or slope) and depth, and add aggregate as necessary.

# Level an Area

**1** **BUILD THE STRIKE-OFF GUIDES.** Secure an 8-ft. length of ¾-in. PVC pipe to a slightly longer piece of 1×4 lumber (see DO IT RIGHT, left). You'll need two of these assemblies, which you'll place parallel to each other, 4 ft. to 6 ft. apart across a section of the work area and 4 in. below the finished area's intended grade. Use your level to ensure the strike-off guides follow the slope (if any) of your excavated area, then secure them in place using 8-in. wooden stakes, a rubber mallet, and 6d common or duplex nails.

**2** **POUR THE SAND.** Add a layer of washed sand on top of the aggregate base, whether from 60-lb. bags or by using your wheelbarrow or cart to haul it from a bulk pile in the yard. Ease the work of spreading it by opening bags or dumping loads in several locations within the excavated area, between the strike-off guides. Rake the sand to a consistent depth and visually level it. It's okay if the sand is slightly higher than the top of the strike-off guides.

**3** **STRIKE IT OFF.** Use the straight (narrow) edge of a 2×4 that easily spans across the PVC strike-off guides. With a helper, move the 2×4 back and forth as you work it down the length of the PVC guides, scraping (or screeding) the sand to a consistent level. Work from each end toward the middle, moving the excess sand you've accumulated there to the next

section. Gather and remove the final bit of excess sand. When two adjacent sections are finished, lift out the guides, fill the voids left by the strike-off guides, and smooth the surface.

**4** **WORK IN SECTIONS.** Narrow sections 4 ft. to 6 ft. wide are easier to screed than wider areas. Divide your work area into roughly equal sections. As you complete one section, move one of the PVC strike-off guides to the next location, level it, and stake it into place.

# Painting a Room

A fresh **COAT OF COLOR** gives any room a new personality

PAINTING A ROOM HAS THE SAME FEEL-GOOD POTENTIAL as shopping for new clothes. There's plenty of excitement about choosing the right color combinations and about the way you're going to feel when you're done.

Like other paint projects, this is one that can be done solo. But it's faster and more fun with two people. In terms of planning, you'll need to decide if you want to paint the trim as well as the walls and ceiling. It's best to get trim, doors, and windows painted before you begin to paint the ceiling and walls.

FIXING CRACKS     PAINTING TRIM     CUTTING IN     CEILINGS & WALLS

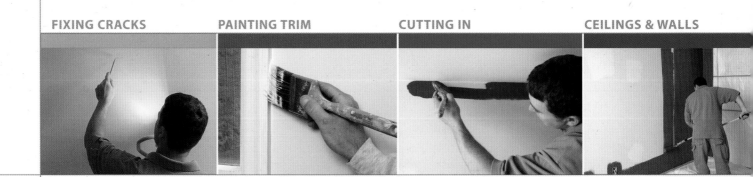

▶ **DO IT RIGHT**

**Acoustic or popcorn ceiling** texture can easily be ruined by using the wrong type of paint, applying too much paint, or excessive rolling. Use oil-based paint and a long-nap roller. Or use an airless sprayer, following the manufacturer's instructions.

◆ **DO IT NOW**

**Dress for success!** Wear old sneakers, painter's pants, a long-sleeve T-shirt, and a painter's cap. When using a roller, wear goggles to protect your eyes (and eyeglasses) from paint-roller spray.

✛ **WHAT CAN GO WRONG**

**A new roller can shed** some fuzz and leave it behind as you roll on your paint. To prevent this, wrap a new roller cover with masking tape. When you peel off the tape nearly all of the loose stuff comes off with the tape.

# Tools & Gear

*Painting a room can require as little as a roller and tray, a paintbrush, and a drop cloth. But with a few inexpensive extras, you'll get top-notch results. This extra gear will also make the job go faster and easier.*

**CLEANING SUPPLIES.** Wall and ceiling surfaces may be dirtier than you think, and any deposits of dust or grime can prevent paint from adhering well. For quick, thorough cleaning, you'll need a vacuum, sponges, a bucket, rags, and a household cleaner that won't leave a soapy residue.

**REPAIR TOOLS.** Have a putty knife handy for applying spackling compound and a caulking gun for applying caulk.

**ROLLER, EXTENSION POLE & TRAY.** Each painter needs a 9-in. roller with a screw-in extension pole. If you're painting with partners, get an extra tray.

**3-IN. NYLON-POLYESTER BRUSH.** This is what you'll use to paint trim and to cut in around windows and doors and along corners.

**STEPLADDER.** You'll need a sturdy stepstool or a stepladder for repair work and painting above windows and doors.

**DROP CLOTH.** A canvas drop cloth will protect the floor where you're painting. If there's wall-to-wall carpet on the floor, put down a double layer.

**SCREWDRIVERS.** To remove door hardware and outlet covers, you'll need a screwdriver for Phillips® head and slotted screws.

# What to Buy

**1| REPAIR SUPPLIES.** In any room, you can expect to find small cracks and holes in wall and ceiling surfaces. To repair these areas, buy some spackling compound and acrylic painter's caulk. Caulk is mainly for filling cracks between trim and wall or ceiling surfaces. Spackling compound is for other cracks and holes.

**2| PRIMER & PAINT.** Choose an interior primer or primer/sealer compatible with the top coat you'll be using. If your top coat will be a color other than white or light tan, ask the dealer to tint the primer so that its color is similar to the color of the top coat. Choose a high-quality interior acrylic-latex paint as your wall and ceiling top coat. You can go with a standard color or have the dealer custom-tint the paint for you. You'll need to select either a flat or eggshell sheen. To figure out how much you need, measure your room and record how many doors and windows you have. Someone at the paint store can then help you figure out how much paint you'll need.

**3| ROLLER COVERS.** You'll need one for each painter. Buy thin-nap (³⁄₈-in. or ¹⁄₂-in.) covers, which are best for smooth surfaces. The best roller covers have beveled edges to minimize roller tracks.

**4| PROTECTION.** Make sure to have a roll of painter's plastic drop cloth to cover furniture, chandeliers, and other items that need protection from paint drips. For personal protection, don't forget a painter's cap and goggles.

**5| PAINTER'S TAPE.** Painter's masking tape is what you want. Get a ³⁄₄-in. roll and a 2-in. roll. Other masking products might also help to prevent paint spills from getting where they shouldn't. You can also buy pregummed paper or lightweight plastic drapes with tape from your paint supplier.

## WHAT CAN GO WRONG

**M**ildew can prevent paint from adhering to a surface. This mold is often found in damp locations like bathrooms, laundry rooms, or areas with little or no air circulation. **Telltale signs:** moldy smell and dark, blotchy deposits. **What to do:** Sponge or spray on a 1:1 solution of laundry bleach and water. Let stand 5 minutes, then wipe down and neutralize with water or a water-vinegar solution. Repeat if necessary.

### ◼ LINGO

For painters, *boxing* isn't about trading punches. It's a strategy for avoiding subtle color differences. If you plan to use more than one gallon of paint to paint a room, mix the next gallon with the last half of the one you are using in a large plastic bucket.

# Cleaning & Caulking

**1** **PREPARE THE ROOM.** Clear out everything you can. Remove outlet covers and apply painter's tape over switches and receptacles. Consolidate any remaining furniture in the center of the room and protect it with plastic drop cloths. Cover the floor with canvas drop cloths. Don't forget to cover any built-in furniture and any ceiling fans.

**2** **FIND THEN FIX CRACKS & HOLES.** It's easier to discover cracks and depressions when you shine a bright light across the surface. Fill holes and cracks with spackling compound. Sand the repair area smooth after the compound dries. If you're doing a lot of sanding, put a box fan in a window to draw dust-laden air outside.

**3** **CAULK THE CRACKS.** Scrape out any cracked or dried caulk where moldings meet walls or ceilings. An old screwdriver makes a good scraping tool; a painter's 5-in-1 tool works even better. Apply a ⅛-in.-dia. bead of caulk along all trim/wall junctures that have open cracks, smooth the bead with a wetted fingertip, and allow it to skin over before painting.

**4** **PAINT THE TRIM FIRST.** If your plan is to paint walls, ceiling, and trim, then it's best to get the trim painted first, along with the room's windows and doors. When you're ready to start on the ceiling and

walls, mask off the trim with painter's tape or pregummed masking paper. Don't forget to protect interior window sills from roller drips. And don't forget to clean the walls and ceiling before you start painting.

**1**

**2**

**3**

**4**

# Cutting & Rolling

**5** **CUT IN THE CEILING.** Always paint the ceiling before the walls. Using a 3-in. paintbrush, apply a band of paint on the ceiling where it meets the wall. You can cut in the ceiling all around the room or work on one section at a time. When there's a pair of painters working, one can cut in with a brush while the other begins to roll.

**6** **LET'S ROLL!** Screw the roller extension into your roller. Dip into your paint tray and roll out the paint on the tray's slanted surface until the nap is evenly coated. Begin rolling the ceiling next to the wall, where you've cut in with the brush. Then roll a big "W" pattern in an area about 3 ft. square. Fill in the open areas in the W, then move on and repeat the process.

**7** **CUT IN THE WALLS.** Use your 3-in. brush to cut in one wall at a time. Brush a band of paint down the corners, around window and door openings, and above the baseboard. If the walls are being painted a different color than the ceiling, take more care when cutting in along these corners.

**8** **ROLL THE WALLS.** Work from one end of a wall to the other. Start your roller at the top of the wall, then roll straight up and down just until you've applied an even coat. When you're finished, peel off the masking tape, clean up the room, and put away your gear. Wow! Your new room looks great.

**5**

**6**

**7**

**8**

Big color in a little space. If having fun is part of the program, a bold color will get the message across.

Orange may not be the first color that comes to mind for a bedroom, but why not? This shade looks fresh paired with white ceiling and trim—and with shades of blue, the complementary color of orange.

Green can go with any color. This shade of green leans toward red rather than yellow to give it a softness that goes well with rich orange-golds and purple-browns. White trim keeps the look of the room bright.

**Wake-up call.** Builders play it safe and give most rooms the all-white or off-white treatment. If your plans are to cover the walls with bright artwork or install curtains and window treatments in contrasting colors, these highlights look good against a neutral background. But a bold color on walls and/or ceilings is still the most dramatic way to wake up a bland room. A contrasting trim color looks nice, too.

Just one color paired with white can transform a bathroom beyond the ordinary. Take a look and you'll see that white predominates, making it easier to select fixtures and accessories. Add mint-green paint and the bathroom instantly looks clean, cheery, and stylish.

You may want to balance a rich wall color with a light ceiling. This lovely red-toned dark lavender gets a lift from the white ceiling and trim and from the yellow-toned pine floorboards.

Paint can add details that don't exist in the three-dimensional world. Paint trims a round window and low doorway—and a moon—at the entrance to an understair playspace for kids. Blue paint indicates the sloped ceiling inside and so may dissuade taller folk from entering.

A pale pink would have been the choice for a serene ambience, but fuchsia walls give a bedroom a sophistication that balances the frothy bedlinens.

A classic, slate-blue color is a perfect choice for a bedroom in a traditionally styled house. The color is kept just to the wainscoting to keep the room bright, and true white trim reinforces the crisp, serene look.

# Strié & Chambray

Dragging a glaze using **DRY-BRUSH TECHNIQUES** opens a world of painting possibilities

LOOKING FOR AN EASY WAY to add interest to a painted room? Look no further than the decorative painting technique called strié or dragging. Using this technique, a colored glaze is applied over a base coat of eggshell or semigloss paint. Then the wet glaze is immediately worked with a dry brush to create a delicate and detailed vertical pattern. A half-height wall, such as the area below a chair rail, is a particularly good candidate for dragging, because you can easily drag your brush from top to bottom without getting on a ladder.

PREP THE WALL    ROLL ON THE GLAZE    TEXTURE TECHNIQUE    YOU'RE DONE!

Strié, also known as dragging or striating, is a decorative technique that involves dragging a dry brush vertically over a freshly applied glaze to expose some of the base coat color below. Chambray is similar but you follow up with a horizontal pass to produce a woven texture.

# Tools & Gear

**STEPLADDER.** While not required for this wainscot application, you'll need this if your work takes you up to the ceiling.

**CANVAS DROP CLOTH.** Protect your floors with a canvas drop cloth. Plastic is too slippery underfoot. If your floor is carpeted, double or triple the protection to prevent spills from leaking through the canvas.

**PAINT ROLLER & TRAY.** Plastic trays seem easier to clean and don't rust. A 4-in. roller worked fine for this wainscoting project, but for a full-height wall, use a standard 9-in. roller.

**PAINTBRUSHES.** For texturing the glaze, you need a 3-in. or wider brush with relatively stiff, coarse bristles. Specialty brushes like the one above are also available where paint supplies are sold.

### ▶ DO IT RIGHT

**New roller covers,** even quality ones, shed fuzz, which ends up on your wall in the wet paint. To minimize the problem press tape onto the roller and then peel off loose material.

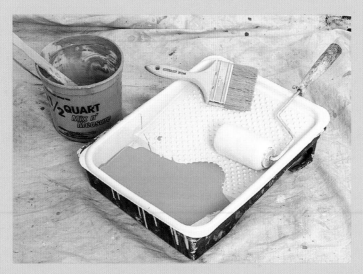

## WHAT'S DIFFERENT?

**O**il-based paints and glazes have been preferred by most professional decorative painters chiefly because of the longer "open" time—a period that the glaze stays wet enough to work with a sponge, rag, or other texturing tools. But if you don't like to work with alkyd finishes, don't worry. You can mix an extender (paint conditioner) into water-based glaze to increase its open time.

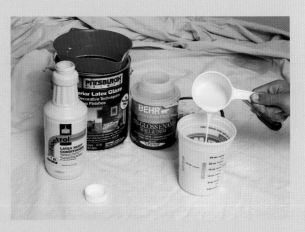

# What to Buy

**1| PAINTER'S TAPE.** Painter's tape is designed to seal well at the edges so paint won't bleed underneath, but it will not pull off any paint or damage surfaces when it is removed. Use medium-tack tape on painted trim that has cured for at least 30 days and low-tack tape on freshly painted trim.

**2| GLAZING LIQUID.** Glazing liquid has a paint-like consistency and is available in acrylic (water-based) and alkyd (oil-based) versions. When mixed with paint, the resulting glaze produces a somewhat translucent finish that allows the color of the base coat to show through. The higher the glaze-to-paint ratio is, the more translucent the finish will be.

**3| PAINT.** You need two colors: typically a light color base coat in eggshell sheen and a darker color you'll use to tint the glazing liquid.

**4| PAINT THINNER.** You'll need this for thinning glaze, dampening rags to remove drips, and cleaning brushes only if you're using an alkyd glaze.

**5| PAINT-MIXING BUCKET.** Washable plastic buckets with volume measurements make it easy to measure the right proportions of paint and glaze.

## COOL TOOL

**Keep your paint** and roller fresh in a covered paint tray while you brush out each rolled section, or even during a coffee or lunch break. You'll find these plastic trays at your paint store.

**For consistent results,** it's important to keep your texturing brush dry. Wipe the glaze off the bristles with a damp rag as you complete each pass. If you're texturing a large area it may even be necessary to clean the brush.

# Four Simple Steps

**1** **PREPARE THE WALL.** Remove any cover plates and mask the fixture. Complete any needed trim or wall repairs, prime them, and paint the trim (if planned). Mask trim to protect it during wall painting. Burnish the tape with a fingernail to make sure the tape is well adhered at the edge. Roll on a base coat of eggshell or semigloss latex paint.

**2** **MIX & APPLY GLAZE.** Pour 1 part paint and 1 part glazing liquid into a paint bucket and mix well. Use a medium-nap roller (⅜ in. to ½-in.) to apply the glaze over a 3-ft.-wide area from the top to the bottom of the wall, which in this case is from the masked chair rail molding to masked base molding. No need to cut in with a brush.

**3** **TEXTURE THE PAINT.** Immediately fill in the unpainted areas at the very top and very bottom with the strie or dragging brush. Then drag the brush down the wall from top to bottom in a single pass, maintaining even pressure. Overlap the previously brushed area very slightly to avoid creating a noticeable transition from one pass to the next. Roll and brush your way along the wall the same way.

**4** **REMOVE MASKING TAPE.** As you complete each wall, remove the masking tape. Always pull at a low angle and slowly to avoid pulling any paint off the trim with the tape. If necessary, touch up any areas where paint may have bled under the tape.

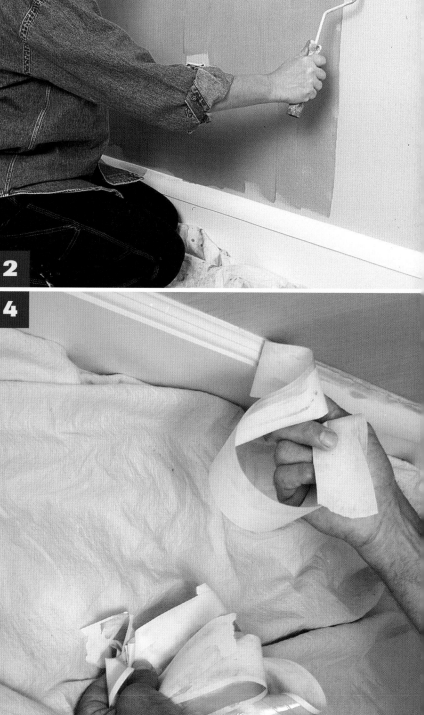

**Wide blue stripes made with the strié technique add a soft, fabric look to the wall in a child's room.**

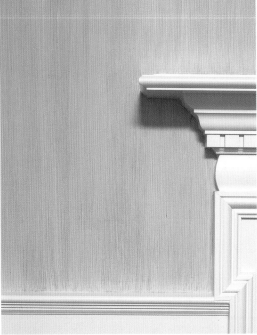

**This vertical strié pattern above the wainscoting and mantel looks very much like rough, natural silk.**

**In this close-up you can clearly see the detail of the technique shown in the photo on the facing page.**

**Walls painted with the chambray technique (that's strié done with two passes at right angles) really do look like woven fabric.**

# Weave walls anywhere.
The strié wainscoting shown in the step-by-step pages represents only one of almost limitless possibilities for this technique. While well suited to walls, strié is also effective on doors, tabletops, and other surfaces. Experiment with different "tools," such as a flagging brush, a cellulose sponge, or a rag. Each tool produces a unique pattern. For a more dramatic effect, try using contrasting colors for your base coat and glaze. You can even combine techniques such as strié and stripes. As with most decorative painting, practice on paper before committing your design to your wall.

A cheery alcove is finished with an apple-green glaze dragged over a white base coat. This airy finish makes a nice backdrop for the dark dresser.

# Painting Trim

To make a good room look great, transform **MOLDINGS, WINDOWS & DOORS** with fresh coats of paint

STAINED TRIM MAY BE JUST RIGHT for a cabin or lodge, where rustic seems right. But paint is the way to go if you want a room's moldings, windows, and doors to really pop. Trim colors that contrast with walls and ceilings might suit your style in one room, while a more subtle color change might be right somewhere else in the house. (For some design ideas, see p. 74.) Either way, this painting project calls for some smart prep work and a combination of tricks and proven techniques to get the pro results you want. Let's get started!

**PREP STEPS**   **TRIM TEST**   **GET THE DOORS DONE**   **WINDOW VIEW**

# Tools & Gear

**SCREWDRIVER.** A 4-in-1 driver is just the ticket for removing hardware.

**HAMMER & NAILSET.** To set trim nails, you'll need a 16-ounce hammer and a $\frac{1}{32}$-in. or $\frac{2}{32}$-in. nailset.

**PUTTY KNIFE OR 5-IN-1 TOOL.** Either tool will spackle and fill nail holes but the 5-in-1 is much more versatile. It can open paint cans, scrape out cracks, help clean your roller, and apply putty, too.

**WINDOW SCRAPER.** This small scraper is what you need for removing dried paint from window glass. Make sure you have at least a 10-pack of razor blades designed for use in the scraper.

**TAPING KNIFE.** The 5-in. taping and finishing knife has a special application unrelated to its primary purpose: It's used in combination with a window scraper to maintain a frame-to-glass seal when removing paint from windows. (See WHAT CAN GO WRONG on p. 72.)

**CAULKING GUN.** Get the kind with a quick-release button and an integral wire for breaking the seal on caulk cartridges.

**TRIM BRUSH.** If you don't have a good one, buy a new one. Size-wise, 2 in. is a good all-purpose width. Some people prefer the angled-tip over the standard. Some use both. If you need to paint wide trim (like a broad cornice molding or tall baseboard), a 3-in. brush will speed the work.

**STEPLADDER.** A necessity for reaching ceiling moldings.

**All-purpose primers** and primer-sealers recommended for drywall and bare wood are not the best sealers to use on interior trim that has been stained and varnished. You're better off using a primer formulated for use on stained and varnished surfaces.

## ▶ DO IT RIGHT

**You know it's not a good idea** to paint yourself into a corner, but did you know that there's a painting sequence for doors and windows that will help you get better results? Here are the rules:

1 | Paint from the inside out.

2 | Paint detailed areas before flat surfaces.

3 | Paint parallel with the length or grain of wood, not across or against it.

## COOL TOOL

**W**agner® **Glass Mask system** lays down a clear masking film on a windowpane. It's spaced $\frac{1}{8}$-in. away from the frame to allow paint to extend onto the glass. This frame-to-pane seal prevents condensation or rain from getting into this joint, which causes paint failure and eventually rot. Then the tool's scraper head easily removes the film (along with any paint on it) but leaves $\frac{1}{8}$-in.-wide band of paint on the pane perimeter.

# What to Buy

**1| CAULK.** Acrylic-latex caulk is what you want. A single cartridge will be more than enough for a room.

**2| WOOD PUTTY OR PATCHING COMPOUND.** To be sure you're getting the right goop, read the label and product description. Look for the words "non-shrinking" and "fast-drying."

**3| ABRASIVES & DEGLOSSER.** 120-grit aluminum oxide sandpaper will do a good job of scuffing up the surface of varnish or semigloss paint. Half-a-dozen 9x11 sheets will handle an average-size room. Deglosser, also called liquid sandpaper, does a chemical scuff-up on varnished surfaces. Use this if your trim is ornately contoured (difficult to sand) or coated with high-gloss varnish. Deglosser is available where paint is sold.

**4| PAINTER'S TAPE.** Depending on your circumstances you may need low-tack painter's tape for freshly painted or wallpapered walls, medium-tack painter's tape for floors and any hardware, and regular high-tack masking tape for carpeting.

**5| PRIMER-SEALER.** When repairs or sanding exposes raw wood, a primer-sealer compatible with the top coat provides the base paint needed for a good bond. Painting over stained or varnished trim? Use a stain-killing, bonding primer. Primer can be tinted to approximate trim color.

**6| PAINT.** Buy a good-quality semigloss trim paint. Latex paint will be fine for most trimwork; look for the words "100% acrylic" on the label.

**7| PAINT BUCKETS.** Plastic paint buckets are inexpensive and allow you to carry around just the right amount of paint.

**8| OTHER STUFF.** Have plenty of clean rags on hand. If your paint store has them in stock, a plastic paint-can spout makes it easier to avoid drips when you pour paint from the can.

## PAINTING DOUBLE-HUNG WINDOWS

**M**ost modern double-hung windows have removable sashes. If you prefer, you can remove each sash, set it up on sawhorses, and paint it "on the flat." To paint a double-hung window in place, the best strategy is to overlap the windows, paint about half of each, and then reverse the overlap, as shown in the drawings.

### SASHES FIRST, THEN JAMBS

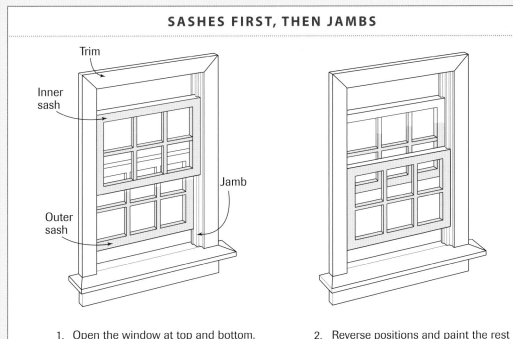

Trim

Inner sash

Outer sash

Jamb

1. Open the window at top and bottom. Paint all of inner sash and half of outer sash.

2. Reverse positions and paint the rest of the outer sash. Paint the jamb last.

# Painting Trim

**1** **PROTECT THE FLOOR.** Lay down a drop cloth and mask the floor perimeter. Use medium-tack painter's tape on wood floors but regular masking tape on carpeting. If you are not painting the ceiling or walls, mask these surfaces with low-tack painter's tape or pregummed masking paper.

**2** **SAND TRIM & SET NAILS.** Scuff-sand all trim using 120-grit abrasive to remove the shininess of semigloss or gloss finishes (paint or varnish). To improve the bond on glossy or detailed surfaces, brush on deglosser, following the manufacturer's instructions. Use a nail set and hammer to drive nail heads about ⅛ in. below the surface.

**3** **APPLY THE PRIMER COAT.** Brush primer on all stained, varnished, and unfinished wood surfaces. Previously painted surfaces do not need to be primed. Work from the top down; do the crown molding first, then the chair rail, and finally the baseboard.

**4** **CAULK & PAINT.** Apply a thin (⅛-in.) bead of caulk to seal cracks at trim joints and between trim and wall or ceiling surfaces. Immediately smooth the caulk with a wetted finger. Use a putty knife to press nonshrinking spackle or wood putty into nail holes and other depressions or damaged areas and sand dried repair spots lightly. Brush on two coats of paint, following the directions on the can about recoating time.

**1**

**2**

**3**

**4**

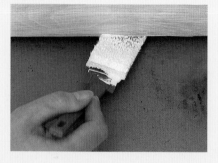

# Painting a Frame & Panel Door

**5** **PREPARE THE DOOR.** If a doorknob and its cover plate are easy to remove, take them off the door by unscrewing the installation screws. Slide heavy paper or a canvas drop cloth under the door. Wedge the door partway open by inserting folded paper or wood shims under the door's bottom edge. Then sand and degloss the door as described for trim.

**6** **APPLY THE PRIMER COAT.** Begin by painting the interior panels. Coat the molded perimeter of each panel first, then paint the flat central area. After painting the panels, coat the stiles, rails, and door edges. Always work from the inside out.

**7** **WIPE PAINT OFF HINGES.** Taking off a door and removing hinges, or even masking them, is not necessary if you immediately wipe paint off the hinges with a damp cloth wrapped over the blade of a putty knife or 5-in-1 tool. Reposition the cloth over the blade each time you wipe.

**8** **APPLY TOP COATS.** When the primer coat has dried completely, it's time to top coat. Two coats will give you a pro appearance. Use a 2-in. paintbrush, and paint from the inside out, starting with the panels. When the last coat has dried, reinstall the doorknob. Nice work!

**5**

**6**

**7**

**8**

# Painting a Window

**9** **REMOVE HARDWARE & SAND.** Remove sash lock hardware and store hardware and screws in a plastic sandwich bag. Also remove and store any window treatment hardware from window jambs. Sand and degloss stained or varnished wood as described for trim.

**10** **PAINT THE SASH.** By switching the positions of inner and outer sashes, you can paint one half of the outer sash, then the other. Always begin with the innermost mullions and work your way out towards the outer sash frame. Bend the bristles to get paint into corners, and avoid overloading the brush with paint.

**11** **PAINT THE FRAME & CASING.** With both sashes lowered, coat the head jamb and window trim. Avoid getting any primer or paint on metal or plastic channels. Lower the sash to paint the upper half of the channels and, when the channels are dry, raise the sash to paint the lower half.

**12** **CLEAN THE GLASS.** Use a fresh blade in your scraper and hold the tool tilted up about 30 degrees from the glass. Doing this minimizes the chance of scratching the glass. To prevent scraping all the paint off the glass and loosing the water seal it provides, hold a 5-in. taping knife or similar tool on the glass and against the frame while you scrape.

**9**

**10**

**11**

**12**

*Above:* Pink glows when accompanied by gold and purple paint. The rule here is that a change in surface allows for a change in color, except at the modest baseboard, which accepts the wall color.

*Above right:* He may have outgrown light blue, but a kid still needs some color. Royal blue trim brightens up a white sleeping/ music niche and adds flair to a tall baseboard.

## Be subtle or dramatic. Paint can be used to make trim blend into the background or to amplify its impact. Possibilities range from painting trim the identical color of the walls to a color that is in contrast to wall colors. Most paint manufacturers have color schemes that take the guesswork out of what colors go well together. The palettes typically include recommendations for walls, trim, and one or more accent colors. You'll also find online tools that allow you to "paint" a particular type of room with wall, ceiling, trim, and accent colors.

Paint chips are no match for a color painted in real life because lighting and existing materials have a huge impact. You might not pair green window trim with a red door on paper, but it looks great in this kitchen because colors are muted versions of their primary cousins and because they contrast or complement colors in the existing tile floor.

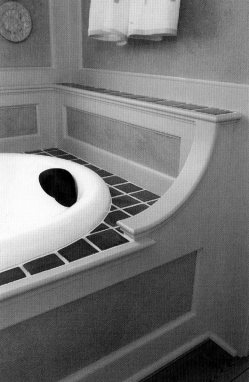

Colors of the ocean inspire a palette for a seaside bathroom. The chartreuse trim adds a glow to cool-colored blue tile and faux-painted panels.

# Colonial Casing

**Passageways are important! Use some CLASSIC CASING to dress up the transition between rooms**

MANY NEWER HOMES HAVE NOTHING more than drywall surrounding passageways between rooms. Fortunately, trimming out these openings is easy. And since our eyes are drawn to passageways, creating an attractive room transition will add lots of architectural impact.

This project features mitered corners. Think of the casing as a large-scale picture frame that allows the molding's profile to wrap around the opening. Whether you choose to leave the trim natural or paint it, the techniques shown here will give you first-class results.

| MEASURE | INSTALL THE JAMBS | LAY OUT THE REVEAL | INSTALL THE CASINGS |

▶ **LINGO**

When installing casing around an opening, don't completely cover the edge of the jambs. Instead, leave a "reveal" about $1/8$ in. wide. Believe it or not, this little ledge makes a big difference in the project's final appearance.

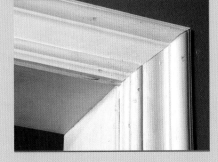

❖ **COOL TOOL**

**A rip guide is a** circular saw accessory that costs little but helps a lot. The guide fits into slots in the saw's base and has a short fence that rides against the edge of the board you're cutting. You can adjust the guide to rip boards of different widths. Make sure the guide you buy is sized to fit your saw.

# Tools & Gear

*Keep your basic tool kit handy because you'll need a hammer, tape measure, and nail set, as well as the tools listed below.*

**CIRCULAR SAW.** This is the tool you'll use to cut the wood jambs that will line the inside of the passageway. To help you cut straight, fit your saw with a rip guide (see COOL TOOL at left).

**DRILL & BIT.** A cordless drill is fine for this project. You'll need a $1/16$-in.-dia. bit to go with it.

**MITER BOX.** Since good miter joints are important here, make sure you have a good-quality miter box or a chopsaw. Both tools will give you the exact 45-degree cuts this project requires.

**COMBINATION SQUARE.** Thanks to its adjustable blade, this square is great for marking the reveal lines on your jambs (see LINGO at left).

**FRAMING SQUARE.** With its long blades, this tool makes it easy to test door openings for square.

**FOUR-FOOT LEVEL.** You'll need a 4-ft. level to make sure your head jamb is level and your side jambs are plumb. Use a 2-ft. level for narrower openings.

**SAWHORSES.** Set up a pair of horses and a 2x10 or 2x12 crosspiece to support your miter box.

**STEPLADDER OR STOOL.** One is essential. If you're working with a helper, get two ways to step up and you'll have an easy time installing the top casing.

**CAULKING GUN.** Have your gun ready as you near the end of the project, so you can seal small cracks in preparation for painting.

**TRIM BRUSH.** If you've completed other projects in this book, you already know how important a good trim brush can be. A brush that's about 3 in. wide offers the best combination of control and painting speed.

# What to Buy

**1| JAMB STOCK.** For this project, you'll need to cut a head jamb and two side jambs to line the inside of the passageway. Measure your opening and get three pieces of 1x6 pine, giving yourself a few extra inches on each piece. Buy only boards that are flat and straight. We used preprimed pine for this project to save time on painting.

**2| MOLDING.** If you spend some time in the molding aisle at your home center, you're sure to find a pleasing casing profile. There are quite a few choices. The casing we used is 3 in. wide and comes preprimed. Assuming your passageway opening is around 7 ft. tall, you'll need to buy four 8-ft. pieces (for side casings) and two head casing pieces at least 12 in. longer than the width of the opening.

**3| SHIMS.** You'll probably need shims to make the head casing level and the side casings plumb. Buy a small package of tapered wood shims.

**4| FINISH NAILS.** Get some 8d finish nails for installing jambs and 6d finish nails for the trim.

**5| CAULK & WOOD PUTTY.** Acrylic latex caulk is the best stuff to use for filling gaps in joints and between the molding and the wall. To fill nail holes, get wood putty.

**6| SANDPAPER.** Several sheets of 120-grit sandpaper should handle the smoothing work you'll need to do prior to painting.

**7| PAINT & PRIMER.** Use a fast-drying interior primer and good-quality semigloss trim paint.

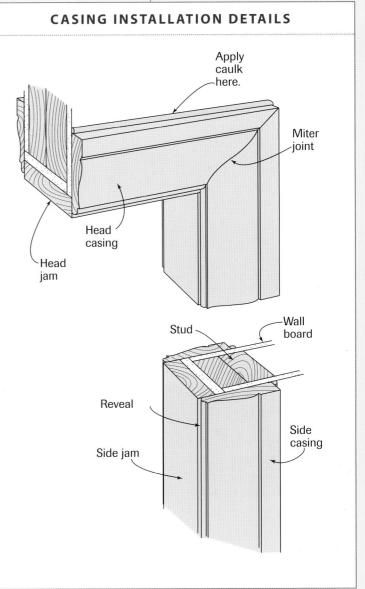

**CASING INSTALLATION DETAILS**

Apply caulk here.

Miter joint

Head casing

Head jamb

Stud

Wall board

Reveal

Side casing

Side jam

# Prepare the Jamb

**1** **CHECK FOR SQUARE, STRAIGHT & PLUMB.** If the existing opening isn't true, you'll need to insert shims beneath your jambs to make the opening square and get surfaces plumb and level. Put a framing square in each corner to see if it's out of square. Then use your 4-ft. level to check both sides of the opening for plumb and the top of the opening for level. Mark where you think your new jambs will need to be shimmed out.

**2** **MEASURE FOR JAMB WIDTH.** It's important to cut your jambs about ⅛ in. wider than the wall thickness. This ensures that your molding will lie flat against the wall. Drywall-finished openings in most houses are about 4¾ in. thick. Measure wall thickness in several places, and add ⅛ in. to the largest width you get.

**3** **RIP YOUR JAMBS TO WIDTH.** Mark a piece of 1x6 jamb stock to the width you need. With your circular saw unplugged, adjust the saw's rip guide so you'll be cutting your jambs to the right width. Not sure? No problem. Rip a test piece of scrap wood, and see if it measures up. When you know the setting is right, rip all three pieces of jamb stock to width.

**4** **CUT & INSTALL THE HEAD JAMB.** Cut the head jamb to length for a snug fit. If the top of the opening came out level (step 1), you can simply nail the jamb against the drywall. If not, insert shims as necessary to bring the bottom face of the jamb into level. Always

insert shims in pairs, from opposite sides of the opening. Make sure the jamb is centered side to side, then drive a pair of 8d finish nails next to the shim. Keep checking for level, add shims in the gap as necessary, and nail about every 24 in.

**DO IT FAST**

**Using a table saw,** you can quickly and precisely rip boards to exact width and crosscut them to length. A portable saw like this one will soon become indispensable if you do a lot of trim and carpentry projects. Look for a model that comes with its own stand.

**DO IT RIGHT**

**Molding can easily split** when you nail it close to the end of a piece. To avoid this problem, predrill nail holes using a $1/16$-in. bit.

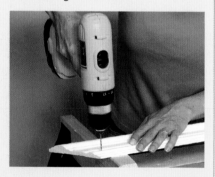

# Install the Casing

**5** **CUT & INSTALL THE SIDE JAMBS.** Measure from the head jamb to the floor on both sides, and cut a side jamb for each side. Shim one or both jambs if necessary, then install with pairs of 8d nails about every 24 in. Cut the shims off flush with jamb edges, using a utility knife or a handsaw.

**6** **LAY OUT THE REVEAL.** To lay out the reveal, set a combination square to $1/8$ in. Place a pencil in the notch in the end of the square's blade and run the square around the edges of your jambs.

**7** **INSTALL THE SIDE CASINGS.** Cut each piece to rough length, and hold it in place against its reveal line. Mark for the miter cut at the top reveal line. Using your combination square, extend the

miter line across the molding, then make the cut on your miter saw. Attach each side casing with pairs of 6d nails about every 24 in. Drive one nail into the jamb edge and the other through the drywall into the framing.

**8** **INSTALL THE HEAD CASING.** Cut the head casing to rough length and miter-cut one end. Hold the piece upside-down against the wall, with the tip of the miter cut touching the tip of the mating miter. (Have a helper hold the piece if you can't reach both ends.) This allows you to mark accurately for the remaining miter cut. Cut and

install the casing, then take a break. You still need to set nails below the surface, fill holes, caulk joints, sand, and paint. But the toughest carpentry work is done, and your passageway already looks great.

**5**

**6**

**7**

**8**

This door casing has Colonial origins and classic staying power. The flat section of the molding lends strength and mass. The outer contours add detail and delicacy.

When the bottom of a window jamb lacks a flat stool, as shown above, the best trim strategy often calls for miter joints at all four corners. The natural finish theme extends to the built-in desk.

The view is the star performer in this entryway, so a modest molding makes a fitting frame. Neutral tones for walls and trim make the most of this outdoor portrait.

## Mitered trim treatments that include mitered corners can look great around windows, doors, passageways, and even built-in cabinetry. There are dozens of different molding profiles that look distinctive when their contours are "wrapped" around a corner with well-made miter joints.

An easy way to add width and detail to a standard mitered casing is to add a simple band molding around the outside edge of the casing. Even if you go without this embellishment, take a clue from the blue hue. This textured wall finish looks great with the white, semigloss paint used on the trim.

# Wainscot

**Thin TONGUE-AND-GROOVE BOARDS** make a durable, great-looking wall that's easy to install

**A**SOLID-WOOD WAINSCOT is a great upgrade for almost any wall. Apart from the beauty it adds, there are practical benefits, too. Wood stands up well to the hard knocks that come from chairs, kids, and wayward feet. No wonder wainscots are popular in entryways, mudrooms, breakfast nooks, and bathrooms.

The beadboard wainscot we're building here is a traditional treatment that's easy to do. If the wall surface is smooth and flat, you can install the ⅜-in.-thick beadboard with panel adhesive. There's very little nailing to do until we get to the baseboard and cap parts of the project. You've probably got your wainscot room picked out already, so get your tape measure out and let's get started.

**LAY IT OUT**     **FIT THE INSIDE CORNERS**     **THEN THE OUTSIDE CORNERS**  **BASEBOARD & CAP**

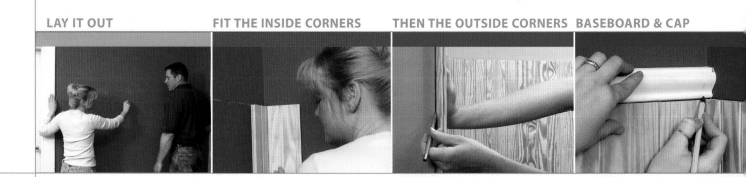

**There's no rule** about how high to make a wainscot as long as you don't divide the wall in half, which can look awkward. The room shown in this project has 9-ft. walls, and the wainscot is 5 ft. high for a farmhouse look.

**You don't need** to know stud locations to install the beadboard, but you do for the cap molding. An easy way to confirm stud locations is to drive a finish nail through the drywall in the spot where you think a stud may be. It's easy to tell when you hit a stud and when you don't. Do your test-nailing below the top edge of the wainscot, and make a pencil mark where you find each stud.

# Tools & Gear

*Keep your basic tool kit handy because you'll need a hammer, tape measure, and nail set.*

**DRILL & BIT.** Predrilling your nail holes will help to avoid splitting the wood. A cordless drill and 1/16-in. bit will do the job.

**CHOPSAW OR MITER BOX.** Either of these tools will handle the precise crosscuts and miters you need to make when installing the cap, baseboard, base cap, and shoe trim. A chopsaw is the faster way to go.

**CIRCULAR SAW.** Put a finish-cutting blade in your saw; you'll need it for cutting beadboard and baseboard pieces.

**BLOCK PLANE.** This small handplane will help you fine-tune the fit of outside corners.

**ROUND FILE.** You'll need a "rat-tail" file to fine-tune the cope joints in the cap moldings.

**FOUR-FOOT LEVEL.** You'll need a 4-ft. level to scribe level lines for the top of the wainscot.

**CHALKLINE.** This is to extend the level lines you make with the 4-ft. level.

**CAULKING GUN.** You'll use this to dispense construction adhesive and caulk.

**COPING SAW.** This small saw has a thin blade held in a C-shaped frame. You'll need it to cope the chair rail and (if you don't have a jigsaw) for making the cutouts for electrical switch and outlet boxes.

# What to Buy

**1| BEADBOARD.** $^3/_8$-in.-thick tongue-and-groove beadboard (also called beaded board) used in this project is available in different widths; $3^1/_8$ in. and $5^1/_4$ in. are the most common. For this project, we used $3^1/_8$-in.-wide boards. At home centers, beadboard paneling comes packed in bundles of boards that are 4 ft. or 8 ft. long. At lumberyards, it's sold in 2-ft. length increments. To calculate how much to buy, add up the length of your walls and subtract the window and door widths. Divide the result by the width of your beaded boards. For example, if you have 480 in. of wall length, 480 divided by 3 means you'll need about 160 boards that are $3^1/_8$ in. wide, or 92 boards in $5^1/_4$-in. width.

## PUTTING IT ALL TOGETHER

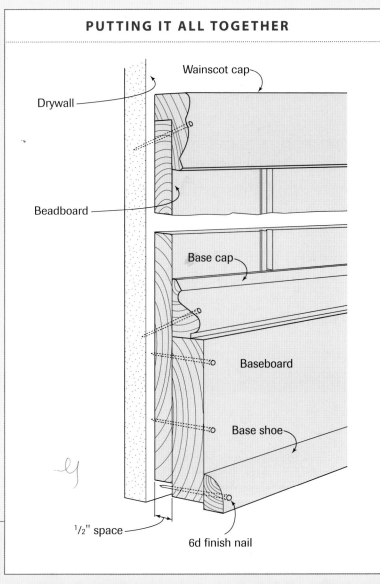

Wainscot cap

Drywall

Beadboard

Base cap

Baseboard

Base shoe

$^1/_2$" space

6d finish nail

**2| WAINSCOT CAP.** This molding fits over the top of the beadboard. Several styles are available—just make sure you get a cap molding designed to fit over $^3/_8$-in.-thick boards.

**3| BASEBOARD, BASE CAP & SHOE.** To go with the wide casings and traditional moldings in this old house, the bottom of the wainscot is covered with a 1x8 baseboard along with base cap and shoe. Your plan might call for a different baseboard height with or without the shoe and/or cap. Or you might choose a molded, one-piece baseboard.

**4| FINISH NAILS.** You'll need 4d ($1^1/_2$-in.) finish nails to install the base cap, 8d ($2^1/_2$-in.) nails for the baseboard, and 1-in. brads for the base shoe.

**5| SANDPAPER.** Use 120-grit sandpaper to sand putty patches for molding that will be painted.

**6| CONSTRUCTION ADHESIVE.** Several cartridges should give you enough for an average-sized room.

**7| YELLOW GLUE.** Have this wood glue on hand for gluing miters and molding together.

**8| CAULK & PUTTY.** Paintable latex acrylic caulk is the type you want. You'll use it to fill gaps and cover seams. The putty is for filling nail holes.

**9| PRIMER & PAINT.** If you plan to paint your molding, get primer recommended for use on bare wood. Also get some acrylic semigloss paint for interior trim.

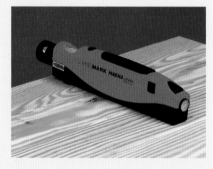

# Install the First Walls

**1** **LAY OUT THE TOP OF THE WAINSCOT.** Mark the height of the wainscot in one corner of the room, then use your level to draw a level line about 4 ft. long. Have a helper hold a chalkline at the other corner, exactly covering the line. Snap the line and check that it is level. Mark level lines on all walls.

**2** **CUT BOARDS TO LENGTH.** Keep in mind that the cap will overlap the tops of the boards, and the baseboard will cover bottom board edges. There's no need to make your cuts supersmooth or to land exactly on the layout line.

**3** **BEGIN AT A CORNER.** Start at the room's most visible inside corner. Apply construction adhesive to the back of a board, then press the board in place, with the tongue butted into the corner. Install the other corner piece, this time with the groove butting into the corner, covering the tongue. Next, work your way out from the corner, installing one board after another. Make sure to fit the tongue-and-groove joints together. Stop when you get two boards away from a doorway or another inside corner.

**4** **FIT THE LAST INSIDE CORNER PIECE.** At runs that end at doorways or inside corners, put the second-to-last board into place without adhesive. Measure the space where the final board has to fit, then measure at the top and bottom of the wainscot, in case the cut needs to taper slightly. Transfer your measurements to the last board, and cut along the line with a jigsaw or a circular saw. Test-fit the last two boards. If necessary, fine-tune the fit by planing the edge of the last board with a block plane.

**1**

**2**

**3**

**4**

### ▶ DO IT RIGHT

**When you encounter** an outlet box, mark where you have to notch your boards and cut the notches with a jigsaw or coping saw. You'll also need to install ⅜-in. box extenders. Ask for these at your home center or hardware store. To install an extender, turn the power off, remove the cover plate, and unscrew the receptacle or switch from the box. Without disconnecting the wires, install the extender and reattach the receptacle or switch.

# Corners, Caps & Baseboards

**5** **INSTALL THE LAST TWO INSIDE CORNER PIECES.** Spread adhesive on the last two pieces, and press them into place. Don't worry if there's a small gap between the molding and the corner; you'll cover it with caulk later.

**6** **MARK FOR AN OUTSIDE CORNER.** When you get to a piece that will have to be cut to meet an outside corner, put it in place and mark the cut along its back. Use a jigsaw or circular saw to make the cut, taking care to stay on the "waste" side of the line. Then

smooth the cut with a block plane. Plane up to the line, but don't plane the line away. You want the piece to extend just slightly past the corner to ensure a tight joint. Install the piece when you're done.

**7** **INSTALL THE SECOND OUTSIDE CORNER PIECE.** Mark the overlapping corner piece by holding it in place, as you did in step 6, then cut it and install it. You can plane for the final fit after the piece is in place. To close up the corner joint, use some yellow glue. If necessary, you can drive a few ¾-in. brads, too. Take a break when you get all your boards on the wall. Great job so far.

**8** **INSTALL THE BASEBOARD & CAP, THEN FINISH UP.** Install the baseboard, base cap, and shoe moldings. The cap molding that tops off the wainscot is also installed with cope joints at inside corners and miter joints at outside corners. The only difference is that you need to trim off the notch to butt a cap piece against the wall. Mark the cut, then make it with a coping saw. Now it's time to call in the finishing crew. Caulk the seams, fill the nail holes, sand, and paint.

**Above: This painted beadboard makes a durable finished wall in an informal dining area.**

**Above right: Don't think that a small space can't take wainscot. This bathroom tucked under the roof actually looks bigger paneled with an all-white wainscot and fixtures. Make sure your baseboard has enough height to balance the look of wainscot, as it does here.**

**Beadboard adds** durability and visual interest just about anywhere in your home. In addition to being used for wainscot paneling, beadboard is the traditional material for porch ceilings, for example.

Today, the beadboard look doesn't mean you have to install individual tongue-and-groove strips. As an alternative, you can use 4-ft. by 8-ft. sheets of beaded plywood.

Here's another take on how to handle the horizontal trim that caps a wainscot. Around a tub—and on the ceiling, where humidity is high—painted beadboard provides a tougher surface than painted drywall, and it adds a traditional flair.

This sunroom shows how versatile beaded tongue-and-groove boards can be. They are used floor to ceiling, as well as on the ceiling itself. The boards also make a shoe-resistant surface on a bench fitted with custom-made cushions.

# Crowning Touch

**This intricate CORNICE MOLDING looks like plaster, but it's made from lightweight foam and can simply be glued in place**

A N INTRICATELY DETAILED CORNICE can be the perfect topper for a room with a noble purpose, a high ceiling, or both. And if you take advantage of the lightweight foam moldings available today, this trim treatment can be far easier to accomplish than the finished results suggest. The urethane foam used in this type of molding makes the material much lighter than wood, so it's easier to handle. Foam molding won't split, crack, or warp, either, and it comes with a factory-applied coat of primer. A number of different profiles are available, so you can find something that suits your style. Once you do, plan to have a helper for this project because you'll need someone to hold up the other end.

CUT THE FIRST MITERS　　ADD THE STICKY STUFF　　NAIL IT UP　　CAULK & FINISH

**WHAT'S DIFFERENT?**

**If you need to buy** a caulking gun, avoid the cheapest models. As with other tools, a little extra money can buy you a lot of extra value. A top-notch gun will have a larger handle to give you some extra leverage for squeezing the caulk out. Two other features to look for: A built-in rod you can use to pierce the seal on a caulk canister and a built-in snip for cutting the plastic tip.

# Tools & Gear

*Keep your basic tool kit handy because you'll need a hammer, nail set, and tape measure for this project.*

**MITER BOX.** To make smooth, accurate cuts in the crown molding, you'll need a miter box that comes with its own fine-tooth saw. To cut wide moldings like the one used in this project, you may need to attach a tall plywood auxiliary fence to your miter box. Check out COOL TOOL on the facing page.

**CAULKING GUN.** You'll need one to dispense the adhesive that bonds the molding to the wall and ceiling.

**PUTTY KNIFE.** Get a putty knife with a small (1-in.-wide) and flexible blade; you'll need it to push wood putty into nail holes and gaps in joints.

**STEPLADDERS.** You'll need one 6-ft. ladder for you and one for your helper. It's time to walk next door and borrow that extra ladder.

**TRIM BRUSH.** The foam trim for this project comes preprimed, but it will still require primer and finish coats of paint. Get a top-quality trim brush that's about 3 in. wide.

# What to Buy

**1 | CROWN MOLDING.** The molding used in this project is a crown dentil molding that extends 3³⁄₈ in. across the ceiling and 4 in. down the wall. It comes in 16-ft. lengths. Some foam-molding profiles are available in only one or two lengths. As a result, you may have to buy a bit more than you need.

**2 | CONSTRUCTION ADHESIVE.** Make sure to get the goop recommended by the molding manufacturer. This construction adhesive comes in caulk-type canisters. You'll need one canister for each 16-ft. length of molding.

**3 | NAILS OR SCREWS.** Use 8d finish nails to install the molding on gypsum wallboard. If your room has plaster walls, buy 2¹⁄₂-in. trim head screws. Add a cordless drill and a square trim-head screw bit to your tools and gear list.

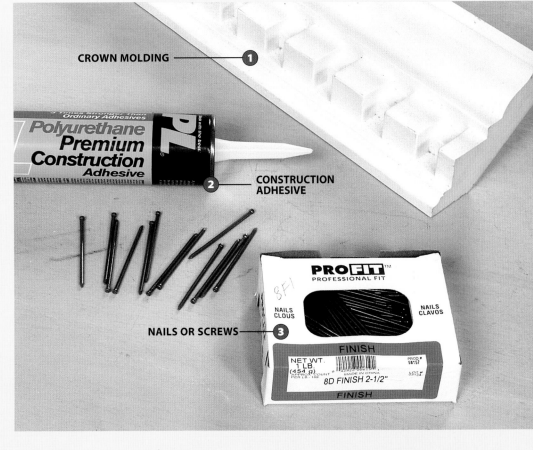

CROWN MOLDING — 1

CONSTRUCTION ADHESIVE — 2

NAILS OR SCREWS — 3

**4 | FILLER & CAULK.** You will have gaps in molding joints and between the molding and ceiling and wall surfaces. Buy the filler and caulk recommended by the molding manufacturer.

**5 | PRIMER & PAINT.** Buy a water-based interior primer and a latex semigloss trim paint. Top-quality latex paints say "100% acrylic" on the label.

## COOL TOOL

**Whether you are using** a standard miter box like the one shown here or a motorized version, you can improve your tool by adding a plywood auxiliary fence. The wood fence adds some extra height that is helpful when cutting larger moldings. A piece of ¹⁄₂-in. plywood about 5 in. high and 2 ft. long should do the trick. If your saw has holes in its metal fence, you can drive screws through these holes to mount your auxiliary fence. If not, drill your own holes or mount your auxiliary fence with double-sided tape. Before using the saw, use a square to make sure the fence is at a right angle to the base, and cut through the wooden fence at 45 degrees to the left and 45 degrees to the right.

## Making the Cuts

**1** **START WITH OUTSIDE CORNER MITERS.** Dentil molding looks best when it turns outside corners with a full dentil. Begin by cutting each piece about 3 in. longer than it needs to be. To cut the right side of the miter, set the blade 45 degrees to your right. Place the molding upside down, extending left of the blade. (Pretend the base of your miter box is the ceiling and the fence is the wall.) Make the cut so it goes through the right front corner of a dentil. Next, swing the blade to the left and cut the mating piece.

## ▪▪ DO IT FAST

**Left, right, upside down!** Your brain can blow a fuse trying to think through every miter cut. So think them through just once. Take four short pieces of molding and follow steps 1 and 6 to create a sample outside miter joint (if you need one) and a sample inside miter joint. Label each sample piece—"left inside," etc. Before slicing through that expensive molding, you can hold a sample in position on the saw to make sure the cut is the one you really need.

**2** **MITER THE OPPOSITE ENDS.** If the piece ends midwall, cut it square on the end so the next piece can butt right against it. Otherwise, set up your miter box and molding to make either another outside miter or an inside miter joint at the opposite end of each piece you cut in step 1. Use your sample joints to confirm that the blade is angled the right way. When you're measuring for a miter cut on the opposite end, remember that it's better to cut a piece too long rather than too short.

**3** **TEST-FIT, THEN BUTTER UP.** Temporarily tack the pieces you've cut into place by driving finish nails only partway into the wall. Confirm that joints fit together. Then put a squiggly line of construction adhesive on the top and bottom edges that will contact the ceiling and wall. Also put adhesive on outside miter joints.

**4** **NAIL IT UP.** Drive 8d nails about every 16 in. Use the same spacing if you're driving trim-head screws into plaster walls and ceilings. Place your fasteners in the thin areas of the molding, not in the dentils. Don't worry if you aren't fastening into studs or ceiling joists. The fasteners just need to hold the molding in place until the adhesive sets.

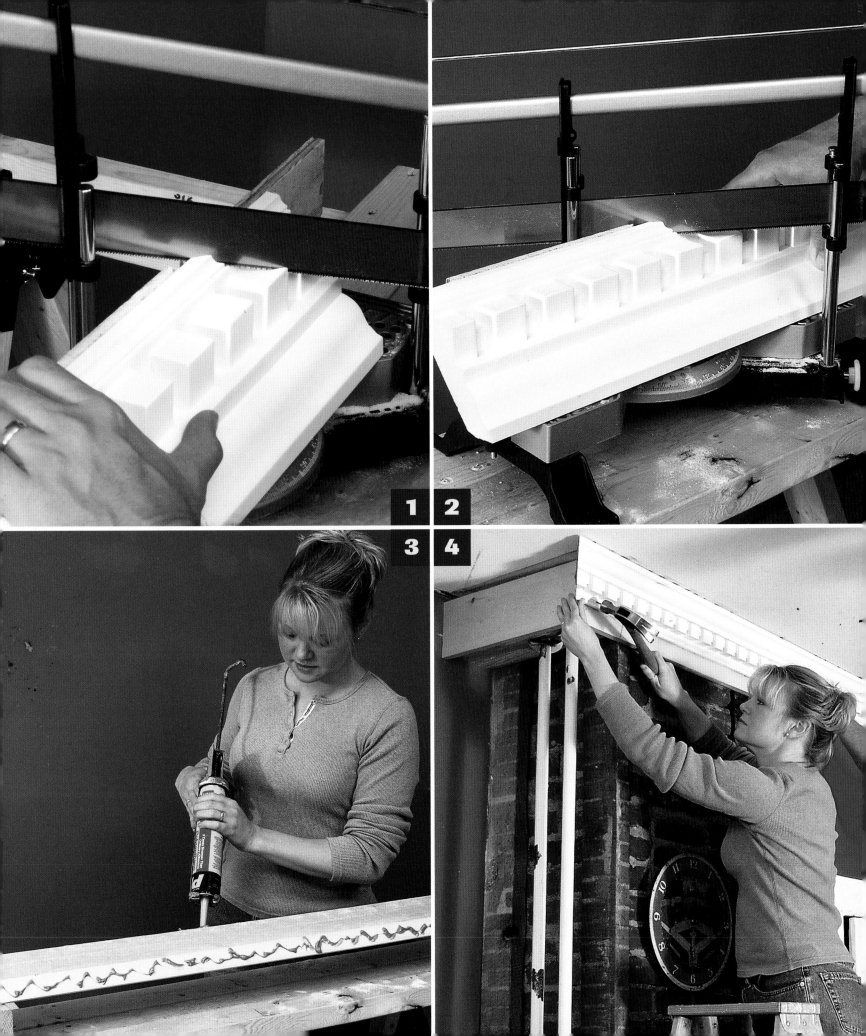

**1** **2**

**3** **4**

**▶ DO IT RIGHT**

**Foam molding cuts** easily, but avoid powering your way through each cut with rapid strokes. This tends to create rough edges. Instead, just let the saw's weight do the cutting, and slice through the molding with smooth, slow strokes.

**◆ DO IT NOW**

**It's smart to cut molding** to rough length before you position it on the miter box for final cutting; this gives you a more manageable length to maneuver. A short "toolbox-size" handsaw is a good tool for making these cuts. Just what is rough length, anyway? It's anywhere from 2 in. to 6 in. more than what the final length will be.

# Putting It Up

**5** **MARK FOR "MIRROR-IMAGE" INSIDE MITERS.** Just like outside miters, inside miters require symmetrical, "mirror-image" miter cuts to be made in the joining pieces. Measure how much of the dentil detail remains on each inside miter you've already cut and installed. Then transfer this measurement to the molding you need to cut to complete the joint.

**6** **CUT INSIDE CORNERS.** To cut the right side of an inside corner, swing the blade 45 degrees to the left and position the molding upside down on the left side of the saw. Do the reverse to cut the right side of an inside miter. Before you make each miter cut, make sure the blade is positioned on the "waste" side of the marks you made in the previous step.

**7** **MATCH UP THE BUTT JOINTS.** Where lengths of molding butt together, the dentil pattern needs to remain as uniform as possible. To maintain this uniformity, you'll probably need to square-cut the molding between two corner joints and insert a "right-size" piece to give you correct dentil spacing. Measure, mark, and cut the pieces you need to get the best dentil pattern spacing.

**8** **INSTALL REMAINING PIECES, THEN FINISH UP.** Work your way around the room, cutting and installing all remaining pieces of molding. Then set all nails, fill holes with putty, and caulk all gaps between sections of molding and between molding and wall or ceiling surfaces. Smooth rough surfaces and sharp edges with sandpaper, then finish with primer and trim paint.

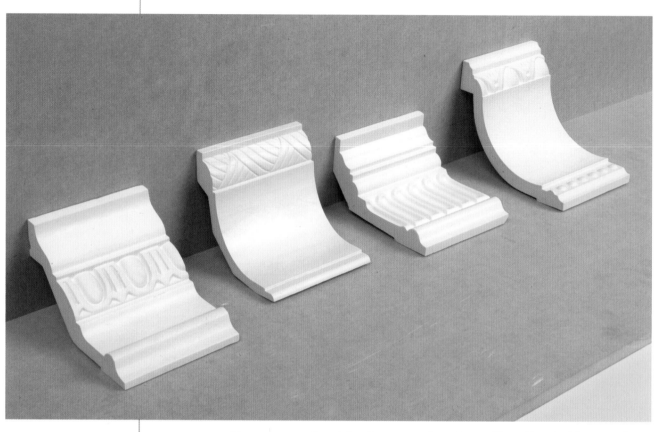

These cross-sections taken from several cornice profiles tell the inside story of plastic's appeal as a molding material. The core is made from foam that's dense but light and dimensionally stable. The outer "show" surface can be formed to include intricate details, and the factory-applied primer provides a smooth base for finish coats of paint.

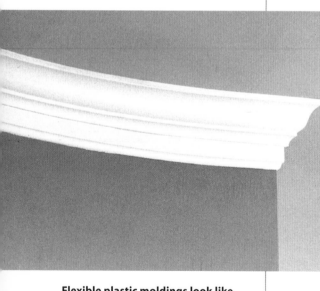

Flexible plastic moldings look like wood or plaster but can bend to fit against curved walls. Available in different profiles, these moldings come preprimed. But don't add finish coats of paint until after the molding is in place.

# It's as good as wood, so it's easy to understand why plastic moldings are becoming more and more popular. They're lighter than wood versions, and they don't warp, split, or bow out of shape. Easy to cut and install, these moldings can look just like painted wood or plaster when your installation work is done. You can even get plastic moldings with a factory-applied finish that looks remarkably like real wood. As the selection of plastic moldings grows, so do your design possibilities. Here are a few ideas to get you started.

The cornice in this kitchen proves that two coves are better than one. The small cove in the oak molding used to trim out the top of the wall cabinets is echoed by the cove profile in the larger molding.

Yes that's plastic! Some urethane molding profiles, including this crown, are available with a surface finish that looks like real wood. You can even stain this molding any color you like as long as you use a nonpenetrating stain.

# Building a Better Baseboard

This **THREE-PIECE TRIM** treatment is a lot easier to install than it looks

**N**OBODY LIKES GETTING STUCK in an ugly pair of shoes. That's why every room in your house deserves a nice baseboard to dress up the bottom of the wall and create a pleasing transition where the floor stops and the wall begins. The three-piece baseboard we're building here is a great upgrade in any room that's hampered by skimpy base molding. And here's something interesting you'll discover when you tackle this project: The three-piece design of the baseboard can actually make it easier to install than some one-piece baseboards, especially if you're dealing with irregular wall and floor surfaces. Let's get started . . .

**ROOM & BOARD**      **MAKING MITERS**      **COPING SKILLS**      **FINAL SAND**

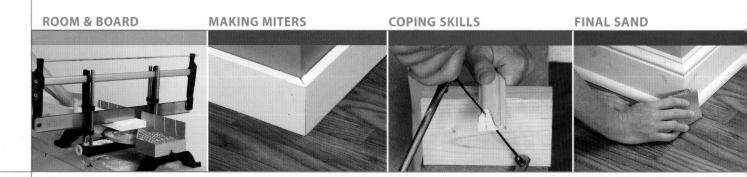

**Combination square or** angle square? Both work for laying out square or 45-degree angles. The angle square has calibrations for laying out loads of other angles, too. And this thick, durable square also works well as a guide for making square cuts with your circular saw.

**The combination square** has a ruler that slides in the handle, making it ideal for marking lines and reveals. The best combination squares have a built-in level and a scribing point that stows in the handle.

# Tools & Gear

*Keep your basic tool kit handy because you'll need a hammer, tape measure, and nail set. Also gather up the tools listed below.*

**DRILL & BIT.** You'll need a corded or cordless drill equipped with a $1/16$-in. bit to predrill nail holes for scarf joints.

**MITER BOX.** You'll use a miter box to make exact cuts in trim pieces. A good miter box like the one used in this project comes with its own fine-tooth saw and costs about $40.

**SQUARE.** Either a combination square or an angle square will do. See "WHAT'S DIFFERENT?" at left.

**COPING SAW.** This small saw has a thin blade designed for cutting curves. You'll need it to cut the cope joints in cap molding pieces. Since these blades break easily, make sure you've got several spare blades on hand.

**FILES.** With a small, flat file and a tapered, round "rat-tail" file you can fine-tune the fit of your cope joints.

**CAULKING GUN.** You'll use this to dispense the caulk to seal the joint between wall and casing.

**TRIM BRUSH.** Your new trim deserves a nice finish. Apply it with a high-quality trim brush that's 2 in. to 3 in. wide. If you're using oil-based finish, make sure to use a natural-bristle brush or a synthetic brush recommended for use with oil or alkyd finishes.

## DO IT RIGHT

**L**ook closely at an unfinished board and you may notice a series of ripples running across the surface. These are caused by planer blades during the milling process. When you apply paint or varnish, these surface irregularities can become quite noticeable. That's why it's smart to sand the wood surface smooth before you use a board to trim a room. Start with 80-grit sandpaper, and finish up with 120-grit sandpaper. A belt sander gets the job done quickly, but a random-orbit sander will also work.

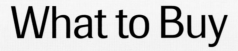

CAP
MOLDING ② —

① — BASEBOARD

③ — SHOE
MOLDING

# What to Buy

**1 BASEBOARD.** The baseboard will be 1x4, 1x6, or 1x8 (this project used 1x4). You can use either #2 pine or finger-jointed boards that are preprimed (as shown here). To compile your lumber order, measure each wall length and subtract door openings. Add some extra (about 10%) to make sure you'll have enough. You'll need cap molding and shoe molding of the same lengths.

**2 CAP MOLDING.** This molding creates a graceful transition between the baseboard and wall. "Caps" come in several profiles and heights. Find one that looks good on the top edge of your baseboard.

**3 SHOE MOLDING.** Shoe molding closes up the gap between the baseboard and floor. It comes in several thicknesses and heights. Here we used molding that's ½ in. thick at the bottom and ¾ in. high.

**4 FINISH NAILS.** You'll need 8d (2½-in.) finish nails for the baseboard, 4d (1½-in.) nails for the cap, and 1-in. brads for the shoe molding.

**5 SANDPAPER.** Use 120-grit sandpaper to sand putty patches for molding that will be painted.

**6 WOOD GLUE & PUTTY.** Yellow wood glue will be used at miter joints. Putty is for filling nail holes.

**7 CAULK.** Buy a paintable latex acrylic caulk, so you can fill small gaps between the wall and the top of the baseboard.

**8 PRIMER & PAINT.** Use a good-quality primer under two coats of semigloss trim paint.

## PLANNING THE JOB

**A good prep step** for this project is to draw a plan view of the room and identify what lengths of trim you need and which joints go where. For example, all three baseboard trim pieces will butt against a door casing. On inside corners, the two boards simply butt together, while the cap and shoe moldings need to meet with cope joints. On outside corners, all pieces meet each other with miter joints. And along the length of a wall, there should be an angled scarf joint where one piece of molding ends and another joins it to continue the molding run.

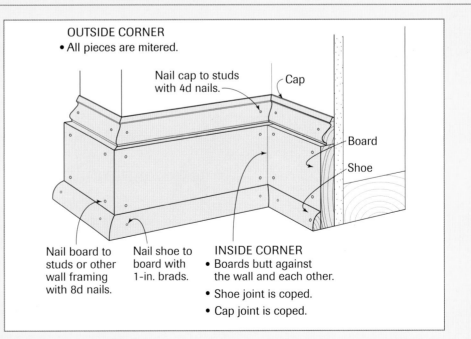

OUTSIDE CORNER
• All pieces are mitered.

Nail cap to studs
with 4d nails.

Cap

Board

Shoe

Nail board to
studs or other
wall framing
with 8d nails.

Nail shoe to
board with
1-in. brads.

INSIDE CORNER
• Boards butt against
the wall and each other.
• Shoe joint is coped.
• Cap joint is coped.

An electronic stud finder will help you locate studs, joists, and other framing members quickly behind wall and ceiling surfaces. You can pencil these locations on the wall or ceiling and know where you have to drive a nail to hit solid backing.

**+ WHAT CAN GO WRONG**

When you're nailing trim, it's easy to forget how easily a hammer blow can dent the wood. You can avoid this damage by remembering not to drive finish nails all the way in. Instead, leave the head of the nail proud of the wood surface (slightly above it), then set it below the surface using your hammer and a nail set.

# Install the Board

**1** GET THE FIRST BOARD UP! After marking stud locations on the wall just above where the baseboard will be installed, you can cut and install your first board. Make it a board that simply butts against the wall. If a baseboard heater gets in the way, stop the board about ⅛ in.

away from the edge of the unit. Cut the board to length on your miter saw. Install each board by driving two 8d finish nails at each stud location.

**2** INSTALL SOME MORE. Cut and install as many butt-jointed pieces as you can. If you need more than one board to cover a wall, go to the next step. To mark a board that fits against door casing, try this trick: Make a board-sized notch in a small, rectangular piece of plywood or pine. Put the baseboard in place, letting one end run past the door casing. Hold the jig against the casing and over the board, then mark your cut line along the edge of the jig.

**3** USE SCARF JOINTS AS NEEDED. If you need to install more than one board along a wall, cut a 45-degree scarf joint like the pros do; it's less noticeable than a butt joint. Try to locate the scarf joint near a stud. Set your miter saw to make a 45-degree cut. Cut and install one board, then the other, taking care to glue and align the joint. Take note: Scarf joints also work for cap and shoe molding.

**4** COMPLETE OUTSIDE CORNERS. Don't measure for these miter cuts; it's more accurate to hold the board in its installed position and mark the outside miter cut right against the corner of the wall. Use an angle square or a combination square to mark the

miter cut on the edge of the board. Position the board carefully in your miter box so that the entire blade is on the "waste" side of the cut. Install each outside corner as you mark and cut it.

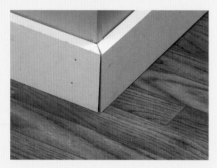
# Install Cap & Shoe

**5**   **INSTALL THE FIRST CAP PIECE.** Square-cut the first piece to fit between two inside corners. Install the cap by driving 1-in. brads into each stud. Try this tip: Angle the nail downward so the cap will be pulled tightly against the top of the board.

**6**   **COPE THE CAP.** Cut the next cap piece about 6 in. longer than it needs to be. On your miter saw, make a 45-degree cut on the end to be coped as if you were cutting an inside miter joint. Next, cut along this profile with your coping saw. Angle the blade back to remove all the wood that could stop the profile from fitting tightly against the mating piece. Don't worry if you have to stop cutting in one direction and start cutting in another.

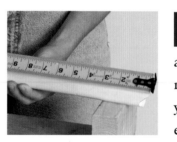

**7**   **TUNE THE FIT & FASTEN THE PIECE.** Test-fit the cope against a scrap of cap. Using a file, fine-tune the fit of the joint. When it's right, measure, mark, and cut the cap piece so you can nail it in place. The opposite end will be either a butt joint (to fit against the wall or a door casing), a scarf joint (to join another length of cap molding), or an outside miter joint (to end at an outside corner of the wall). Repeat these last two steps until you've finished installing all the cap molding.

**8**   **MAKE THE SHOE FIT.** Install the shoe molding one piece at a time, working your way around the room as you did with board and cap pieces. All shoe joints can be mitered, and you can begin the installation at an inside corner. To install each piece, hold it firmly against the floor and drive the nail at a slight downward angle into the baseboard (not the floor).

**9**   **FINISH UP.** With cutting and nailing done, set all nail heads just below the wood surface, fill the holes with putty, sand surfaces smooth, and apply paint. While you're sanding the nail holes, use the sandpaper to slightly round over all outside miter joints.

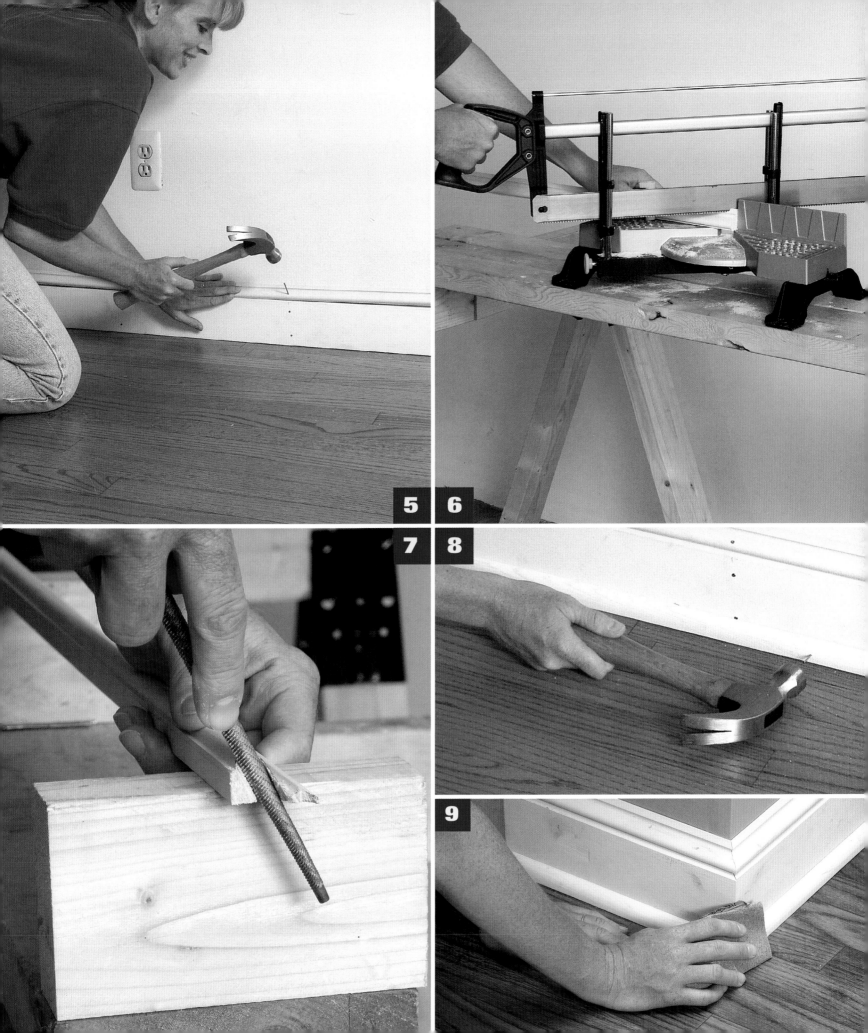

**5** **6**

**7** **8**

**9**

This built-in cabinet features an integral baseboard plinth that's beefy enough to offer a traditional, well-heeled appearance. Flat baseboard is trimmed with shoe molding and a base cap.

**As the name suggests, baseboard** can be thought of as the basis or beginning for any room's trim treatment. That's why you'll want to make sure the style and proportions of your baseboard relate well to other molding details, including built-in cabinetry. The design ideas shown here will help you get this dialog started.

A deep baseboard anchors this paneled wall, and provides plenty of space for installing receptacles. Make sure that door-jamb casing is deep enough so that the baseboard— and paneling in this case—can butt against it comfortably.

In this room, the baseboard was kept simple so the eye would naturally be drawn to the elaborate crown molding. Carpeted rooms should never use a shoe molding. Install baseboard before carpeting and butt the carpet to the baseboard.

It's not every day that you see baseboard and baseboard cap finished with contrasting colors, but why not? It's a cheery detail in this busy family home.

# Mantelpiece

With or without a fireplace, **MITERED MOLDINGS** make this ornate shelf fit for trophies, trinkets & other treasures

ADMIT IT: YOU'VE BEEN ADMIRING these ornate display shelves in your favorite home-furnishing catalogs. But in the time it takes to order a factory-made shelf and get it shipped to your home, you could build and finish several of these shelves yourself. The materials for the shelf shown here will cost you less than $15, so you'll save loads of money. And since you're in charge, you can design mantelpiece shelves in any size and style you like by combining different moldings with the square-edged boards used to make top and bottom pieces. Finish up with your choice of paint, stain, or varnish, and you'll give this project a unique style that can't be found in any catalog.

CUTTING CROWN          GLUE               SAND & FINISH          HANG IT!

**Planning to finish** the shelf differently from the crown? Perhaps an oak shelf with a clear finish or stained and varnished pine? To speed the process, sand and finish the shelf and paint the crown before assembly so you'll just have to touch up at the end.

## ❖ COOL TOOL

**It's called a palm sander** because it fits in one hand, leaving the other free to hold the work. Palm sanders take a quarter-sheet of sandpaper and make quick work of jobs like smoothing the shelf. You can even use it to make nicely rounded edges.

# Tools & Gear

*Keep your basic tool kit handy because you'll need a hammer, tape measure, and nail set.*

**MITER BOX.** To miter the molding you'll need a miter box. A good miter box like the one used in this project comes with its own fine-tooth saw and costs about $40. Avoid cheaper wooden or plastic boxes that have slotted sides. If you want pro-level speed and precision, get a chopsaw .

**COMBINATION SQUARE.** This adjustable square is a versatile layout tool. For this project, you'll use a combination square to mark where the top of the molding meets the bottom of the shelf board.

**DRILL.** You'll need one to predrill holes for the hanger screws.

**CIRCULAR SAW.** You'll need this power saw to cut the shelf board to size. To ensure smooth cuts, make sure you've got a finish-cutting blade in your saw.

**PAINTBRUSH & RAGS.** Your display shelf deserves a fine finish. A good-quality 3-in. paintbrush is what you need to apply primer and paint or stain and varnish. If you're using oil-base paint or varnish, make sure to use a natural-bristle brush or a synthetic brush recommended for use with oil or alkyd finishes. If your finishing plans involve applying stain or varnish, also get a few clean, soft rags.

## DO IT RIGHT

**To prep your miter box** for the cutting work in this project, anchor the box to a workbench or to sawhorses with some screws. Most miter boxes have holes in the feet or base for screwdown attachment. The other prep step involves attaching a plywood auxiliary fence to your saw's standard fence. A higher fence that you can cut into will help you get more exact cuts in your molding (see COOL TOOL on p. 99).

# What to Buy

**1 CROWN MOLDING.** The molding used for this project is
$9/16$ in. thick and $4^5/8$ in. wide. You'll find crown molding in different sizes and shapes at your home center or lumberyard.
Choose any profile you like as long as the overall width of
the molding is at least $3^1/2$ in. Molding is usually sold by the
foot. Get a piece that's straight and at least 1 ft. longer than
the planned length of your finished shelf.

**2 5/4 X 6 PINE.** A 5/4 x 6 pine board is really about 1 in.
thick and $5^1/2$ in. wide. Look for a straight, flat, knot-free piece
that's as long as you want your shelf to be.

**3 BRADS.** These tiny nails are for fastening the molding to
the underside of the shelf. Buy a small box of 1-in. brads.

**4 YELLOW GLUE.** This woodworking glue will bond the
molding pieces to each other and to the shelf. The brads just
hold things together until the glue sets.

**5 SANDPAPER.** Buy a couple of sheets of 120 grit for
rounding the shelf edges and sanding putty patches smooth.

**6 WOOD PUTTY.** Make sure you have some putty on hand
for filling brad holes and small gaps in joints.

**7 FINISH.** For a painted finish, get interior primer and semi-

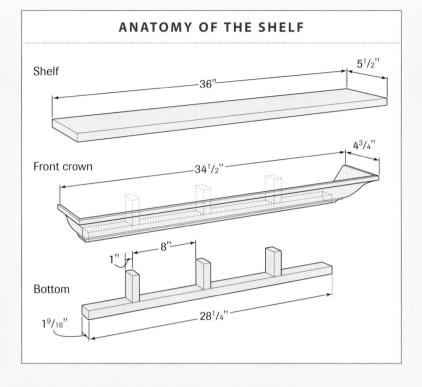

**ANATOMY OF THE SHELF**

gloss trim paint. Use polyurethane varnish for a clear finish. Stain
or tinted varnish are other finishing options.

**8 FLUSH-MOUNT HARDWARE.** One piece of each interlocking
pair mounts on the wall; the other is fastened to the back of the
finished shelf. You'll need two sets of flush-mount hardware for
this project.

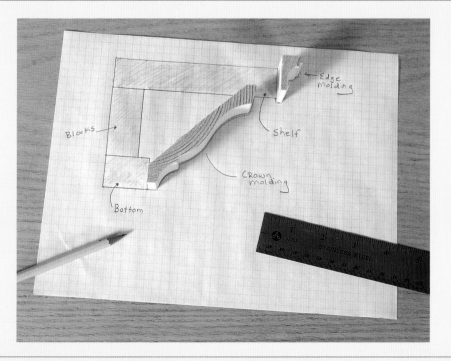

## DESIGN YOUR SHELF

**You can design a mantelpiece** shelf with
a single molding or combine different
moldings to build up a larger and more elaborate architectural detail. Here's a design strategy
that's easy and fun: Using your miter box, slice
off an inch or so of the molding or moldings
you plan to use. Place these molding cross
sections on a piece of graph paper, combining
them with the full-scale section drawings of
the other parts of your mantelpiece—the shelf,
bottom, and backer blocks. This exercise will
show you what the completed mantelpiece
profile will look like and what the dimensions
of the parts need to be.

▶ **DO IT RIGHT**

**The proportions** of your display shelf will depend on the size of the crown molding you plan to use. To get an exact idea of how high and deep the molding is when it's installed, cut off a small section and place it against a framing square, as shown in the drawing. Now you'll have an easy time determining what the width of the shelf should be.

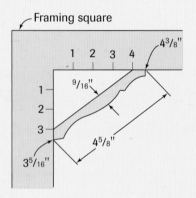

Framing square
1 2 3 4
4³⁄₈"
9⁄₁₆"
1
2
3
4⁵⁄₈"
3⁵⁄₁₆"

# Attach the Front Crown

**1** **CUT & MARK THE SHELF BOARD.** Using a circular saw, cut the 5/4 x 6 stock to the length you choose—36 in. is shown here. Then decide how far over the crown molding you want the shelf board to extend—¾ in. in this case. Use your combination square to mark the underside of the shelf board, showing where the top edge of each molding piece will fit.

**2** **CUT THE FRONT MOLDING PIECE.** Make the miter cut for the left side of the front molding piece. To do this, put the molding upside down on the left side of the saw, and swing the blade 45 degrees to your right. Align the blade with your cut line, and make the cut. Holding the front molding piece in its installed position on the shelf board, mark where the opposite miter needs to be cut. Reverse the setup of your first miter to cut this opposite one.

**3** **ATTACH THE FRONT CROWN.** Start 1-in. brads into the molding, orienting them so they will go straight into the bottom of the shelf board. Put yellow glue on the narrow top edge of the molding. Holding the molding in place along your layout line, drive and set the nails.

**4** **CUT THE SIDE MOLDING PIECES.** Cut outside miters on the two pieces of molding that join the front piece. Put each piece in place, and mark where they cross the back of the shelf. Square-cut both side pieces to length.

**1**

**2**

**3**

**4**

⊘ **UPGRADE**

**Prefer the look of natural wood?**
If so, you can make your mantelpiece shelf from oak crown molding and an oak shelf board. Both of these ingredients are in stock at most home centers and lumberyards. Finish the project with a couple of coats of polyurethane varnish. Oak is a lot harder than pine, so predrill all your brad and nail holes.

⬤ **NEED A HAND?**

**Want to give the edges** of your shelf a gentle curve? You can do this by using a block plane. Adjust the blade to take a light cut (you can test this on scrap stock), then plane the ends of the shelf first, followed by the shelf's front edges. You'll still need to complete the smoothing at the shelf edges with sandpaper, but the block plane treatment adds a nice handcrafted touch.

# Finish It Up

**5** **CUT & INSTALL THE BOTTOM PIECE.** Using a circular saw, cut your bottom board to its finished width. Square-cut one end of the board, and hold it in place along the bottom edge of the front molding. Mark it so you can cut it to final length, then make the cut using your miter box. Attach the bottom to the front molding piece with glue and 1-in. brads.

**6** **INSTALL SIDE MOLDINGS & BLOCKS.** Attach the side molding pieces with glue and brads. Make sure to spread glue generously on miter joints, then fasten the side pieces to the shelf board and the bottom. To bridge the gap between the shelf board and the bottom, cut three blocks. Space them evenly apart, and install them with glue and 6d finish nails.

**7** **FILL, SAND & FINISH.** Fill all nail holes with wood putty; also putty up any gaps between joints. When the filler has hardened, give your shelf a thorough sanding. The shelf edges will look great if you just cup a folded piece of sandpaper in your hands and run it along the top and bottom edges. Apply primer and two coats of trim paint.

**8** **HANG IT UP.** Lightly pencil a level line on the wall where you want the top of the shelf to be. Screw your hanger hardware to the back edge of the shelf board and to the wall. Fasten into studs if possible; otherwise, attach hanger brackets to the wall with screws and drywall anchors. Install your mantelpiece, then collect some treasures and curios to show off on this special shelf.

**5** **6**

**7** **8**

One shelf can have two finishes. The top of this display shelf is a cherry board finished with clear varnish. The molding detail below is painted in an antique blue color.

Building your own mantelpiece gives you the opportunity to get the proportions right. This example fits nicely over the fireplace. Its earth-toned finish was inspired by the brickwork.

## The great thing about making your own mantelpiece shelves is that you can custom-design each one to fit a particular space and express your own sense of style. With some mitering mastery and a selection of your favorite molding profiles, the possibilities are limitless. In fact, if you've finished installing the crown molding in a room, you may have enough left over to build a matching shelf or two.

Think of all the uses...displaying your most beautiful candlesticks in the dining room or your favorite perfumes in the powder room. How about two shelves, or even several, perhaps of different lengths, to create a striking display of collectibles in the living room? Or let a plant or two take advantage of a sunny wall by giving them a shelf to perch on.

Who says you need a fireplace? This mantlepiece can overlook a hot bath instead of a hearth. The trim treatment on the bottom of the shelf includes a stock crown molding above a dentil molding. Bringing a green tile from the wall to the paint store ensured a color match for the shelf.

White is right when you want to create a classic appearance, even in a small display shelf. Use the same molding detail to build shelves in different sizes—this gives you plenty of possibilities for creating a unique wallscape.

# Painted Cabinets

**Brush on a MAJOR MAKEOVER,** then complete the transformation with new hinges and handles

I F YOU'RE FAMILIAR WITH THE WORKING END of a paintbrush and roller, then you already have the skills to give your kitchen one of the most dramatic makeovers possible—at the lowest possible cost. Go lighter or brighter, cool it down, or spice it up—with color alone, you can give your whole kitchen a new look. Replace the pulls, handles, and hinges, and you'll create an even greater impact. Be sure to clean your surfaces thoroughly first, then apply the paint, attach your new hardware, and get ready for compliments.

SAND THE SURFACES        APPLY THE PAINT              REMOUNT THE DOORS          ADD NEW HARDWARE

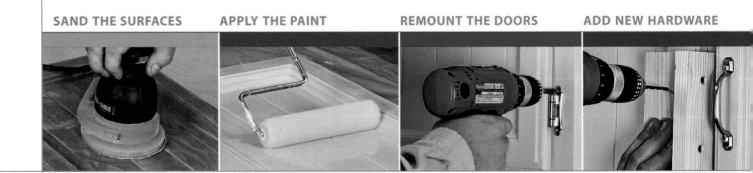

▶ **DO** IT RIGHT

**To get a smooth, roller-mark-free** finish on painted surfaces, use the "striking off" technique the pros use. After you've rolled the entire surface with paint, go back and position the roller at the top of the surface. Then roll it all the way down the length in one continuous stroke. Start back at the top, right next to the area you just rolled. Repeat as needed to strike off the whole surface.

❖ COOL TOOL

**If you're sanding your cabinets** by hand, use a sanding block to evenly distribute pressure. A sanding block is easy to make: Just wrap a third of a sheet of sandpaper around a 5-in. section of a 1x4.

# Tools & Gear

*If you've done any painting in your home, you'll probably have most of the tools you need to paint cabinets. The only specialty tools involved are for removing and adding hardware.*

**CLEANING SUPPLIES.** To get a good paint bond, you'll need to clean your cabinets thoroughly. A bucket and stiff bristle brush coupled with some trisodium phosphate (TSP) work well to remove built-up dirt. Be sure to wear rubber gloves and eye protection when working with TSP.

**PAINTER'S TAPE, DROP CLOTHS, LATEX GLOVES & RAGS.** Keep paint off walls, floors, and countertops with painter's tape and drop cloths—keep it off your hands by wearing gloves. You'll also want rags on hand to handle spills.

**STEPLADDER.** Reach the tops of wall cabinets with a stepladder when cleaning, priming, or painting.

**AWL.** The sharp point of an awl lets you indent screw locations for hardware. The indent also serves as a starting point for a drill bit.

**SCREWDRIVER OR CORDLESS DRILL/DRIVER.** You can remove and install doors and hardware with a screwdriver, but a drill/driver will speed up the job.

**SELF-CENTERING DRILL BIT.** This nifty drill accessory makes it easy to drill perfectly centered mounting holes for hinges.

**COMBINATION SQUARE.** The square's adjustable blade makes it the perfect tool for positioning hardware quickly and accurately.

**RANDOM-ORBIT SANDER & 150-GRIT SANDPAPER.** Cabinets need to be roughed up to give primer and paint something to "bite" into. A random-orbit sander works best since it won't leave tiny swirl marks like an orbital sander might.

**SMALL ROLLER & PAINT TRAY.** The fastest way to apply paint to cabinets is to roll it on. A small 3-in. to 4-in. foam roller is ideal for this.

**FOAM BRUSHES.** Even if you use a roller, you'll still need a 2-in. foam brush to handle edges and details—like the molded edges of raised panels.

**PUTTY KNIFE.** This tool is useful for filling holes with putty and scraping away old paint.

## WHAT'S DIFFERENT?

**S**ealers (often referred to as sanding sealers) are intended for use on bare wood only. Primers, on the other hand, can be applied to previously painted wood. Primers do a couple of things: They seal any open pores and help lock in stains. They also provide a better foundation for new paint because they are formulated to adhere or "bite" into the old paint better than a new coat of paint can.

# What to Buy

*The supplies you'll need to paint your cabinets are inexpensive. What can cost a bit, though, is the hardware. Your total price tag will depend on how many pieces you need and the cost per item.*

**1| PUTTY OR FILLER.** You'll need this to fill in the holes used to mount your old hardware. Solvent-based fillers are the best since they shrink less and dry quicker than water-based fillers. Ask for help before buying though—not all solvent-based fillers accept paint well.

**2| PRIMER & PAINT.** To choose a primer and paint for your cabinets, ask for help at your local hardware store or home center. The type you use will depend on the existing finish. Oil-based primers usually bond better with old finishes than water-based primers do—but they also have a strong odor and take longer to dry. You can cover either with latex enamel paint. Enamel will create a tougher finish that's more resistant to staining and chipping than regular latex paint will.

**3| NEW HARDWARE.** You'll need one pair of hinges for every door and either a pull or knob for each drawer and door. This can get expensive—especially if you choose high-end hardware. But since most hardware stores and home centers have pulls and knobs that cost less than two bucks apiece, you can keep hardware costs below $100 with some wise shopping. If you like the current position of your knobs and pulls, try to find new hardware that matches up with the old mounting holes. If you find suitable hardware, you can skip filling in the old holes in the drawers and doors with putty.

### TYPES OF HINGES

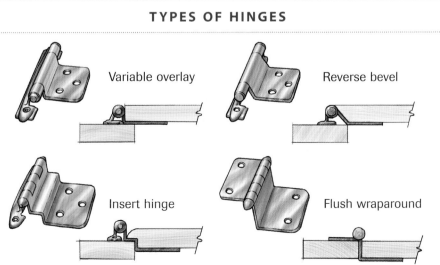

Variable overlay

Reverse bevel

Insert hinge

Flush wraparound

## WHAT CAN GO WRONG?

**Though many cabinet door hinges** are similar in appearance, they are not all the same. Make sure you know what type you need before purchasing new hinges. If you want to keep the same type, take an old hinge with you to the store to help find a replacement. If you're thinking about upgrading your hardware, now is a good time to do it.

# Prep for Painting

**1** **REMOVE DOORS, DRAWERS & HARDWARE.** Since you'll want to reinstall the doors and drawers later in their original locations, label each part. Drawers can usually be removed by pulling them out and lifting up to disengage the rollers. Label each drawer by writing a position code on masking tape stuck to the drawer bottom. See DO IT RIGHT, left, for labeling doors. Use a screwdriver or cordless drill/driver to remove all knobs, pulls, hinges, and catches.

**2** **CLEAN ALL SURFACES.** Before you reach for your paint, take the time to prepare the cabinet surfaces so you'll get the best paint bond possible. This is a crucial step since paint can't bond with dirty surfaces. Start by cleaning the doors, drawer fronts, and face frames with a solution of TSP and water. Follow the manufacturer's recommendations for the right mix. TSP is a strong detergent, so wear rubber gloves and eye protection as you clean. A stiff bristle brush will help scour away stubborn kitchen dirt. Allow the parts to dry overnight.

**3** **SAND GLOSSY SURFACES.** When the cabinet parts are completely dry, sand all surfaces lightly with 150-grit open-coat sandpaper wrapped around a sanding block. You don't need to sand down to bare wood—in fact, that's the last thing you want to do. All you want to do here is scuff the surface enough to give the paint something to "bite" into. A random-orbit sander will make quick work of this tedious job.

**4** **FILL HARDWARE HOLES.** Next, if you're not reusing the hardware mounting holes, fill these holes and imperfections (dings, dents, etc.) by pressing putty or filler into the holes with a putty knife. (If

you're reusing hardware, leave the holes for the screws unfilled.) Apply enough putty so it's a bit proud of the surface. After the putty has dried for the recommended amount of time, use a sanding block to sand the putty flush with the surface.

## + WHAT CAN GO WRONG

**If you plan on reusing** existing hardware holes, you may find one that has been stripped. To solve this problem, just dip the end of one or two wooden toothpicks in glue and insert into the hole. Trim off the excess with your utility knife and drive in the screw. The screw threads will "bite" into the toothpicks for a solid grip.

## ▶ DO IT RIGHT

**A simple drilling jig** is just a ¼-in. piece of wood. Cleats on both faces help position the jig for drilling. Pick a location for the hardware, then measure the distance up from the bottom of the door or drawer and offset from the adjacent edge. Transfer these measurements to the jig, then drill the desired-size mounting hole at this spot. Position the jig on the corner of a door or drawer so the cleats butt up against the edges of the part. Drill through the hole in the jig and your hardware will be perfectly aligned.

# Prime, Paint & Finish

**5** **MASK OFF SURFACES.** Before you paint the face frames, you'll likely need to mask off adjacent areas, such as walls, countertops, and the floor. Painter's tape lets you mask off large areas quickly. Use drop cloths to protect the countertops and floor.

**6** **PRIME ALL SURFACES.** Using a small foam roller, prime the backs of the doors. While they're drying, prime the cabinet face frames, drawer fronts, and the sides of any end cabinets. Once the doors are dry (usually within an hour or two), flip them over and prime the front.

**7** **PAINT ALL SURFACES.** After the primer has dried overnight, use the same procedure to paint the face frames, doors, drawer fronts, and cabinet sides with the finish coat. If you're painting dark cabinets a light color, you'll likely discover that you need two to three coats for good coverage. If you do need multiple coats, consult the recommended drying times on the can of paint.

**8** **INSTALL NEW HINGES.** An accurate way to install hinges—if you're not using the existing holes—is with a combination square. Determine how far in you want the hinges from the cabinet edge. Set the blade of the square to that distance and mark it. By using this method to position each hinge, all hinges—and cabinet doors—will be in alignment. Use a self-centering bit in the drill/driver to drill pilot holes, then secure the hinges to the doors with screws.

**9** **INSTALL THE DOORS & ADD PULLS AND KNOBS.** Now you can mount the doors to the cabinets. Center one door at a time in the opening then drill mounting holes with a self-centering bit, using the hinge as your guide. Drive the supplied screws into the holes to secure the doors to the cabinets. Repeat for the remaining doors, taking care to align them with each other. All that's left is to add the hardware. Use a drilling jig (see DO IT RIGHT, left) to guide your drill bit. When you've drilled all the holes, attach the knobs and pulls with the screws provided.

**5 6**

**7 8**

**9**

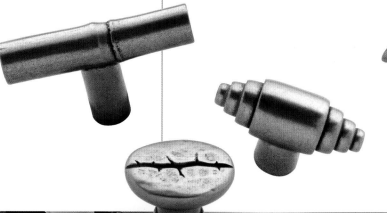

**Give your fingers something to "smile" about every time you pull on one of these fun-shaped knobs. Molded in smooth metal, these intriguing shapes blend utility with whimsy.**

**The kitchen is a great place to mix and match—as long as different looks complement, not compete. Here, warm oak cabinets frame the food prep area while their sage-painted cousins define the window wall and sink.**

# A dash of color or an unexpected texture or shape can add an engaging dimension to an otherwise ho-hum kitchen. You can define a part of the kitchen, accent an asset, or hide flaws, all with a few sweeps of the brush or roller. You might not think that something as small as a knob can have such a large impact on the overall look of a kitchen—but it can. New hardware is one of the easiest ways to spruce up your cabinets.

File this entry under "bright ideas." These curved pulls evoke memories of card catalogues from the libraries of our youth. The labels allow you to easily locate whatever it is you're searching for—and you won't need the Dewey® decimal system to find it!

Get a handle on new textures for adding visual interest. The surprise of fine leather (stitched over stainless steel frames) will make every drawer opening something special for the eye and hand.

Give your cabinets an antique look that doesn't take years to achieve. A sand-through finish like the one on this cabinet door will give your kitchen a warm, lived-in feel.

**An off-white paint creates the perfect creamy tone that will lighten up a kitchen and accept almost any style of hardware. Leaving the cabinets light lets you introduce color to the walls, countertop, and floor.**

**Bring a subtle touch of the outdoors to the kitchen with nature-themed pulls and handles, like these engraved metal beauties.**

**A glazed finish, textured glass, and gleaming pewter knobs set the stage for showing off collections— and the cabinets themselves.**

Hand-hammered surfaces combine with fanciful flowers to produce authentic, rustic knobs and pulls. Accents like these can add just the right touch to your kitchen.

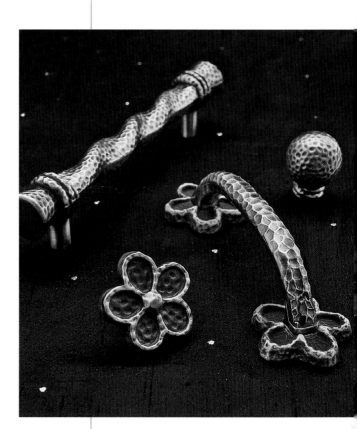

For splashes of color and design, ceramics really shine. Whether patterns or solids, pastels or punchy brights, they're a great option for bringing cachet to cabinets.

Warm wood and cool metal give a double-texture appeal to these handles. The wood softens a contemporary room, while the metal adds a modern touch to traditional decor.

# Cabinet Refacing

**REFACE** your cabinets and **REPLACE** doors and drawer fronts for a new kitchen without the cost of new cabinets

I F YOUR KITCHEN CABINETS work fine but look tired, don't replace them—reface them! With roll-on self-stick veneer on the cabinets and new doors and drawer fronts to match, you'll put a fresh face on old cabinets in short order. Add new knobs and pulls to complete the transformation. It's a major makeover project that won't break your bank. All you need for a new-look kitchen is a steady hand, a little patience, and modest carpentry skills.

COVER THE ENDS     APPLY THE VENEER     ADD NEW DRAWER FRONTS    MOUNT THE NEW DOORS

**Although it's used primarily** to bond plastic laminate to countertops, a laminate roller is an ideal tool for pressing self-adhesive veneer in place. A metal handle coupled with a hard rubber roller lets you exert firm, even pressure to guarantee a good bond. If you don't have a laminate roller, your best bet is to use an ordinary rolling pin.

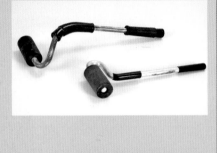

**There's no better time to** upgrade your cabinets with distinctive molding and trim than when you're refacing. Most refacing suppliers offer decorative matching trim such as crown molding, dentil molding, and even decorative valences for over your kitchen sink or range.

# Tools & Gear

*Basic carpentry tools are all you need to reface your cabinets. Specialty tools, like the laminate trimmer, will make the job easier.*

**TAPE MEASURE.** Refacing requires accurate measuring—not only to order parts but also to lay out the veneer for cutting, marking trim for cuts, and mounting doors, drawers, and hardware.

**COMBINATION SQUARE.** You'll use this four-in-one tool along with a utility knife to cut perfect joints where veneer strips meet.

**BLOCK PLANE.** The low-angle blade on this plane makes it easy to trim end panels and veneer without worrying about grain direction.

**HAMMER & NAIL SET.** End panels and trim are attached with brads and a hammer. Use a nail set to drive brads below the surface so you can add putty to hide the holes.

**SCISSORS & UTILITY KNIFE.** You can cut self-stick veneer with ordinary scissors, and it's easy to trim to size with a utility knife. Make sure you have sharp blades handy.

**PRYBAR.** If your old drawer fronts are nailed to the false fronts, a prybar will separate them.

**SCREWDRIVER OR CORDLESS DRILL/DRIVER.** You can attach drawer fronts, doors, and hardware with a screwdriver or a drill/driver fitted with a screwdriver bit. With the amount of assembly required for the average kitchen, the drill/driver is your best bet.

**DRILL & BITS.** If you don't have access to a drill/driver, use a standard power drill and bit set to drill the numerous holes you'll need for mounting the drawer fronts, doors, and hardware.

**LAMINATE TRIMMER WITH FLUSH-TRIM BIT.** This is the best tool for trimming veneer and end panels. The diminutive size of the router lets it go places its larger cousins can't.

**PUTTY & PUTTY KNIFE.** Fill old hardware holes in face frames using putty and a putty knife.

**CIRCULAR OR SABER SAW.** The panels that cover exposed cabinet ends will need to be cut to size. Likewise, you'll have to cut any molding to fit—use either a circular saw or saber saw.

**SANDING BLOCK & 150-GRIT SANDPAPER.** Smooth putty-filled holes flat with a sanding block wrapped with 150-grit sandpaper.

**HANDSAW.** You'll need a handsaw to trim the lips off the old drawer fronts if they're the three-sided variety (see DO IT RIGHT, p. 144).

**TRISODIUM PHOSPHATE (TSP).** Use this solution to clean your cabinets before refacing.

**GLUE OR CONSTRUCTION ADHESIVE.** Either works well for attaching end panels to cabinets.

**CLAMPS.** Use spring clamps and a wooden cleat to ensure uniform height on all your doors.

# What to Buy

**1| SELF-ADHESIVE VENEER.** The self-adhesive veneer sold by most refacing suppliers comes in large, flexible rolls, typically 24 in. by 96 in. The general rule of thumb for ordering rolls is you'll need one roll for roughly every 10 doors. So if you have 25 doors, you'll need three rolls.

**2| DOORS & DRAWER FRONTS.** The doors and drawer fronts for your cabinets will have to be made to fit your kitchen. Since these are custom parts, expect to wait 3 to 5 weeks for delivery. Follow the manufacturer's ordering directions and double-check your order before placing it. You won't get a refund on a custom order. Use the screws recommended by the manufacturer to attach the drawer fronts.

**3| END PANELS (IF NECESSARY).** In most kitchens, one or more of the cabinets will be exposed on the end. These are covered with matching panels, typically 1/4-in. hardwood plywood, that you'll cut to fit. It's available in a variety of sizes to cover base, wall, and pantry-type cabinets.

**4| MOLDING.** If you don't want to add decorative molding, you'll likely need some simple cove and/or quarter-round moldings to serve as transitions between your cabinets and the adjacent walls and ceiling. Most refacing suppliers stock a variety of shapes and sizes of moldings finished to match the other refacing supplies.

**5| HINGES.** You can reuse your old hinges, but now's a good time to pick up some new ones for a fresh look. If your old doors required a catch to keep the door closed, consider upgrading to self-closing hinges—no catch required.

**6| DOOR & DRAWER PULLS.** In general, knobs are used for doors and pulls for drawers. But it's your kitchen, so you can do whatever you want (see Design Options, pp. 146–149, for more on hardware options).

## DO IT RIGHT

**T**he most common, and costly, mistake when refacing cabinets is ordering wrong-size parts. To avoid this, you must measure accurately, carefully compile a list of what you'll need, and then double-check it. Start by making a rough sketch of the kitchen cabinets. Label each with an alphanumeric code starting with "W" for wall cabinets and "B" for base cabinets. Follow the refacing manufacturer's directions for measuring doors and drawers. Most will ask you to measure the openings, and then add a specified amount to each measurement. Record the opening size for each cabinet, then add the designated amount. Double-check your measurements and your math before placing your order.

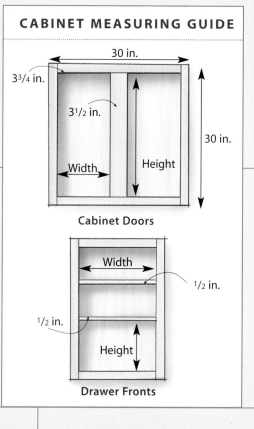

**CABINET MEASURING GUIDE**

30 in.

3 3/4 in.

3 1/2 in.

30 in.

Width

Height

**Cabinet Doors**

Width

1/2 in.

1/2 in.

Height

**Drawer Fronts**

# Reface the Cabinets

**1** **REMOVE THE OLD DOORS & DRAWERS.** The first step to giving your cabinet a new face is to pull out the drawers and remove the old doors. A drill/driver fitted with a screwdriver bit will make quick work of removing the doors. Label the drawers with a pencil mark on bottom so you'll know where to return them after you've put on the new fronts.

**2** **PREP THE SURFACES.** Once you remove the doors, you'll need to prep the face frames before you apply the veneer. Start by filling any old hardware mounting holes with putty, leaving it a bit proud of the hole. Once the putty has dried, sand it flat. Clean the surface with a mild solution of TSP, following the manufacturer's directions. Allow this to dry and then scuff sand the face frame with sandpaper wrapped around a sanding block. You're not trying to remove the old surface here, just roughen it up slightly to give the adhesive on the veneer something to "grab" onto.

**3** **ATTACH THE END PANELS & TRIM.** Cover the exposed cabinet ends with 1/4-in. matching plywood panels. Measure carefully and cut the plywood slightly oversize with a circular saw. Apply glue or a bead of construction adhesive to the back of the panel about 2 in. in from the edge around the perimeter of the panel. Attach the panel to the cabinet with brads and a hammer. Then use a block plane or laminate trimmer to trim the edges of the panels flush with the face frame.

**4** **APPLY VENEER TO THE STILES.** Apply veneer to the vertical portions of the face frames (the stiles) first. Measure each stile and cut a piece of veneer roughly 1/2 in. to 3/4 in. wider and 2 in. longer than your measurement. Then cut the veneer to size with scissors. Peel off the backing and carefully center the veneer on the stile. Press the veneer in place with a laminate roller. Repeat for all the remaining stiles. When done, go back and trim off excess veneer with a utility knife. The edges of the stile will act as a straightedge to guide your cuts.

## COOL TOOL

**Self-centering drill bits** are ideal for mounting cabinet doors. When the bit is inserted in a hinge hole and depressed, an inner sleeve retracts up into an outer sleeve (1). This positions the twist bit so it can drill a perfectly centered hole for the hinge screw (2).

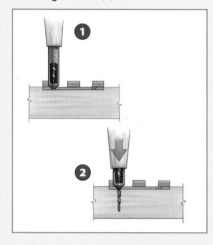

## ▶ DO IT RIGHT

**If the front of the drawer** forms a side of the drawer box instead of being mounted to a separate piece that makes up the side, you'll need to cut off the lips of the drawer front with a handsaw. This will allow the box to slide all the way into the cabinet. You'll attach your new drawer front to the box front.

# Add Doors & Drawer Fronts

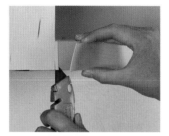

**5** **APPLY VENEER TO THE RAILS & TRIM.** Measure and cut veneer for the horizontal pieces (the rails) just as you did for the stiles. Again, cut the pieces 1/2 in. to 3/4 in. wider and 2 in. longer than needed. Apply veneer to the rails, following the steps you used for the stiles. Now position a combination square so its blade is aligned with the inside edge of the stile. Then use a utility knife to cut through the overlapping layers of veneer on the rail and stile. Carefully peel the end of the rail piece back and remove the waste underneath. Press the rail end back to create a flawless joint. Repeat for all rail pieces.

**6** **REMOVE OLD DRAWER FRONTS.** If your drawers are four-sided, remove the screws that hold on the "false" front. If the false front is held in place with brads, use a prybar and hammer to remove it. If your drawers are three-sided, cut off the drawer lips (see DO IT RIGHT, left).

**7** **ATTACH NEW DRAWER FRONTS.** To attach each new drawer front, first drill oversize holes in the inside front of the drawer. (If applicable, you can reuse the existing screw holes.) Drive two screws through these holes to attach the new front. Leave the screws friction-tight. Install the drawer in the cabinet, check the alignment, and tighten the screws after making any necessary adjustments.

**8** **ATTACH THE DOORS.** Mount the hinges (see "Painted Cabinets," step 8, p. 132). To ensure that all doors are installed at the same height, clamp a cleat (use a section of a 1x2) to the bottom of the first cabinet. Set a door on the cleat, center it, and drill holes for the mounting screws. Drive the screws in. Repeat for the remaining doors.

**9** **ADD HARDWARE.** Measure each drawer and door for the hardware, mark the location, and then drill the holes for knobs and pulls. Attach the knobs and pulls using the hardware provided.

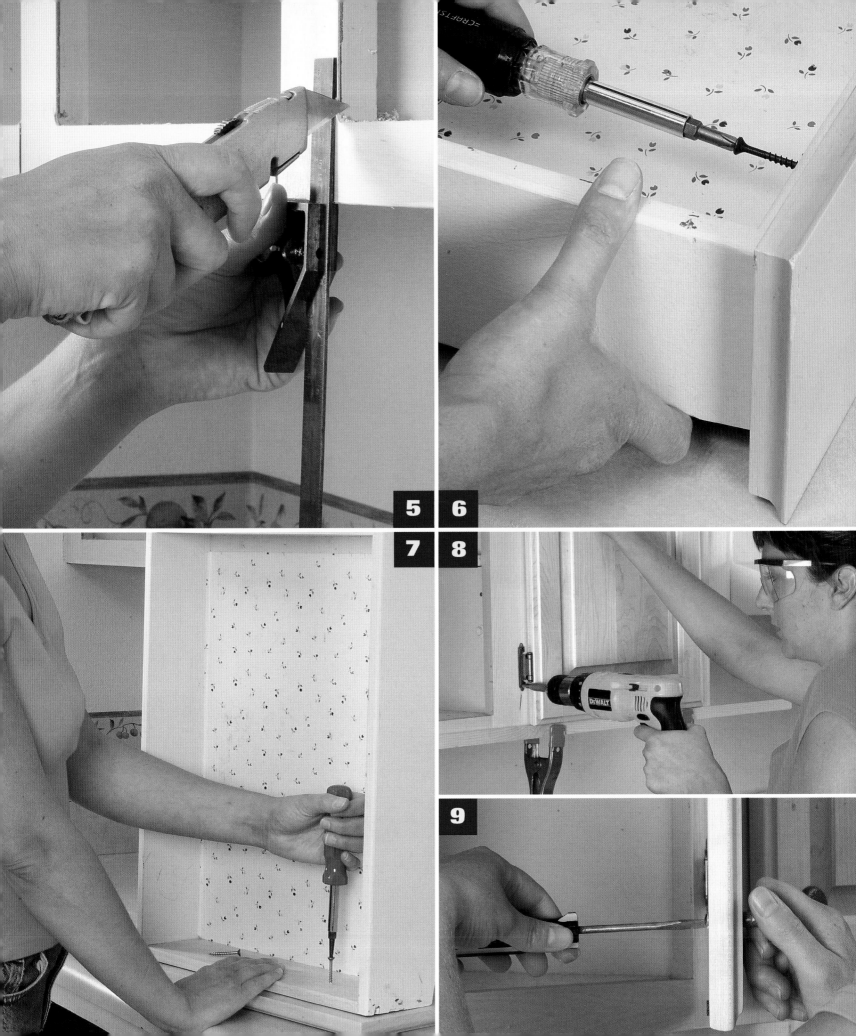

The clean lines of the doors and drawers and the inviting warmth of cherry give this kitchen a simple Shaker look. The dark-toned, understated hardware complements both the countertop hue and the feel of the kitchen.

**Creating a new look** for your kitchen doesn't have to involve a lot of time or a lot of money. In lieu of a major renovation, simply try a little face-lift. Updating the drawer fronts and faces on your old cabinets can make your kitchen look brand new again. Switch out worn knobs and pulls for more up-to-date ceramic, metal, or hand-painted designs. Mix and match to create your own personal statement.

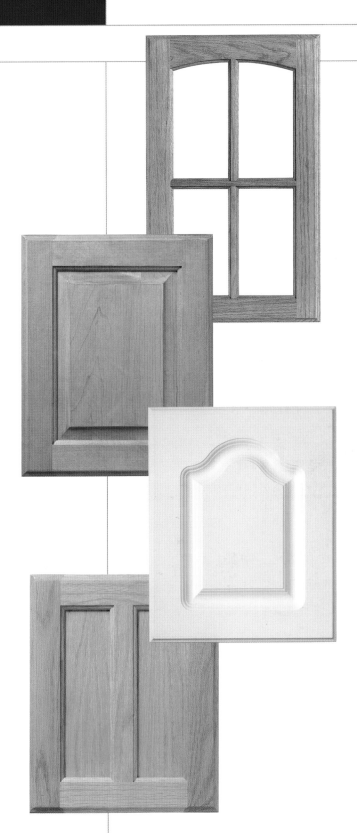

Reflecting the history, heritage, and culture of native North America, these knobs and pulls are inspired by totem art and the natural beauty of the Pacific Northwest.

The hardest part of refacing cabinets just might be choosing the right doors. Traditional or contemporary, light or dark, there are door styles and finishes to suit any taste.

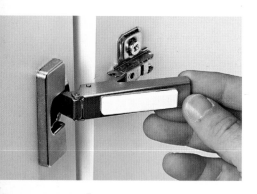

**Upgrade your hinges when you replace cabinet doors. Four types (from top): cup type, no-adjustment type, adjustable, and traditional butt hinge.**

Nothing "heavy" about these metals: from classic simplicity to unexpected whimsy, whether shiny or matte-finished, this hardware is anything but ordinary.

Here are just three of the myriad refacing woods and styles available (clockwise from left): cherry frame-and-panel, unfinished paint-grade maple, and pickled maple.

A beadboard finish and glass door fronts give this kitchen an updated country look. The light cabinets and walls make this cheery room seem larger than it is.

# Cabinet Organizers

Make your cabinets work harder with slide-out shelves and other
**INGENIOUS ORGANIZERS**

KITCHEN STORAGE SPACE IS LIKE MONEY: For most people, there can never be too much. But there are easy ways to make the most of what you have—without knocking out walls or adding cabinets. A great way to maximize your space is with pull-out bins and shelves. These handy helpers install quickly and yield a lifetime of benefits. If you're tired of getting down on your knees to access those hard-to-reach items, make your kitchen work better and smarter. Invest just a little time and money now, and you'll wonder how you ever managed without these essential extras.

MARK MOUNTING HOLES    DRILL MOUNTING HOLES        ATTACH SLIDING RAILS        INSTALL PULL-OUTS

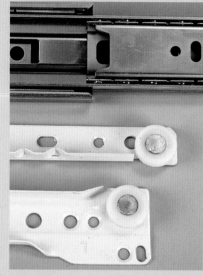

### ⊛ WHAT'S DIFFERENT?

**The difference between** a $20 pull-out bin or shelving unit and a $50 model often has to do with the materials used to make the slides. Economy slides use plastic parts and rollers that glide along thin, stamped metal tracks. More costly slides use ball bearings that roll effortlessly along an extruded or machined track. Since pull-out shelving and bins get a lot of use in the kitchen, it makes fiscal sense to invest in ball-bearing construction.

### ▶ LINGO

**A full-extension slide allows a bin, drawer, or shelf to open the same amount or more than the length of the slide. This provides total access to the contents. A standard slide travels only three-quarters the length of the slide, which limits access to the contents at the rear of the drawer, bin, or shelf.**

# Tools & Gear

*The tools you'll need to install cabinet organizers are simple and few. Odds are you have most of them on hand already.*

**TAPE MEASURE.** You'll need one of these to measure cabinets before ordering organizers and then to place them inside the cabinets. A 12-in. tape is long enough, and its small size makes it easy to use inside cabinets.

**AWL.** This is the perfect tool for marking hole locations for screws. Not only does it mark the location, but its sharp point also makes a depression that serves as a starting point for a drill bit.

**DRILL & BITS.** To mount an organizer inside a cabinet, you'll need a drill and bits to drill holes for the mounting screws. A small drill bit set is all that's needed.

**SCREWDRIVERS.** You'll find that it's generally easier to install mounting screws inside a cabinet with a screwdriver than with a drill/driver because of the limited space. Have both standard and Phillips head screwdrivers on hand.

**LEVEL.** One of the best ways to keep a shelf or bin sliding smoothly is to mount it level in the first place. A small torpedo level works best in the confined interior of a cabinet.

**WOOD FILLER OR PUTTY.** If you have old hardware holes to fill, or inadvertently drill a hole in the wrong spot, use putty to fill the hole. On finished cabinets, the crayon-like wax fillers work best. Just rub the tip over the hole to fill it and wipe away any excess with a clean cloth.

**PUTTY KNIFE.** A putty knife is also a necessity if you want to fill in holes properly. For example, if you remove the hinges from a door to attach the door to a pull-out bracket, you'll want to fill the old hinge-mounting screws in the cabinet.

# What to Buy

*The cabinet organizers you buy will depend on which cabinets you want to organize, the size of the cabinets, and the organizers available. The two most commonly used organizers are pull-out bins and pull-out shelving.*

**1| PULL-OUT BINS.** Pull-out bins are generally the easiest type of organizer to fit and install. That's because most attach to the inside bottom of the cabinet. All you have to do is find a bin that's smaller than your cabinet opening—even by a few inches. Pull-out bins are available with one, two, or three bins. The three-bin units typically have triangle-shaped bins and are used as recycling centers.

**2| PULL-OUT SHELVING.** Buying pull-out shelving can be tricky because some shelving units are adjustable over a certain width and others aren't. Keep in mind that the dimensions of the unit you buy must match your cabinet. Most shelving units ride on separate slides that are mounted to the sides of the cabinet interior. You can find preassembled double-shelf units that attach to the bottom of the cabinet, but you can't adjust the shelf height as you can with separate shelves. The downside to separate shelves is that if they aren't mounted level and parallel to each other, the shelf may bind. Pull-out shelving is available with shallow wood drawers, plastic-coated wire baskets, chrome wire baskets, and even wicker baskets.

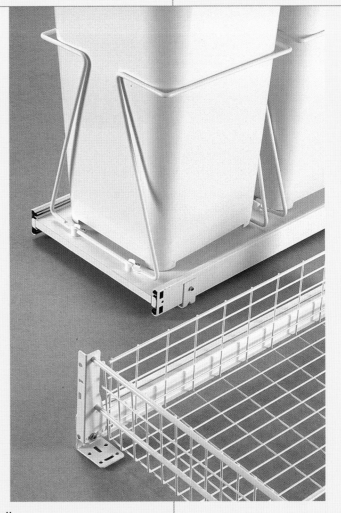

## DO IT RIGHT

**M**ost cabinet accessories are adjustable only over a very small range. So it's critical that the accessory to be installed matches the cabinet space. Before you even start looking at cabinet organizers, measure the openings of all the cabinets you want to organize. Measure each opening carefully, positioning your tape measure inside the face frames (if applicable) or inside the cabinet. Take each measurement a couple of times to double-check for accuracy. If possible, have someone help you take the measurements. It's easier to read the tape if you're not holding both ends.

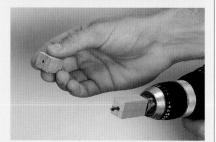

**A wooden stop** will keep you from drilling through a cabinet part and ruining it. Using the same bit you'll use to drill your mounting hole, drill a hole through a short scrap of wood (say a 2-in.-long section of a 1x4). Then cut the scrap to length so it fits over the drill bit, exposing only the length of bit needed to drill to the desired depth.

**Want the convenience** of a pull-out bin without the hassle of first opening a cabinet door? Most cabinet-accessory manufacturers sell optional brackets that allow you to attach the existing cabinet door directly to the pull-out mechanism. With these brackets installed, you simply pull out the door to access the contents.

# Install Bins

**1** **REMOVE DOORS.** Removing the cabinet doors will give you some extra room to work in the confined space inside a cabinet. Have a helper steady each door while you remove the hinge-mounting screws with a screwdriver. Set the doors aside. Thread the screws back into the mounting holes so you won't lose them. For frameless cabinets that use 32mm hinges, you can often simply loosen a screw and press a release lever to disconnect the hinge flap from the side of the cabinet.

**2** **LOCATE MOUNTING HOLES WITH A TEMPLATE.** The first step in mounting a pull-out bin is to locate and mark the center of the cabinet with a tape measure and pencil. Then position the manufacturer-

supplied template so it's centered on this mark. Mark the mounting holes in the bottom of the cabinet by pressing through the paper template with an awl. This will leave a small depression in the cabinet bottom that will make it easy to start your drill bit at the proper screw locations.

**3** **DRILL HOLES FOR THE MOUNTING MECHANISM.** Once you've marked the hole locations, remove the template, chuck the recommended size bit in your drill, and drill the holes.

**4** **ATTACH THE RAILS TO THE CABINET.** Use the screws provided to secure the bin base or bin rails (as shown here) to the cabinet base. If separate rails are used, measure between them in a couple of places to make sure they're parallel. If they're not, loosen the screws, adjust as necessary, and retighten.

**5** **ADD THE PULL-OUT MECHANISM.** Extend the rails as far as they will go and align the pull-out mechanism with their ends. A helper can make the job much easier. In most cases, the mechanism will have a set of tabs that fit in openings in the rails. Once in place, test the operation to make sure it's smooth. Finally, place the bin or bins inside the mechanism.

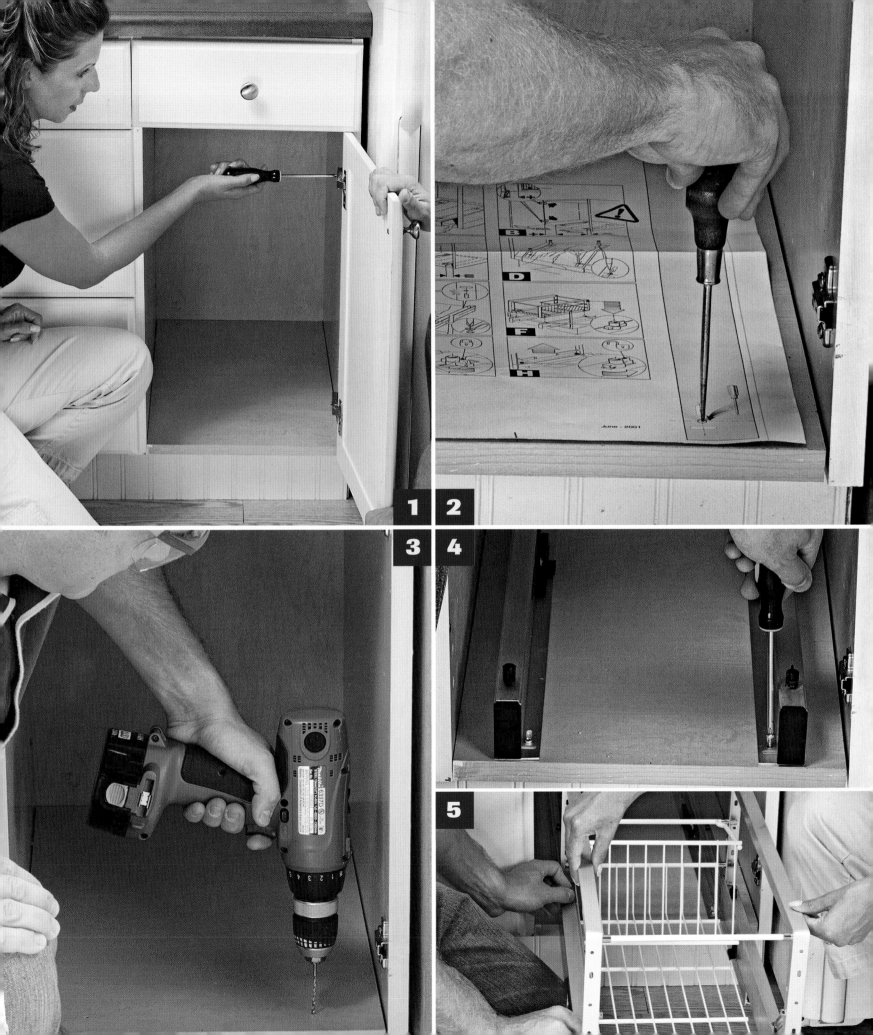

**Pull-out shelves can bind** if the brackets are not level with each other or if they aren't parallel. Check for level by first cutting a scrap of wood to fit between the brackets. Place the scrap so that it spans the front end of the brackets, and rest a torpedo level on the scrap. Adjust as necessary and repeat for the back end. Check for parallel by measuring from bracket to bracket at the front and back. If the measurements aren't equal, add shims behind the end with the larger measurement.

**To add a shelf** above the unit you just installed, cut a scrap of wood to match the desired distance between the shelves and place it on top of the lower shelf unit. Then place the template on top of the scrap and mark the mounting holes with an awl. Repeat for the opposite side, then proceed as you did for the first shelf.

# Install Shelves

**1** **SEPARATE THE DRAWER FROM THE SLIDE BRACKETS.** Remove any doors to make shelf installation easier. Most slides used for pull-out shelves consist of two halves: One half attaches to the cabinet side, the other to the shelf. As a general rule of thumb, you'll need to separate these parts for installation. Check the directions to see if this is necessary.

**2** **LOCATE & DRILL MOUNTING HOLES.** Use the template provided with the shelving unit to accurately locate the slides on opposite sides of the cabinet interior. If you're installing more than one shelf in a cabinet, start with the bottom shelf. Position the template as directed and press through the paper with an awl to mark the hole locations. Then drill holes at these locations with the recommended size drill bit.

**3** **ATTACH THE SLIDES.** After drilling the holes, attach the slides to the inside faces of the cabinet. If the slides are adjustable they may require some assembly at this time—you may need to remove screws and remount them in different holes to achieve the desired width. Secure the slides to the cabinets with the screws provided. Set a torpedo level on top of each slide, and readjust if necessary.

**4** **ADD THE SLIDING SHELF TO THE SLIDES.** Extend the slides and drop the shelf onto them. For the wire basket shown here, tabs on the bottom of the basket snap into openings on the slides. In most cases, there will be some kind of device to lock the parts together. Test the pull-out action and adjust the slide positions as necessary to get smooth action (see WHAT CAN GO WRONG, left).

Transform a common problem—the under-counter mess of cleaning items—into an accessible, neat solution. This clever pull-out accommodates tall spray bottles, sponges, and more.

Convenience is having a trash can right where you need it, when you need it, and then tucked invisibly away when you don't.

## Cabinets overflowing? Patience worn thin trying to find things? "Get organized" is easier said than done—but easy to do with accessories that help you keep things in their place and out of your way. From swivel-out pantry shelves to hide-away trash bins, space-saver organizers not only help you use the space you have, but also help make kitchen time more pleasant. Maximize your space with these ingenious helpers.

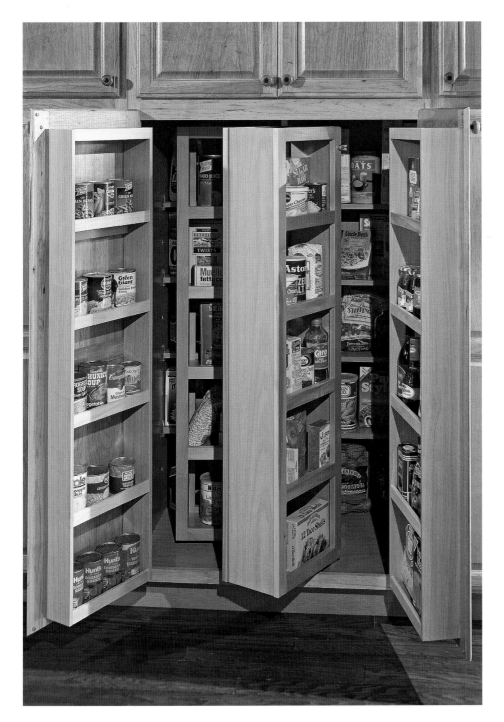

Hide-and-seek is no fun when you're searching for olive oil (or pancake mix or raisins). Stop the game with this handy center-mount pantry, which offers four easy-access tiers of storage that can be viewed from multiple sides.

Pantry shelves that just sit motionless aren't giving a full measure of service. Shelves that open out and swivel like these can easily double your storage space for food items. Since you can see almost all the contents at a glance, there's no need for the classic kitchen contortion: down on your knees, groping for something at the back of a dark shelf.

As you open the door to this corner cabinet, the half-circle wooden trays rotate out individually to give instant access to the contents.

Don't let space go to waste. This shelving unit allows for a pull-out drawer for most-often-used pots and pans. Heavy pots or those not used as frequently stay put on the bottom of the cabinet.

Unleash the storage potential of your under-sink cabinet doors to keep things neat and within reach. The shallow top shelf is ideal for scrubbing/cleaning devices, while the bottom is tall enough for bottles and boxes.

Want to double the usefulness of your utensil drawer? Try this double-decker unit. The top element slides to permit access to all the tools and kitchen gadgets underneath.

These handsome units are really multitaskers—the airflow around the wicker baskets keeps produce fresh longer, while the pull-out mechanism keeps everything out of your way until you need it.

Organization is the spice of life with this pull-out spice drawer. Tiers of slanted platforms allow for easy viewing and place your favorite seasonings right at your fingertips.

# Tile
# Backsplash

This **TILE TRANSFORMATION** is a great way to brighten up a dull kitchen with color and texture

ERE'S A PROJECT that does triple duty in function, form, and ease of accomplishment. A tile backsplash not only protects your walls from water, grease, and grime, but it can also add visual punch to a ho-hum kitchen. What's more, it's one of the simplest tiling jobs you can take on, so it's a great project for beginners. Just stroll the tile aisle of your local home center to browse the myriad colors, patterns, and textures available. Then use the detailed steps here to create a new accent for your kitchen that only *looks* difficult and expensive.

INSTALL BACKER BOARD    APPLY THE MORTAR        SET THE TILES         APPLY THE GROUT

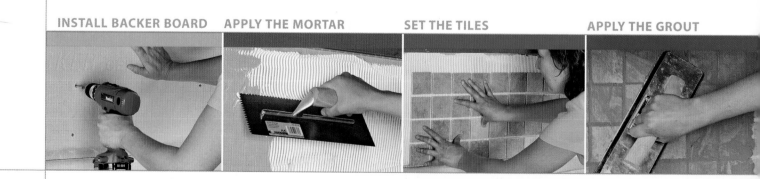

**Between the backer board** and the tile, tiling a backsplash will add 1/2 in. or more to the thickness of your wall. This means anything mounted in an electrical box needs to be extended in order to be flush with the tile. That's where box extenders come in. These plastic rectangles are available in various thicknesses.

**Gravity works against you** when you're tiling a wall. To fight gravity's pull on the tiles, use strips of masking tape to help hold tiles in place until the mortar sets up.

# Tools & Gear

*There are three distinct types of tools you'll need to install tile: tile-cutting tools, mortar tools, and grout tools. Which ones you'll use will depend on the type of tile you're installing and the obstacles you'll need to work around.*

**NOTCHED TROWEL.** Use this tool to apply thin-set mortar. The evenly spaced notches on the edges range from 1/8 in. to 3/8 in. in size.

**GROUT FLOAT.** This rubber-faced tool is similar to a notched trowel and is used to force grout into the spaces between the tiles. When held at an angle, it's also useful for scraping off excess grout.

**SPONGE & RAGS.** You'll need a sponge to wipe off the grout after it's dried to a haze and clean rags to buff the tiles clean after sponging.

**TILE SPACERS.** Cross-shaped plastic tile spacers can be inserted between each tile to ensure consistent spacing and even grout joints between the tiles. Spacers are available in different sizes to create varying-width joint lines.

**TILE CUTTER.** You can easily cut straight lines on smooth, glazed tiles with a tile cutter.

**TILE NIPPERS.** These pliers-like tools remove tiny bits of tile by nipping away at the edges.

**RUBBER-FACED MALLET.** This is the best tool for setting or "bedding" tile in thin-set mortar.

**STUD FINDER & CORDLESS DRILL/DRIVER.** Use a stud finder to locate the wall studs and a drill/driver to drive the special screws that secure the backer board to the studs.

**MASKING TAPE, MESH TAPE & DROP CLOTH.** Seal electrical receptacles with masking tape, and use mesh tape to hide seams in the backer board. A drop cloth will protect your counters.

**SMALL BRUSH.** It's easiest to apply grout sealer to thin grout lines with a small brush.

## UPGRADE

**S**pecialty **"decorator" tiles** that are colorful, embossed, or made from small pieces (mosaics) can be very expensive. Instead of covering an entire backsplash with these, savvy homeowners sprinkle them throughout a backsplash as an inexpensive accent or to add a spark of color.

# What to Buy

**1| BACKER BOARD.** Often referred to as cement board, backer board is a thin sheet of cement-like material that you attach to the wall to create a smooth surface for the tile. It also prevents the water in thin-set mortar from damaging your wall. Backer board comes in 1/4-in. and 1/2-in. thicknesses. Quarter-inch board is much easier to work with because it can be cut by first scribing a line and then snapping it to length. The thicker 1/2-in. type must be cut with a power saw fitted with a masonry or diamond-coated blade.

**2| BACKER BOARD FASTENERS.** Backer board manufacturers recommend securing the board to your wall with corrosion-resistant screws or nails with a minimum length of 1 1/4 in. A good option is to use ribbed countersinking screws, which are designed to self-drill to the depth necessary for the screw to sit flush with the backer board.

**3| TILE.** Ceramic tile is the most common type of tile used in backsplashes. It cuts easily and is available in an array of colors, patterns, and textures. Porcelain is a special type of ceramic tile that is much harder and, therefore, harder to cut. If you're planning to install porcelain tile, plan also to buy or rent a motorized tile saw. As a general rule, wall tiles look best when they're 4 in. square or smaller. Mosaic tiles—in which a web-like backing is adhered to the back of small tiles to ensure uniform spacing—also look great on a backsplash. When you purchase tile, make sure to select boxes of tiles that were made in the same batch. Look for identical lot and shade numbers marked on the sides of each box of tiles to ensure uniform color and overall appearance. You'll also need some bullnose tiles, which have one rounded, glazed side, for the edges and top of your backsplash.

**4| THIN-SET MORTAR.** Thin-set mortar is the "glue" that bonds tile to a backer board or wall. You can buy it in dry form and mix it with water into an oatmeal-like consistency, or buy it premixed, in which case all you need to do is trowel it on. Premixed mortar tends to be stickier than mixed mortar and works especially well for wall tile. Its extra grip helps fight gravity.

**5| GROUT.** You'll find grout labeled as either sanded or unsanded. Use unsanded grout to fill fine gaps less than 1/16 in. wide. For wider gaps, use grout that has sand added to it to serve as filler. Grout colors are almost as varied as the tiles themselves.

**6| GROUT SEALER.** Grout is porous and will stain if not sealed. Consult the grout label for the recommended sealer.

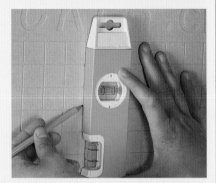

**Wall tile is designed** to be installed level and plumb. Don't depend on your eye for this. Instead, mark vertical and horizontal reference lines on the backer board before tiling. If you have a window above your sink, it's best to draw a centerline on the sink or window as a starting point for the tile. This way you'll end up with an equal amount of tiles on both sides.

**Many wall tiles** have built-in nibs on their sides that space the tiles apart for consistent grout lines. For tiles that don't have these, you'll need to use tile spacers. These plastic pieces let you quickly position tiles with uniform spacing.

# Test, then Tile

**1** **INSTALL BACKER BOARD.** To prepare your backsplash for tile, you'll need to attach a layer of backer board. Start by locating and marking the wall studs with a stud finder. Next, using the screws recommended by the backer board manufacturer, attach the board to the wall studs. If there are any seams, cover them with mesh tape. Apply a thin layer of thin-set mortar over the tape with a trowel. Draw reference lines on the backer board to mark your starting point (see DO IT NOW, left).

**2** **TEST THE PATTERN.** Regardless of the type of tile you've chosen for the backsplash, it's always a good idea to make a test run "dry." This means laying out the sheets of tile on your countertop or worksurface to check how they'll look. You'll often find color, shading, or pattern differences that you'll want to adjust. This is an especially important step when you're working with variegated tiles (like the mosaic tiles shown here), which you'll want to mix and match to get the most pleasing pattern overall.

**3** **APPLY MORTAR.** When you're happy with the tile pattern, use the notched trowel to spread the mortar onto the backer board. Most makers of thin-set mortar suggest a $1/4$-in. notch for tiles 12 in. or less in length; others suggest a $3/16$-in. notch—see the mortar and tile packaging for recommended size. Spread the mortar over an area about 2 ft. square. Avoid working the mortar excessively. What you're looking for here is a consistent layer with no bare spots.

**4** **POSITION A ROW OF TILES.** Now you can begin to lay tiles. Start by positioning the first tile along your marked starting point or reference lines. Since the mortar will probably obscure these, use a level to make sure the first tiles are in alignment. Press down slightly as you lay the tile to force it into the mortar. If you are using spacers, install one between each tile as you place the tiles on the wall.

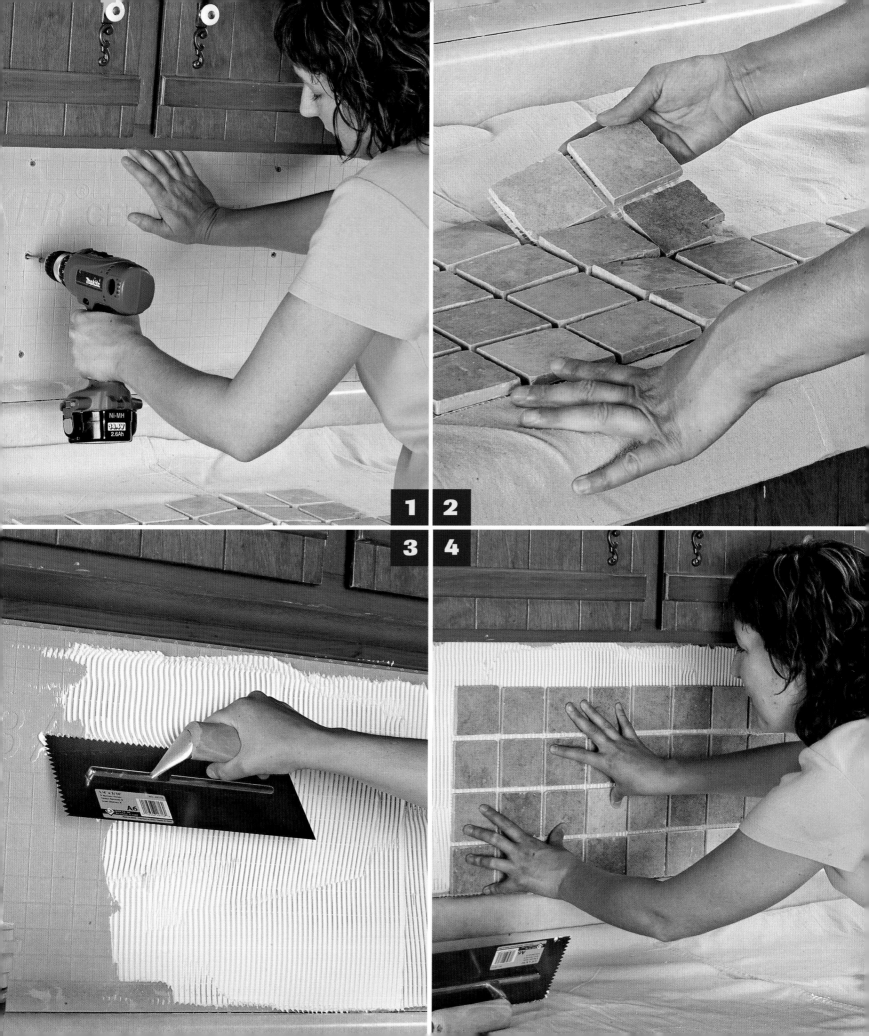

**1**

**2**

**3**

**4**

# Nip, Grout & Clean

**5** **INSTALL PARTIAL & SPECIALTY TILES.**  Place a full tile in the leftover space at the end of a row and scribe a line on the tile where it needs to be cut. Use a tile cutter or motorized tile saw to cut any partial tiles in a straight line. Curved or notched tile can be cut using a tile nipper. Exercise patience here: If you try to nip off too large a piece, you can end up snapping off much more than you wanted. Install partial tiles as you do full tiles. Finish off the sides or tops of the tiled area with bullnose or other specialty tiles.

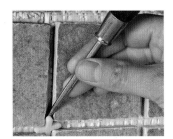 **6** **APPLY GROUT.** Once the tile is in place, and you've waited the recommended time for the mortar to set (typically overnight), you can apply grout. If you've used tile spacers, remove these first by prying them out with an awl or pulling them out with pliers. Mix grout if necessary and then spread it over the tiles with a grout float. Press down on the float to force the grout into the joints.

**7** **SQUEEGEE OFF THE EXCESS.** To remove the excess grout, hold the float at an angle so that the bottom edge acts like a squeegee. Skew the float diagonally as you wipe it across the tiles. This way, the edge of the float can safely span the joints without falling in and squeezing out the grout from the joint. Continue working the area until most of the grout has been removed. Wipe down the float, then go over the area one more time with the float held nearly vertical to scrape off as much grout as possible.

**8** **CLEAN THE TILES.** Remove the remaining grout with a wet sponge. Have a large bucket on hand and refill it with clean water often. Just as you did with the float, wipe the sponge diagonally over the tiles. Wipe over each grout joint only once—repeated wiping can pull the grout right out of the joint. After the grout has dried to a haze (which takes less than an hour), use a soft cloth to buff away the grout film.

**The not-so-humble backsplash** protects the wall from liquids and grime, of course, but it does so much more when the material is versatile tile. Use it to punch up the color in your kitchen, extend the decorating theme of the room, or add a special texture to a plain space. Whatever your taste or budget, there are lots of tiles to choose from.

An embossed tile backsplash blends durability with a touch of elegance.

Thanks to the soft and varied tones of the backsplash tile, the eye is led not to the cooktop or microwave, but to a swath of texture and color.

Fond of flowers? Crazy for critters? A fan of fine art? You can find theme tiles to suit just about any interest. They're just perfect for making a personal statement.

An otherwise plain expanse of solid-surface material gains bold impact from an inset border of background and accent tiles.

With specialty tiles like this raised border, the rustic tones of subtly patterned tile seem more vivid. Borders also draw the eye and define backsplash spaces.

For classic old-world elegance, hand-painted tiles add a rich look (sometimes with prices to match). Use them sparingly for dramatic effect, or concentrate your makeover dollars and enjoy their beauty everywhere.

Glimmering clear-glass tiles are 4-in. squares of fun. The color comes from glaze bonded to the back. They're a bit pricey, but are clearly super as accent tiles.

# Sink & Faucet Upgrade

## Transform the centerpiece of your kitchen with a new SINK & FAUCET

**T**HIS MAKEOVER PROJECT NOT ONLY LOOKS GREAT but also makes your time in the kitchen more enjoyable. The kitchen sink and faucet are the most-used fixtures in the home, so look for replacements that suit your decor and needs. The double-bowl sink and single-handle faucet we've chosen look smart and operate smoothly. With the almost endless array of styles and finishes available today the hardest part of this upgrade will be choosing fixtures to help create the kitchen of your dreams.

REMOVE THE OLD SINK    INSTALL THE FAUCET         INSERT THE NEW SINK BOWL  CONNECT THE PLUMBING

✦ **DO IT NOW**

**Before you begin any** plumbing work, it's best to drain the water from the lines. If your faucet has shut-off valves, close them and open the faucet to drain out any water in the faucet. For faucets without shut-off valves, turn off the water at the main shut-off valve (usually near the water meter) and then open the sink faucet. For best results, open all faucets in your home to completely drain all the water from the lines.

✚ **WHAT CAN GO WRONG**

**An important step** in picking out a sink and faucet combo is to check that the number of holes the faucet requires matches the number of holes in the sink. Also check that the distance between the holes for the faucet match those of the sink. This will save you from the frustrating task of drilling holes into your new sink.

# Tools & Gear

*Many of the tools you'll need to replace a sink and faucet are probably already in your toolbox. There are also a couple of specialty tools that will help make the job easier.*

**ADJUSTABLE WRENCH.** You'll need a wrench to tighten and loosen smaller nuts and fittings.

**SLIP-JOINT PLIERS.** The jaws of the pliers slide in a slot to adjust over a wide range, making them useful for tackling larger nuts and fittings.

**SCREWDRIVERS & NUTDRIVER.** A trusty screwdriver will remove and tighten sink-mounting clips and the screws that secure various faucet parts. Use a nutdriver for sink-mounting clips that have a bolt-type head.

**STRAINER WRENCH OR NEEDLE-NOSE PLIERS.** The business end of a strainer wrench is notched to fit over the X-shaped casting in the bottom of the strainer. Needle-nose pliers can also do the job.

**BASIN WRENCHES.** The long extension arm of a basin wrench allows you to loosen or tighten faucet-mounting nuts in the clear space below a sink. The serrated jaws on the end are self-adjusting—they close to fit around the nut as pressure is applied.

**SOCKET SETS.** A set of ratchets and incremental-sized sockets make quick work of loosening and tightening various nuts and bolts.

**PUTTY KNIVES.** Both the plastic and metal varieties will come in handy to break old sealant bonds between sinks and countertops and to remove old sealant residue.

**RAGS, BUCKET & GLOVES.** Plug up the open end of the waste line with rags, and use a bucket to catch water from the supply lines. Wear work gloves to protect your hands when lifting out your old sink.

## WHAT'S DIFFERENT?

**Pipes can be joined together** with either permanent or temporary fittings. Permanent fittings for copper pipe are soldered, or "sweated," together. The fitting is heated with a propane torch until it's hot enough to melt solder. Solder is flowed into the joint to create a strong, watertight seal. Temporary fittings are used in places that periodically need maintenance or replacement—such as lines and valves to fixtures like faucets. The most common temporary fitting is a compression fitting, which has three parts: a fitting, or body; a ferrule, or compression ring; and a compression nut. The nut and ferrule slip over the pipe, which is inserted into the fitting. Tightening the nut compresses the ferrule into the fitting, creating a watertight joint.

# What to Buy

**1| SINK.** Before you go sink shopping, measure the width and depth of your current sink—you don't want one that doesn't match the opening in your countertop. Unless you want to replumb the waste lines, you should pick a sink that has a similar bowl size and configuration. You'll also need to be aware of the different ways sinks attach to countertops (see SINK-MOUNTING OPTIONS, below). Finally, pick a sink with the same number of holes required for mounting the faucet—a good reason to pick your faucet first.

**2| FAUCET.** First decide if you want one or two handles. Then look at sprayer options—choose from a separate sprayer, a pull-out sprayer, or none at all. You'll also have choices in mountings: Some faucets mount in a single hole in the sink, but many require three. Finally, pick a style that blends with the other elements in your kitchen.

**3| FLEXIBLE SUPPLY LINES.** The simplest way to connect a new faucet to existing supply lines is with flexible supply lines—available wherever plumbing supplies are sold.

**4| SINK TRAP KIT.** If your new sink has the same bowl configuration as your old one, you may be able to use your existing trap and waste fittings (the pipes underneath the sink). Otherwise, you'll need a new plastic sink trap kit to hook up the sink. You may also need extension tubes that run between the strainers and the trap fittings.

**5| TEFLON TAPE & PLUMBER'S PUTTY.** Virtually every plumbing project you tackle will need some type of sealant to prevent leaks. When you shop for your fittings, make sure to pick up some Teflon tape and plumber's putty.

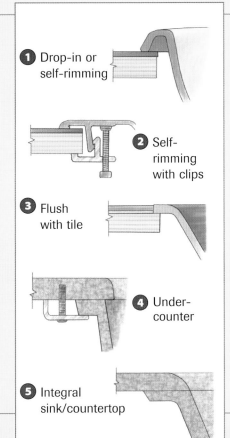

1 Drop-in or self-rimming

2 Self-rimming with clips

3 Flush with tile

4 Under-counter

5 Integral sink/countertop

## SINK-MOUNTING OPTIONS

*Forming a watertight seal between the countertop and sink is critical when mounting a sink. Here are the five most common mounting methods.*

**1| DROP-IN OR SELF-RIMMING.** A true self-rimming or porcelain cast-iron sink relies on its significant weight and a thin layer of sealant to create a seal. When set in place, the weight of the sink squeezes out any excess sealant, forming a watertight seal under the small flat on the rim.

**2| SELF-RIMMING WITH CLIPS.** Although called self-rimming, this style of sink (the common stainless-steel kitchen variety) really isn't. A dozen or so clips hook onto a lip on the underside of the sink and pull the sink tight against the countertop as the screws are tightened.

**3| FLUSH WITH TILE.** For kitchens with a tile countertop, the sink is usually installed first and then the tile is added. The disadvantage here is that the grout surrounding the sink will allow water to seep in, eventually causing the seal between the sink and countertop to fail.

**4| UNDER-COUNTER.** Under-counter sinks are pressed up under a solid-surface countertop and held in place with clips that screw into inserts embedded in the countertop. Silicone caulk is used as a sealant and also serves as an adhesive that helps hold the sink in place.

**5| INTEGRAL SINK/COUNTERTOP.** Forming the sink and the countertop out of the same material and gluing them together is the best way to keep water from seeping between them.

**To prevent sewer gas** from seeping into your home, insert a rag or cloth in the open end of the waste line as soon as the trap has been removed.

**In older sinks,** plumber's putty was typically used to create a seal between the sink and countertop. This created a good seal but, as time wore on, the putty formed a cement-like grip. To prevent damage to your countertop (especially a laminate counter) run the blade of a metal putty knife around the perimeter of the sink to break the old bond before you try to lift out the sink.

# Out with the Old…

**1** **REMOVE THE DOORS FOR BETTER ACCESS.** Since the space under a sink is tight, remove the doors from the sink base cabinet. This way, you won't be constantly bumping into them as you work.

**2** **DISCONNECT THE SUPPLY & WASTE LINES.** Turn off the water supply to the faucet (see DO IT NOW, p. 174). Open the faucet to drain out any water in the pipes. Then use an adjustable wrench to loosen the coupling nuts that connect the supply lines to the faucet—

have a bucket underneath to catch any water in the lines. Next, loosen the slip nuts that connect the trap to the tailpiece and waste line. Then carefully remove the trap and empty it into the bucket, and remove the supply and waste lines.

**3** **REMOVE THE SINK-MOUNTING CLIPS.** Working from underneath the sink, remove any mounting clips, if applicable. Use a screwdriver or nutdriver to loosen the clips, and then disengage them from the sink with your fingers.

**4** **LIFT OUT THE OLD SINK.** Before you lift out the sink, break any existing putty bonds with a putty knife (see DO IT RIGHT, left). Put on a pair of gloves to protect your hands from sharp metal edges, then gently push the sink up from the bottom. As soon as you have enough room, slip your fingers under the lip of the sink and lift it out. If your old sink is cast iron, insert "finger-saver" blocks (thin scraps of lumber or shims) under the rim to prevent the weight of the sink from crushing your fingers. Also, have a partner help lift out and set aside the old sink—cast iron is heavy.

**5** **CLEAN UP THE COUNTERTOP.** With the old sink out, use a plastic putty knife to scrape off any sealant residue. If you must use a metal putty knife, wrap a clean cloth over the end to help prevent the knife edge from scratching your countertop.

# …In with the New

**6** **INSTALL THE FAUCET.** Install the faucet in the sink before you install the whole unit—you'll have better access to the mounting nuts. Place a towel or drop cloth on the countertop. Turn the sink upside down and slide it over on the countertop so it overhangs far enough to let you insert the faucet from underneath. Use the gasket supplied to secure the faucet and tighten the mounting nuts with a screwdriver.

**7** **INSTALL THE STRAINER.** Install the strainer before setting the sink in place. Squeeze out a generous coil of plumber's putty and wrap it around the inside edge of the strainer. Then follow the manufacturer's directions for gasket placement and insert the strainer into the basin hole. Thread on the nut and then tighten the strainer by inserting a pair of needle-nose pliers or a strainer wrench in the bottom of the strainer. You'll get a lot of putty squeezing out as you twist to tighten. Remove the excess and wipe away any putty residue with a clean cloth.

**8** **CREATE A SEAL.** Self-rimming sinks rely on a sealant to keep water on the countertop from seeping under the rim. Apply a continuous 1/2-in.-diameter coil of plumber's putty or a generous bead of silicone caulk around the rim. Alternately, you can apply the sealant to the edge of the sink cutout.

**9** **INSERT & SECURE THE SINK.** Lift up the sink, turn it over, and set it into the sink opening. It should be a snug fit. Press down to squeeze out any excess putty or caulk. Clean up the excess later after tightening the mounting clips, if applicable. If you are using clips, space them out equally on all sides and then tighten them in the sequence recommended by the manufacturer, using a screwdriver or nutdriver.

**10** **RECONNECT & TEST THE LINES.** Reconnect the supply lines to the faucet and sink first, and then connect the waste lines. Before turning on the water, remove the faucet aerator to keep it from clogging with impurities in the system. When the water looks clean, reattach the aerator. If you've installed a pull-out sprayer, attach the counterweight to the sprayer hose so it will retract into the faucet when not in use.

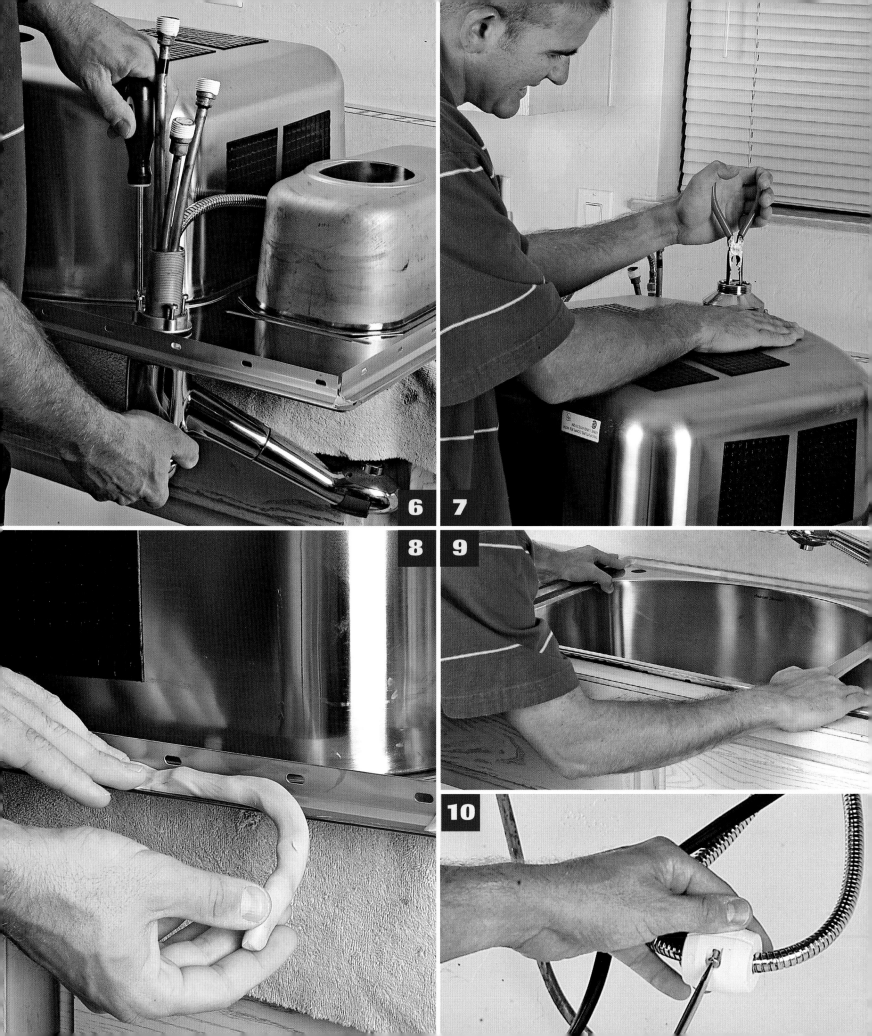

For cooking and cleanup, this double-bowl, front-apron model does double duty because the bowls are about the same size. Recessed tiles at the front add charm to the solid-surface material that cleans like a dream.

A perennial favorite, gleaming stainless steel pleases both the eyes and ears. The sound-deadening feature of this single-bowl model cuts down on noise when the water is turned on.

**Time to throw in** the (dish) towel on the old kitchen sink? Let the most-used plumbing fixture in the house reflect your style with today's abundance of designs. Whether one or two bowls, stainless steel or solid-surface, contemporary or country, today's sinks turn on a gleaming array of good looks and efficient performance.

You'll be surprised at the number of colors available for porcelain sinks. From loganberry to bone to rhapsody blue (shown below) there's a hue for every mood.

Glossy porcelain over lightweight steel puts a fresh finish on this dual-level sink. Wash pots in the deep side, rinse carrots in the other, and enjoy the versatility for years.

For a country kitchen, here's the perfect country sink in vitreous china. From the high backsplash to the distinctive profile, it brings old-fashioned form to 21st-century function.

**This simple ivory-toned faucet offers a nice contrast to the tile mosaic. Many faucet models come with an accompanying water filter.**

**Today's waterworks** pour on the choices: chrome, bronze, or brushed nickel finish; single or double handle; pull-out or deck-mounted sprayer. And don't forget about the soap dispenser. With so many styles to choose from, you're sure to find something that complements your kitchen decor and provides the function you need.

**The gooseneck swoop of this faucet frees up working space under the water flow. The deck-mounted handle, soap dispenser, and sprayer place everything you need right at hand.**

Like things simple and sleek? Consider this faucet with a gooseneck shape for accessibility, a pull-out sprayer for ease, a single-handle lever, and a soap dispenser.

Here's a new twist on a classic style. The upward arch keeps the faucet clear of working hands, while the sprayer stands aside until needed.

A bold bronze finish and intriguing Victorian styling make a strong design statement. Fixtures this stylish take center stage when installed in a simple sink.

# Laminate Tile Floor

Get a **NEW FLOOR** in a snap with laminate flooring that **LOOKS LIKE TILE**

**T**EMPTED BY CERAMIC TILE but turned off by the cost? Let laminate flooring give you the look you want—without the aspects you don't—for your new kitchen floor. Hardworking laminate mimics almost any material you can put under foot: tile, of course, plus hardwood, stone, slate, and more. Laminate easily takes the use—and abuse—of kitchen life, and you can install it over almost any other flooring (except carpeting). With snap-together assembly, installation takes little time, and the result is high impact.

LAY THE UNDERLAYMENT     SNAP TOGETHER FLOORING     INSTALL TRANSITION STRIPS     FINISH OFF WITH TRIM

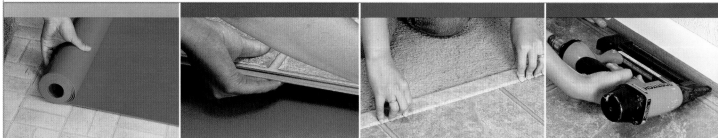

## ▶ LINGO

Unless your foundation is a concrete slab, the floor joists in your kitchen are covered with either tongue-and-groove plywood, particleboard, or oriented-strand board (OSB). This layer is called the subfloor. The subfloor may be covered with an additional layer of underlayment, such as 1/4-in. plywood (for vinyl tile) or cement board (for ceramic tile). The top layer of flooring is installed on top of the underlayment or subfloor. The top layer usually rests on a cushioning layer, such as foam or felt, which, just to confuse you, is also called underlayment.

# Tools & Gear

*Installing laminate flooring requires only basic carpentry tools, plus a few specialty items.*

**PRYBAR, PUTTY KNIVES & PUTTY.** Most flooring manufacturers recommend removing existing baseboard before installing laminate flooring. To keep from harming your walls, this is best done with a prybar and a pair of putty knives, one with a wide blade. You'll also need to fill in any nail holes in your trim with putty.

**TAPE MEASURE.** Measure twice, cut once. A 12-in. tape measure will handle all your measuring needs here.

**COMPASS AND/OR CONTOUR GAUGE (OPTIONAL).** If you need to cut flooring to fit around any obstacles (such as a pipe or molding), you can scribe the flooring to fit with a compass, or define the shape with a contour gauge.

**RUBBER MALLET & TAPPING BLOCK.** Even snap-together flooring requires the occasional whack to create a tight joint. Have a rubber mallet on hand and either buy or rent the tapping block recommended by the manufacturer. A tapping block is milled to match the profile of the flooring so it won't damage the flooring.

**HANDSAW, MITER BOX & HACKSAW.** Instead of cutting around door casings, it's easier to undercut the molding so the flooring can slip under it. A handsaw and a scrap of flooring are all you'll need for the job. Use a handsaw with a miter box to cut trim. If the transition moldings you're installing use a metal track, you'll need a hacksaw to cut it to length.

**UTILITY KNIFE OR SCISSORS.** Either of these trusty tools can easily cut most underlayment.

**CIRCULAR OR SABER SAW.** Laminate flooring is tough to cut with a handsaw. Consider buying, renting, or borrowing a circular or saber saw.

**SCREWDRIVER, CORDLESS DRILL/DRIVER & BITS.** Depending on your subfloor, you might need to drill pilot holes for mounting transition strips. Transition strips are generally screwed to the subfloor. You can do this with a screwdriver or, more preferably, a drill/driver fitted with a screwdriver bit.

SNAP TOGETHER

TONGUE AND GROOVE

## WHAT'S DIFFERENT?

**W**hen laminate flooring was first introduced, the edges of planks were cut with matching tongue-and groove joints. The parts were held together by glue applied at the joint. Although the profiles milled in the edges of snap-together planks resemble a tongue-and-groove joint, there are additional ridges and valleys that force the mating pieces to snap tightly together when assembled.

# What to Buy

**1| UNDERLAYMENT & SEAM TAPE.** You'll need to install underlayment before laying down any laminate flooring. Laminate flooring manufacturers offer a variety of options for this—rolls of foam are the most common. It's important to select the correct type for your subfloor (see WHAT'S DIFFERENT, p. 188). Also, most manufacturers recommend using their brand-specific tape to seal the strips of underlayment together.

**2| LAMINATE FLOORING.** Most laminate flooring is made up of four layers. The top, or wear, layer is cellulose paper that's impregnated with clear melamine resins. Under this is the design layer (a photo or other pattern printed on paper). The middle layer, or core, is usually fiberboard. The bottom, or stability, layer works along with the top layer to create a moisture barrier to help keep the core from warping. Because the core is wood, it's important to buy your flooring in advance of the intended installation date so the planks can acclimate to the room. Most manufacturers recommend placing unopened cartons of flooring in the room where they'll be installed at least 72 hours in advance.

**3| TRANSITION MOLDINGS & TRIM.** You'll need a transition strip wherever your new laminate flooring meets other flooring. For laminate flooring these are usually two-part units: a metal or plastic track that is attached to the subfloor, and a strip that snaps into the track to create a smooth transition. Strips are available to transition to carpet, wood flooring, vinyl, and ceramic tile. Also, whether you removed your old base trim or not, you'll still need some type of trim to conceal the expansion gap between the flooring and wall or old base trim.

**4| INSTALLATION KIT.** Some manufacturers offer kits to make installing their floors easier. Some you can buy and others can be checked out like a library book and returned when the job is finished. Contents usually include a tapping block, a pull bar for pulling planks together at the ends, expansion spacers, and special clamps (if required).

## COOL TOOL

**Sure, you can cut** laminate flooring with a handsaw and a miter box, but a power miter saw will make quick, accurate cuts with little effort. If you don't want to lay out the dough to buy one, you can rent one from most home and rental centers.

## DO IT RIGHT

**Most manufacturers** recommend that you use glue with their snap-together flooring when used on kitchen floors. Water and food spills are common here, and gluing the joints creates a watertight seal that keeps out moisture that can cause the joints to swell.

## ◆ DO IT NOW

**Your subfloor should be level** and free from dips and high spots. Check this with a 4-ft. level at various points in the room. Any depression greater than 3/16 in. should be filled with a leveling compound—a cement-based coating that goes down smoothly and sets up quickly. Most compounds are ready for the next step in the installation process in less than an hour.

## ✳ WHAT'S DIFFERENT?

**All underlayment is not the same.** Closed-cell polyethylene is the most common underlayment for laminate floors. It provides fair cushioning and noise reduction, but offers no barrier to moisture. If you're installing laminate flooring over a concrete floor or over a subfloor that has an uninsulated crawl space below, you'll need a vapor retarder to keep moisture from rising up into the flooring. You can buy either separate sheet plastic for this, or a 2-in-1 foam underlayment, which combines a vapor retarder with a foam cushion.

# Prep the Old Floor

**1** **REMOVE THE BASEBOARD.** Most manufacturers recommend removing your old baseboard before installing flooring. This can be done with a wide-blade putty knife and a prybar. Slip the putty knife behind the baseboard and insert the prybar between the knife and the

trim. The putty knife will prevent the prybar from damaging your wall as you pull off the base. If you plan on reusing the baseboard, use two putty knives and sandwich the prybar between them. The second putty knife will protect the baseboard.

**2** **UNDERCUT THE TRIM AT DOORWAYS.** The next step to prepare for laminate flooring is to undercut the door casings. Place a scrap of laminate flooring on the existing floor to serve as a guide. Lay your handsaw down flat on the scrap and cut through the trim. This will create the perfect gap for the new flooring to slip under.

**3** **CLEAN THE FLOOR THOROUGHLY.** Once you're done making sawdust, use a vacuum to thoroughly clean the floor. Go over it twice, because even small bits of debris trapped under the foam underlayment can cause problems down the road.

**4** **INSTALL THE FOAM UNDERLAYMENT.** Place the cut end of the foam underlayment roll against the wall in one corner of the room and unroll it. Cut it to length with a sharp utility knife or a pair of scissors. To prevent tearing the underlayment as you work, most manufacturers suggest laying one row of foam at a time and then covering it with flooring.

**5** **TAPE THE SEAMS.** When it's time to join together strips of foam underlayment, butt the edges together and use the recommended tape to join the seams. Make sure the foam doesn't overlap.

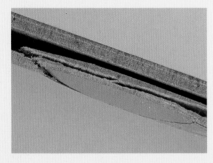

**Laminate flooring needs gaps** around its perimeter so it can expand and contract as the seasons change. The most reliable way to create this gap is to use spacers—either provided in the installation kit or made from scraps of wood.

# Lay the Floor Tiles

**6** **FORM LONG STRIPS.** Both the long edges and the ends of laminate planks snap together. This means you'll have to connect all the planks in a row together end-to-end before you can snap the long edges together. Starting at one wall, snap the planks together until you near the opposite wall. Measure the gap, cut a partial plank, and snap it in place. Make sure to leave the recommended gap at both ends of the strip.

**7** **POSITION THE FIRST STRIP.** Now slide the long strip against the wall, taking care to place spacers every 8 in. to 10 in. and at the end of every plank. Double-check to make sure you've left the appropriate gap at the ends of the strip.

**8** **STAGGER THE JOINTS.** Follow the manufacturer's instructions for staggering the joints. The most common method is to cut the first plank in the second row so it's roughly two-thirds the length of a full plank. The first plank in the third row is cut one-third the length of a full plank. Be sure to cut the end of the plank that butts up against the wall. Form a long strip and snap this onto the first strip. Continue cutting and snapping planks until you reach an obstacle or the opposite wall.

**9** **MARK AROUND OBSTACLES.** You can use a compass to "scribe" around an obstacle, or use a contour gauge to create a template of the obstacle. To scribe with a compass, place a plank as close as possible to the wall. Open the compass so it spans the largest gap between the plank and wall. Set the pencil on the plank and press the point of the compass against the wall. As you guide the compass along the wall, the pencil will copy irregularities onto the plank.

**10** **CUT THE PLANKS AS NEEDED.** Clamp the marked plank to a sawhorse and cut to size with a handsaw, saber saw, or circular saw. For curved cuts, the saber saw works best. To fit the plank around an obstacle (such as a pipe) you'll need to cut it in half at the center of the obstacle, then fit each half around the obstacle.

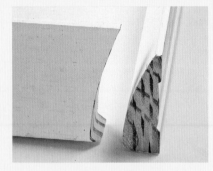

# Add Transition Strips

**11 LAY THE FINAL PLANKS.** When you've laid all the full planks you can and you're near the opposite wall from where you started, you'll likely be left with a space that's not wide enough for a full plank. Measure the distance between the last full board and the wall and cut a plank to fit with a circular or saber saw. As you cut the planks to width, take care to leave an expansion gap.

**12 INSTALL THE TRANSITION TRACK.** Once all the flooring is in place, follow the manufacturer's instructions for cutting the metal or plastic track to fit inside the door opening. Then position the track as directed and fasten it to the subfloor with the screws recommended by the manufacturer.

**13 INSTALL THE TRANSITION STRIP.** With the track in place, follow the manufacturer's directions to cut the transition strip to length. To install the strip, simply position it over the track and snap it in place. Some strips can be stubborn: You may need a rubber mallet to "persuade" them to fit into the track.

**14 ADD THE BASE TRIM.** If you're reinstalling the baseboard, now's the time to nail it back on. To complete the floor, you'll need to add trim to conceal the expansion gap between the flooring and the walls. Measure and cut trim with a handsaw and miter box. Fasten the trim to the wall or existing baseboard with a hammer and nails or with an air nailer (see COOL TOOL, left). When all the trim is in place, fill any nail holes with matching putty.

**Fancy or fundamental,** kitchen floors are made to take daily abuse in stride and still look good. Whether you want the look of wood, tile, or stone, an intricate pattern or a simple design, manufacturers have you covered. There are even options in transition strips and underlayment, so step right up and make your selections.

Quality vinyl flooring is available in colors and patterns (inlaid for durability) galore.

This ceramic tile look-alike is really a patterned laminate. Other laminates mimic stone and concrete or are patterned.

This isn't your grandmother's linoleum. It's made from natural ingredients, but doesn't try to mimic any other substance. And color options are practically limitless! You can even add a decorative border.

Many types of underlayment are available to fit varying subfloors and foundations. Depending on your subflooring, you can choose (from left): a cushioned underlayment with moisture barrier, a foam cushion only, or a cushion with moisture barrier and noise reducer.

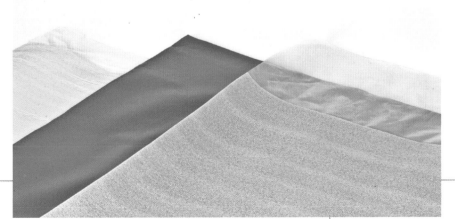

You can find laminate flooring that mimics just about any wood type and finish.

Love the look of wood but not the cost or care? Try laminate flooring. This single-wide plank design has beveled edges on all four sides that create a unique V-groove between planks.

Many transition strips are designed to snap into a U-shaped track (far left). All five common types are made to match the laminate flooring (from left): stair nosing to finish stair edges; T-molding to join two laminate floors; carpet transitions to go from laminate to carpeting; end molding to finish laminate flooring at sliding doors, ceramic tiles, and other areas; hard surface reducers to transition between laminate flooring and lower hard surface floors such as vinyl, wood, or tile.

The wide array of ceramic tiles lets you create your own custom patterns, looks, and themes. Just take your time with installation for lasting looks and performance.

Tile patterns really "pop" in an otherwise solid-colored kitchen. A border defines both the range area and the room's perimeter.

# Painted Vanity Cabinet

Give your bathroom cabinets a new identity with **PAINT & HARDWARE**

F YOU'VE GOT A DARK AND DINGY VANITY CABINET in your bathroom, a little bit of paint, some new hardware, and a touch of imagination can transform it in a weekend. The total cost, even if you don't own a brush, will be less than $50. There's no need to remove the cabinet from the room either—the work can be done in place without making a big mess. We offer three facelift options: a bright contemporary look, antiqued, and sponged. The step-by-step pages will show you how to do each of the decorative treatments.

**REMOVE HARDWARE**  **PREP THE SURFACE**  **APPLY PAINT**  **ANTIQUE OR SPONGE**

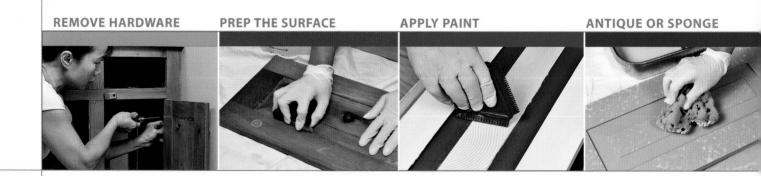

**⊡ LINGO**

Orbital often refers to the action of a power sander. The abrasive sheet or disc is driven in small circles, or orbits. The orbiting action is random to help promote even removal of material and to prevent swirls from showing up on the surface being smoothed.

# Tools & Gear

*Aside from a screwdriver and sander, all you'll need are some basic paint supplies. If you're replacing the old hardware, you may also need a drill/driver to bore new hardware holes.*

**SCREWDRIVERS.** Two sizes for Phillips and flat-head screws will normally do the trick.

**CANVAS DROP CLOTH.** Paper or plastic under the canvas is advisable. Canvas alone will catch drips, but not prevent seep-through from a spill.

**COMBINATION SQUARE.** If you need to measure for new hardware, this tool will come in handy.

**PAINT BRUSHES.** A 1-in. and 2-in. professional-quality sash brush should be all that you need.

**PAINT TRAY.** Buy one that accepts a plastic liner. It will save lots of clean-up time, not to mention lots of mess.

**PAINTER'S COMB.** Available at home centers and paint stores, this rubber tool allows you to remove some of a glaze topcoat to form stripes of varying widths.

**SEA SPONGE.** This type of sponge gives the best results and is widely available at home centers.

**UTILITY KNIFE.** This comes in handy for a number of things, plus you'll need it to cut the sponge if you want to try a sponging treatment.

**SANDER.** A random-orbit sander will speed jobs with large flat areas.

## COOL TOOL

**S**anding dust is a problem when you're working within the home. The best tool for minimizing dust is a shop vacuum that has an electrical outlet built into the vacuum housing. Plug your random-orbit sander into it, turn on the sander, and the vacuum activates. A hose from the vacuum connects directly to the sander (which can also be used with a less-effective dust collection bag).

# What to Buy

**1| SANDING SPONGES AND SANDPAPER.** Medium-grit sanding sponges, which can be used damp, do the job and keep dust to a minimum. Work with a bucket of water nearby so you can rinse the sponge often. For the antiquing effect, however, use 100-grit sandpaper.

**2| LIQUID SANDER.** Provides a quick and sure way to ensure a good bond between paint and a previously varnished surface (see DO IT RIGHT, p. 202). It is noxious though, so only use it if you can provide ventilation with a window and fan.

**3| PAINTER'S MASKING TAPE.** Narrow and wide widths will help with this project.

**4| PRIMER.** An enamel undercoat primer is important if you're painting on bare wood.

**5| PAINT.** Use satin or semi-gloss enamel in the bathroom because it's easier to clean than flat paint.

**6| GLAZE.** All three of the decorative treatments we chose required latex glaze. You don't need a lot, so buy the quart size if available.

**7| NEW HARDWARE.** You may want new hinges, knobs, or pulls. Be aware that if the new hardware's screw holes don't match those of your existing hardware, you will need to drill new holes. Hinges can be difficult to set, so try to buy ones that match your old hinges.

**8| DISPOSABLE GLOVES.** Buy a box of 100. They're cheap and save lots of hand-scrubbing time.

**9| VARNISH.** An acrylic varnish is the best way to protect painted finishes.

**10| PATCHING COMPOUND.** Also called spackling compound. Buy a small container of the quick-drying lightweight indoor variety to fill old screw holes as well as dents and gashes.

## UPGRADE

**If simply changing the finish** of your cabinet isn't dramatic enough, order new doors and drawer fronts in the desired style. Get them unfinished and paint them when you do the cabinets.

**Use liquid sandpaper** (also known as chemical deglosser) to ensure a good bond over varnished surfaces. It's especially effective on hard-to-sand fluted or carved surfaces.

**If you're painting** an unfinished cabinet, knots can bleed through the final finish over time. To prevent this, brush a shellac-based sealer over the knots before priming the cabinet.

# Prepare for Paint

**1** **EMPTY THE CABINET AND REMOVE THE DOORS AND DRAWERS.** Remove all hardware, including hinges, and keep them safe in a bucket if you plan to reuse them later. (If reusing the old hardware, as we did with two of our treatments, you may need to use steel wool to remove rust. Then use a rust-inhibiting primer before painting the pieces.) Protect the floor by spreading a canvas drop cloth over a layer of paper or plastic sheeting.

**2** **SAND LIGHTLY.** You only need to degloss the finish, not remove it, so sand lightly. A random-orbit or palm sander speeds the work, and sponge sanders get into detailed areas, such as on raised-panel doors.

**3** **MASK AND PRIME.** Mask off the walls around the cabinet and the cabinet rails and drawer front edges, too. Then apply a quality enamel undercoat primer with a brush to ensure compatibility between the existing finish and the top coat.

**4** **FILL HOLES YOU'LL NO LONGER NEED.** If your new hardware won't fit into the existing holes on the cabinet base, doors, and drawers, press patching compound into unused holes with a putty knife. A second coat is often required; in that case, allow the first coat to dry, then sand it lightly with a fine-grit sandpaper before you apply an additional coat.

**1**

**2**

**3**

**4**

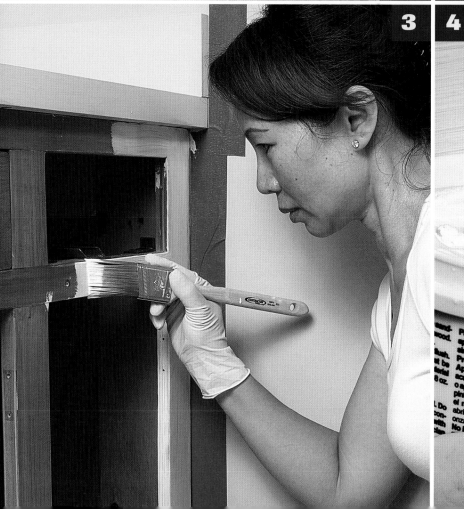

## ▶ DO IT RIGHT

**For a better shot** at one-coat coverage, have the paint dealer tint your primer to approximate (but not match) the color of the topcoat. If the color were to match, you would have difficulty applying the topcoat because it would be hard to see which areas had already been painted.

## ✳ WHAT'S DIFFERENT?

**Crackling creates fine cracks** in the surface of the paint. It can be achieved by brushing on a coat of wood glue (the yellow type) over your acrylic base coat. Then, once it's tacky, an acrylic top coat is brushed on. As the glue layer dries, it will cause the paint to crackle. The crackled surface needs to be protected with varnish.

## ➕ WHAT CAN GO WRONG

**Don't get caught** with paint drips! Removing a dried drip requires slicing it with a razor blade, waiting at least a day for paint to dry, and then some careful sanding. To avoid all that, look carefully for any drips and brush them out. Brushing away from, not toward, inside corners will help.

# Combing & Antiquing

There are many ways to decoratively paint your cabinet, two of which are suggested here: combing (steps 5 and 6) and antiquing (steps 7 and 8).

**5** **APPLY TOP COAT COLOR.** Brush on the top coat, then use accent colors to add some pop. (We used a gloss white enamel top coat and bright green on the door panels.) Painter's tape ensures a neat job. Get a tight tape seal by running a plastic credit card over the tape's edge.

**6** **COMB THE RAISED PANEL.** Start by mixing the color (1 part paint to 3 parts glaze) and applying it with a brush to the surface you want to comb. Then drag a rubber painter's comb over the surface in either straight lines or in wavy patterns as on the door panel shown here.

**7** **START ANTIQUING.** Begin with single coats of varying colors. We used a deep red followed by blue-grey and overcoated with a deep cream color. Varnish between coats and allow each coat of paint or varnish to dry before proceeding to the next.

**8** **SAND LAYERS TO COMPLETE THE ANTIQUE EFFECT.** Use 100-grit and then 150-grit sandpaper to remove paint and to reveal the hidden paint layers. Concentrate on areas that would normally receive wear, such as around hardware and at the cabinet base. When you're done sanding, brush on a solution of 1 part burnt umber (available in acrylic artist's tubes) to 4 parts glaze. Allow the umber glaze to collect in areas that would normally become soiled, such as in grooves, at door edges, and around knobs.

**5**

**6**

**7**

**8**

**If you don't like** what you've done when sponging, combing, or creating other techniques with glaze, simply wipe off the glaze with a damp rag before it dries.

**Painting small objects,** such as knobs, is quicker and easier if you screw them onto a sheet of scrap cardboard before brushing or spraying them. Leave enough space between the knob and cardboard so you can reach the undersides.

# Sponging & Spattering

Sponging (steps 9 and 10) and spattering (step 11) are two more decorative paint techniques that can transform your vanity cabinet.

**9** **PREPARE TO SPONGE.** Choose two or three colors that go well together. We chose a muted green as the base color and sand as the sponge-on color. Use a brush to apply the base color to the surface you want to sponge. Halve the sponge with a utility knife, then cut one of the halves in two so that you end up with one large piece and two smaller pieces. Cut the sponge so that one side of each piece is flat.

**10** **MIX PAINT AND APPLY SPONGE.** Mix 1 part sponge-on color and 4 parts glaze in a bucket and pour it into a paint tray. Lightly load the flat side of the sponge. Tap off excess paint and blot the sponge on a paper towel, then lightly press it to the surface receiving the decorative treatment. Avoid excessive overlapping and rotate the sponge to avoid repetitive patterns. Use the larger piece of sponge for broad flat areas and the smaller pieces for tight corners. Reload the sponge as soon as the imprints become hard to see; continue until the surface is covered.

**11** **DECORATE KNOBS.** Enhance wooden knobs with spattering. Prime the knobs and then apply the base coat color used for your cabinet. Cover the area so you don't spatter everything. Then cut an inexpensive China bristle brush so that ½ in. of bristle remains. Load the brush lightly with an accent color. Spatter the knob by drawing back the bristles and releasing.

**12** **INSTALL NEW HARDWARE (OPTIONAL).** If you decide to replace knobs and pulls, use a combination square to measure and mark for the new holes. Be sure to use the same measures for each door and drawer! Drill the new holes, using a drill bit slightly larger than the screws you'll be using. Then screw on your knobs and pulls. Buy replacement hinges and install them in the original hinge holes.

9 10

11 12

**Styles come and go—**and come back again! Using a decorative paint treatment is a quick and easy way to change the look of your bathroom. Switching out hardware completes the style transformation. On these pages we illustrate two alternate decorative paint treatments in very different styles on the same vanity.

**Antiquing makes new furniture look even better than old. The trick is to be sure the base coat colors complement the top coat. The inexpensive looks-like-glass hardware completes the transformation. Save money and have some fun by mixing reproduction knobs with the original wood knobs (detail, left), distressed to match the cabinet.**

**Tired of the traditional vanity? Convert a piece of furniture to serve the purpose. Here, an old dresser does the job nicely. The drawers were dismantled but the fronts were left in place. The top drawer front pivots forward for storage of small items, and the bottom two drawer fronts are joined to form a door. The finish is crackled.**

Sponging, done with restraint, can look elegant. Choose the right hardware and the effect can be stunning. Other knob and pull options include the spattered approach (top right) and a more contemporary look (bottom right).

# Installing a Tile Floor

**If your bathroom needs a NEW FLOOR,** tile tops the list for durability and creative possibilities

WITHOUT A DOUBT, TILE AND NATURAL STONE are the most beautiful and practical choices for bathroom floors. Large sizes and tight ⅛-in. spacing all but eliminate tile's biggest drawback: dirt-catching grout. Thanks to new tile backer boards and cool tools such as a tile wet saw, tiling a floor is doable for most homeowners. Floors with patterns take a bit more time due to extra planning and cutting. Your first step in this project is to take full advantage of a knowledgeable dealer for design, technical support, and materials. You can handle the rest!

| PREP THE FLOOR | LAY TILE | GROUT IT | APPLY SEALER |

**Use only approved fasteners,** typically either 1¼-in. roofing nails or 1¼-in. no. 8 by 0.375-in. HD self-drilling, corrosion-resistant, ribbed waferhead screws, and drive them flush with the surface.

**When removing existing flooring,** beware that pre-1980 sheet and resilient tile flooring and adhesive may contain asbestos. For testing and other information try your classified directory under laboratories or asbestos abatement contractors, your local or state department of health, or www.epa.gov/asbestos.

# Tools & Gear

*Common carpentry tools, such as a drill/driver, hammer, and prybar, may be required in addition to the following tiling tools.*

**SAFETY GEAR.** You'll be on your knees a lot. Kneepads or a kneeling pad are a must! Wear eye protection when cutting, drilling, and hammering.

**MARGIN TROWEL.** For mixing small quantities of grout and adhesive.

**SCORING TOOL.** Sometimes called a carbide score and snap knife, this tool scores the surface of backer board.

**CHALK LINE.** Extend the chalk-covered string, hold the two ends against the floor, and then lift and release the line to snap a straight line between two points.

**NOTCHED TROWEL.** The notches ensure uniform adhesive thickness and distribution. The depth of the notch should be equal to about two-thirds of the thickness of your tile.

**GROUT TROWEL.** The firm sponge on this tool, which is also called a sponge float, works well to press grout into the joints and to wipe away the excess.

**TILE NIPPERS.** When curved cuts are needed, such as around a toilet flange or heating pipe, nibble away tile with this tool.

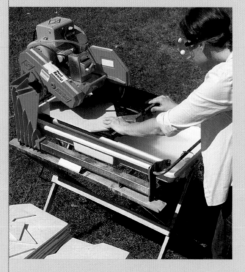

## COOL TOOL

**This table-mounted tile saw** makes cutting tile easy. The tool consists of a motor-driven diamond-grit blade, a sliding table for the tile, and a 45-degree guide for diagonal cuts. A recirculating pump draws water from a pan and squirts it onto the spinning blade to keep it cool and to eliminate any dust while cutting. Have your rental tool dealer demonstrate how to use it safely. Some rental dealers may charge a "usage" fee for the blade but most do not. Avoid companies that ask you to buy the blade outright. Finally, be sure to bring the saw back clean to avoid unnecessary cleaning charges.

# What to Buy

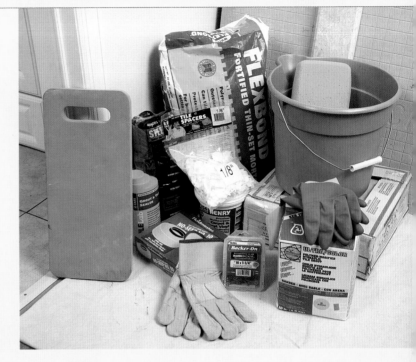

**1| ADHESIVE.** The one you use may vary with the type of tile you choose, so follow the tile manufacturer's and dealer's recommendation for type and quantity. Use this to adhere backer board to the subfloor and tile to the backer board.

**2| BACKER BOARD.** These panels are specifically designed for tile and are a must in wet locations. The Hardibacker® panel we chose has a grid that simplifies tile layout and is easier to cut and handle than cement backer board.

**3| FASTENERS.** Use 2-in. coarse-threaded drywall screws for reinforcing subfloors (1 pound will do it for the average 5-ft. by 8-ft. bathroom) and a 1-pound box of either 1¼-in. no. 8 ribbed waferhead screws or 1¼-in. roofing nails for securing the backer board.

**4| TILE.** Buy or order tile based on your drawing (see PLAN AHEAD, below). Purchase extras to cover mistakes and to have on hand for any future repairs. You may be required to buy full boxes.

**5| TILE SPACERS.** Pick up a bag unless your tiles have spacing lugs on their edges.

**6| GROUT.** Typically a "sanded" version is used for floors and "unsanded" for walls. Go over options with your dealer who can show you samples of dozens of colors and textures.

**7| BUCKET & SPONGE.** A large, firm synthetic sponge works best for cleaning tile surfaces after they are grouted.

**8| SEALER.** Grout, porous tiles, and natural stone flooring must be sealed for water and stain resistance.

**9| SADDLE (OPTIONAL).** Used for the transition between flooring materials at a threshold.

## PLAN AHEAD

**Finalize your tile layout** and tile order on graph paper. Using a scale where ¼ in. equals 1 ft. works well. First, using the paper's gridlines as a guide, draw the tile pattern (here 12-in. by 12-in. tiles with four 4-in. by 4-in. accent tiles). Then draw two perpendicular layout lines across the paper (in red) that meet in the center of the paper (diagonally in this case for a diagonal tile layout). Now draw the room's perimeter, using the perpendicular lines as reference points. Draw in the position of the door threshold and vanity, too. (Typically both layout lines are centered in the room so that the cut tiles at the walls will be equal. In this project, however, the decorative pattern is centered on the threshold, so one layout line is centered on the doorway not the room.)

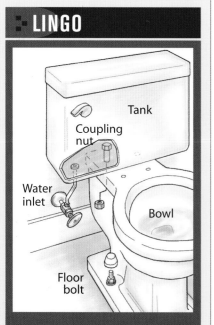

The illustration above identifies the toilet parts you need to know in order to remove and later replace a toilet. You'll need a new wax ring, which comes with installation instructions.

### ▶ DO IT RIGHT

**Nothing makes removing** an old adhered floor easy. The floor scraper (top) has a long handle but can cut into the wood underlayment. A 5-in-1 painter's tool (bottom) works well; a stiff-blade putty knife (not shown) works, too.

# Prepare the Room

**1** **REMOVE THE TOILET TANK.** Shut off the water below the tank, flush, and then sponge the remaining water out of the tank and bowl. Disconnect the water supply from the tank by unscrewing the coupling nut on the water inlet by hand or with groove-joint pliers. Using a large screwdriver, unscrew the tank from the bowl.

**2** **REMOVE THE TOILET BOWL.** Pry off the floor-bolt caps with a flat-bladed screwdriver and remove the nuts that secure the bowl. If they are corroded, you may need to cut the bolts with a hacksaw (inset photo). Lift off the bowl and place it upside down on a padded floor. Put on rubber gloves to scrape the wax off the toilet and flange. Clean the toilet flange and the surrounding floor, and plug the hole with a rag.

**3** **REMOVE TRIM.** If there is shoe molding along the baseboard, remove it using a trim pry bar. If there is no shoe molding, then remove the baseboard or plan to add shoe molding later. Use a piece of ¼-in. plywood or similar wood scrap to protect the wall from damage when you pry off the baseboard.

**4** **REMOVE THE EXISTING FLOORING.** Remove the existing flooring using a floor scraper (unless it's well-adhered vinyl tile, which you can tile directly over). Apply heat with a heat gun to remove stubborn tiles. Then apply adhesive remover to soften the old adhesive so it can be scraped up. Follow the manufacturer's instructions for safety gear and ventilate the room well.

**To cut the hole** for a toilet flange score the necessary circle and score an "X" inside it. Place the panel on two boards positioned just outside the cutout area and break out the circle using a hammer.

**To assure a good bond,** vacuum and sponge-mop the surface of the backer board before applying the thinset setting bed.

# Prepare a Proper Base

**5** **ADD MORE FASTENERS.** To make sure the existing subfloor is as solid as it can be, drive 2-in. coarse-threaded drywall screws through it and into the joists below every 4 in. to 6 in. The existing nail pattern will clue you in to where the joists are. If you find rotted or uneven subflooring, it will need to be removed and replaced with plywood. Call a pro if you're not up to this task.

**6** **CUT BACKER BOARD.** Plan your backer board layout, allowing for a ⅛-in. gap between panels and at cabinets and walls. Stagger joints so that four corners never meet, and don't align joints with joints in the subfloor. Score one side with a carbide score and snap knife, and snap the panel first away from and then toward the scored side. Test-fit all pieces. Mark panel edges on the floor as you remove them so you will know where to spread the adhesive.

**7** **SPREAD ADHESIVE.** Mix adhesive according to the manufacturer's directions. Spread a thin (⅛-in.) layer of adhesive for one board at a time using the straight-edged side of a square-notched trowel. Hold the trowel at a 45-degree angle to create a uniform combed pattern in the final pass.

**8** **INSTALL BACKER BOARD.** Fasten the panels, one at a time, every 8 in. in both directions. The grid on this panel makes spacing fasteners easy. Then, using the same adhesive, apply self-adhering fiberglass tape over the joints. First use a margin trowel to spread adhesive and fill the joints.

Then embed the tape, remove the excess adhesive, and smooth the surface with the trowel. Allow the adhesive to dry overnight before installing the tile.

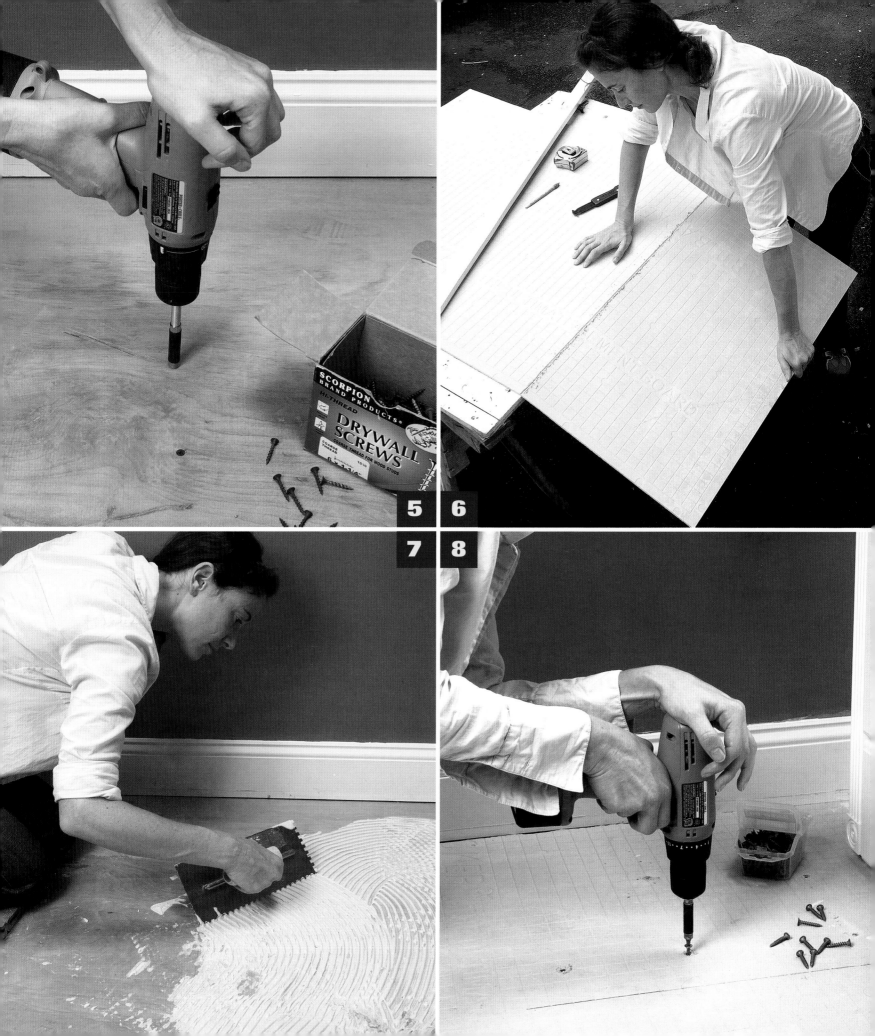

**5**

**6**

**7**

**8**

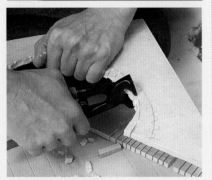
# Plan & Cut

**9**  **SNAP LAYOUT LINES.** To create layout lines, measure the longest walls of the bathroom along the floor and mark the centers. Snap a chalk line through these marks. Mark the center of this line. Then position a carpenter's square at this point and snap a second, perpendicular layout line adjacent to the square. This divides the room into four quadrants (sections). Typically, both lines are centered, but you may decide to base your pattern on a fixture or cabinet. In our case, we centered the accent tiles on the door and between the vanity and toilet.

**10**  **INSTALL A SADDLE.** Set up a diamond blade tile saw, a rental item, and use it to cut a marble saddle to fit between the door jambs. The tile saw is messy, so use it outside or in a garage. Then use the saddle (upside-down) as a height guide when cutting off the stop molding on the door jamb with a handsaw. Spread a thin layer of construction adhesive on the floor and press the saddle into place, centered over the floor transition. Scrape off any excess and clean the saddle and adjacent floor with a damp cloth. Ask your tile dealer about other options for the transition between floors.

**11**  **LAY OUT TILES DRY.** Lay at least two perpendicular courses of tile that extend to the walls using tile spacers but no adhesive. Now you can determine how much will need to be cut from tiles at the perimeter—assuming your walls are square. (In this small powder

room using 12-in. tiles, we positioned all uncut tiles so we could do the cutting all at once.) Use a combination square and pencil to mark the cuts for the perimeter tiles (see also DO IT FAST, left).

**12**  **CUT TILE.** Cut the tiles for courses that abut walls or cabinets. Cut enough for one quadrant of floor at a time. Cut a curve to fit around the toilet flange (see DO IT RIGHT, left). Test-fit all tiles.

**9 10**

**11 12**

**Adhesive consistency is key** to a successful job. Test by placing a tile in adhesive, pressing down, and sliding it about ½ in. to one side and back again. Use a trowel to pry it up and check for adhesive coverage. If there are voids, the adhesive is too dry. Add water and retest. Voids may also occur if the adhesive is not spread thick enough. You may need to adjust your technique or buy a trowel with a deeper notch.

### ▶ DO IT RIGHT

**Place a straightedge** on the surface of the tiles as you go to make sure tiles are even with each other. Make adjustments as needed until the tiles are perfectly straight and flat.

### ◆ DO IT NOW

**Porous tiles,** such as clay and some natural stone, can be stained by grout. Ask your dealer whether you should seal your tile before grouting in such cases.

# Lay Tile!

**13** **SPREAD ADHESIVE.** Mix the floor adhesive as you did in Step 6 and spread a liberal amount over a 10-sq.-ft. area in the quadrant farthest from the door. Use a notched trowel held at a 45-degree angle to comb out the adhesive in one direction.

**14** **LAY TILE.** Starting at the intersection of the layout lines, carefully position the first course of tiles against the line, pressing firmly. Install tile spacers at the corners unless tiles have nubs for automatic spacing. Similarly install the remaining courses in the quadrant. You'll save time if you remove excess adhesive as you work. Keep a damp rag by your side for this purpose.

**15** **LAY CUT TILES.** When all full tiles in the first quadrant are in place, install the cut tiles and mosaic insets. Then follow these instructions to install tiles in the remaining quadrants. Once all tiles are installed, let the adhesive dry overnight—and don't walk on the floor.

**16** **REMOVE EXCESS ADHESIVE.** The next morning, remove the spacers (a screwdriver may help here) and wipe down the floor with a dampened piece of fine steel wool to remove any remaining adhesive on the tile surfaces. Use a utility knife to remove any excess adhesive from the joints. Finish preparing for grout by thoroughly vacuuming the floor.

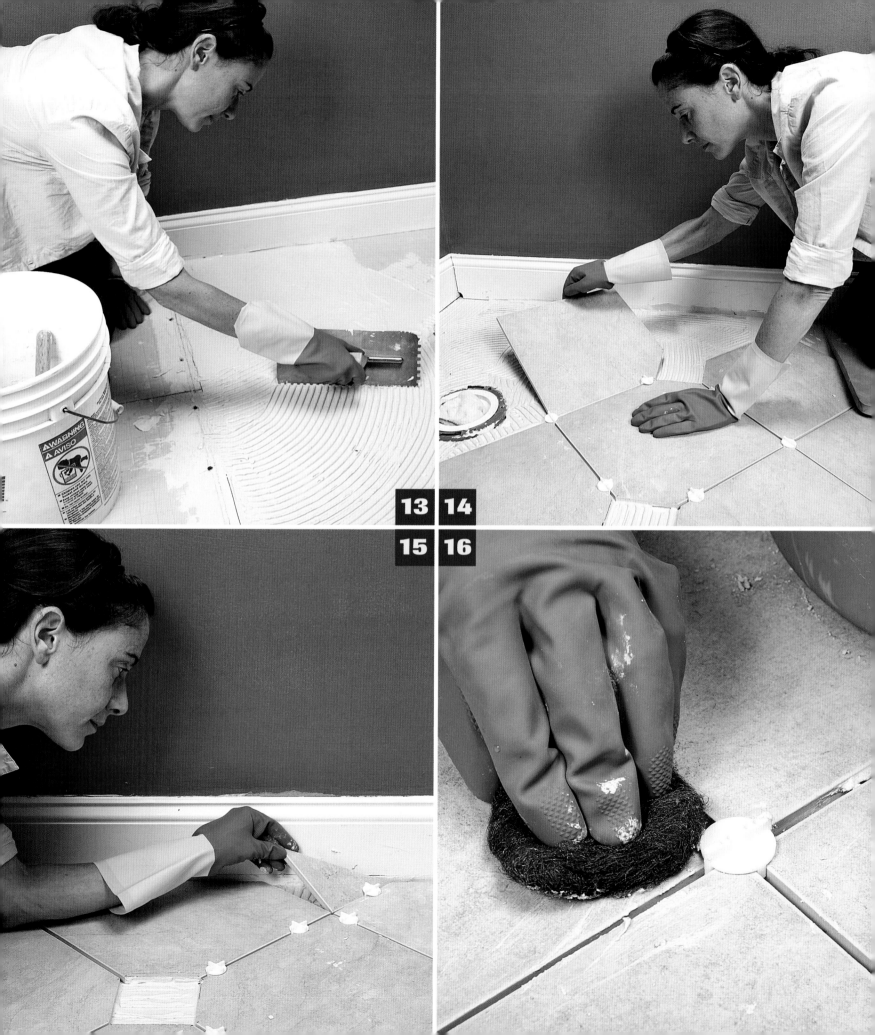

**13 14**

**15 16**

## + WHAT CAN GO WRONG

**Walking or kneeling** on a tile floor before the grout is completely dry can cause cracks in the grout. Minimize the problem by placing plywood boards on the floor. They will distribute your weight over a larger area while applying grout or when you must walk across the room. Use kneepads or a kneeling pad to protect your knees.

# Grout & Finish

**17** **MIX GROUT.** Mix enough grout to do the entire floor at the same time. Add the dry ingredients to the water according to the package directions and mix with a margin trowel. Allow it to rest undisturbed (called slake) for 10 minutes and remix, adding a little more liquid if needed. Allow to slake again. It should be just stiff enough that it won't pour out of the container.

**18** **APPLY GROUT.** Start with the section farthest from the door. Press the grout into the joints with a rubber float held at about a 30-degree angle. Press firmly and spread until every nook and cranny is full. Then wipe off the excess grout, holding the trowel at nearly a 90-degree angle. In both cases, work diagonally to the joints so you don't rake grout out of them.

**19** **CLEAN THE TILE SURFACES.** When the grout is stiff enough so it is not easily disturbed (about 15 minutes), remove any grout on the face of the tiles by wiping them lightly with a large, damp sponge. Rinse the sponge frequently and be sure to wring out all water 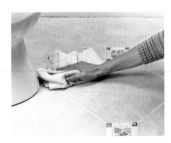 each time. Never allow grout to dry on the tile surface—it is nearly impossible to remove! After a couple hours, polish off the haze with a soft, dry cloth.

**20** **APPLY SEALER.** Wait 72 hours, or for the time recommended by the manufacturer, and seal the grout joints (as well as natural stone or porous tile). It will make the floor more water resistant and less likely to stain. Don't skimp! Flood the floor with sealer, spreading it with a mop or sponge. Wait 10 minutes to wipe up excess sealer with a dry cloth. Reinstall baseboard or shoe molding to cover the cut tile edges.

**17** **18**

**19** **20**

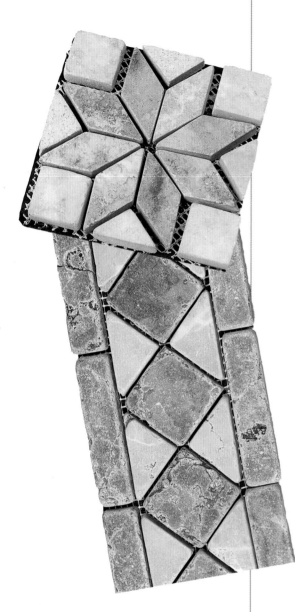

**Mesh backings make installation of small tiles, decorative insets, and borders much easier than setting the tiles individually. Add these for a creative touch—and use them sparingly to keep costs in line with your budget.**

# Tile is timeless.
Its design versatility—and practicality—makes it the perfect choice for a bathroom. Tile can help unify a room or can be used in a way that makes it the focal point. Be sure to do your homework before choosing tile, though—there are literally hundreds of different sizes, types, styles, and colors to pick from. And don't forget about the grout; it can alter the look of a design based on its color and the width of the grout lines.

**This bath features tumbled marble tiles, where all the surfaces and edges have been abraded for a soft, matte finish. A gray grout was selected to match the gray tones in the marble. To make a real statement in your bathroom, apply tiles to the tub surround and walls, as was done here.**

Large tiles, especially when set diagonally, can make a small bath seem bigger. Small tiles, as shown here, create a more cozy look. More grout lines, however, mean more maintenance.

Polished marble gives a formal look. It's beautiful but very slippery when wet. Mosaic insets (see detail photo), grouped in diamond shapes at every other corner, add interest.

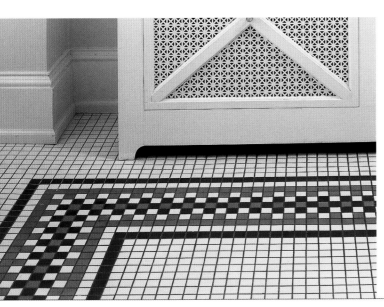

Installing large areas of small tiles is a lot easier with pre-assembled sheets. The borders are preassembled, too.

# Helpful Hang-Ups

## Put bathroom walls to work by installing BARS, HOOKS & PEGS

**T**HE SELECTION AND PLACEMENT of relatively small fittings, such as soap dishes, robe hooks, and towel bars, can have a big impact on how well your bathroom functions. There's nothing worse than spending thousands of dollars remodeling your bathroom only to end up with an awkwardly placed toilet paper holder or a towel hook that's just out of reach of the shower. These little items can affect the design personality of your bath as well. Whether you choose a suite of similarly styled hang-ups or prefer to mix and match, you'll find an enormous selection at your local home center. Installation is a snap thanks to tools like the cordless drill and new stronger, easier-to-install wall anchors.

**MEASURE & LEVEL**      **MARK & DRILL**      **INSTALL THE ANCHORS**      **SECURE THE FIXTURE**

### ⊘ UPGRADE

**If you don't already own them,** add a masonry drill bit set and a driver bit set with a magnetic bit holder to your collection. They allow you to deal with almost any installation more quickly than trying to get by with only a few bits.

### ✛ WHAT CAN GO WRONG

**It doesn't take much torque,** or power, to drive anchors or screws. Overdriving can break the drywall, making the anchor useless. Use a screwdriver if you're just installing a few anchors. For jobs with lots of anchors, you may want to use a drill/driver. Set the clutch to the lowest setting and drive slowly.

# Tools & Gear

*Just the basics for this project!*

**DRILL/DRIVER (PREFERABLY CORDLESS).** Nothing beats the convenience of a cordless drill/driver. It's a worthwhile addition to any tool collection.

**DRILL BITS OF VARIOUS SIZES.** Pick up a drill accessory kit that includes quick-change bits and a magnetic bit holder.

**RETRACTABLE TAPE MEASURE.** A 16-ft. or 20-ft. tape with a 1-in.-wide blade is the most versatile and suffices for most do-it-yourselfers. The extra-wide blade is stiff when extended, allowing you to take longer unsupported measures.

**SPIRIT LEVEL.** Also known as a carpenter's or bubble level, this tool is available in several lengths. A 2-ft. level will do in most cases.

## COOL TOOL

**H**ammer drills (also known as impact drills) are available corded or cordless. They add a fast hammering action to bit rotation. This feature speeds drilling in masonry and tile, as well as in wood. As a bonus, the bits stay cool so they last longer.

# What to Buy

*If you remove or relocate existing hardware, chances are you'll need to repair and paint a wall. Otherwise just pick up the following items:*

**1| BATHROOM ACCESSORIES.** Design lines (suites) usually include a towel bar, towel ring, hooks, and toilet paper holders; some include cup holders and other accessories. When making your selection, keep function and safety in mind. Remember that bars allow towels to dry faster than hooks. And don't install anything where it could poke an eye in the event of a slip and fall.

**2| WALL ANCHORS.** Although hollow-wall anchors are typically included with accessories, they may not be right for your situation. Check the package contents before you leave the store so you save yourself a return trip!

## DO IT RIGHT

**Wall anchors are needed** when you want to attach an item to a surface that doesn't have solid wood behind it—such as in between studs on drywall or on a hollow-core door. For demanding accessories, such as grab bars, use anchors that provide a minimum of 250 lb. deadweight pullout. The Toggler® Snaptoggle® is one such anchor. To install it, simply drill the proper size hole in the drywall, plaster, or other hollow-wall material, using a masonry drill bit. Next, insert the anchor in the hole and pull it tight against the back of the wall. Then push the plastic cap against the wall and bend the straps to break off the excess. You're now ready to screw on your fixture.

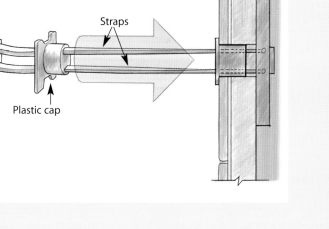

Wall

Straps

Plastic cap

**To prevent a drill bit** from wandering off mark when starting a hole in tile, nick the tile surface with a centering punch. Just a light tap, though, or you may crack the tile!

### ✛ WHAT CAN GO WRONG

**Drilling into tile** (or the grout joint between tiles) with a large-diameter bit may crack the tile. To lessen the chance of this happening, start with a 1/8-in.-diameter bit and increase the bit size one size at a time until you reach the proper size hole for the anchor.

# Install a Towel Bar

**1** **MARK THE LOCATION.** Using a tape measure and a level (or in this case a level that has a ruled edge and enables both tasks), mark the center points for the accessory's mounting plates. Hold a nail through the center of the plate to help position it on the marked center point. Then mark the mounting-hole locations, taking care to put the marks dead center.

**2** **DRILL THE HOLES.** Drill holes as required for the type of wall anchor you are using. For drilling into tile, use a carbide-tipped masonry bit. Start with a pilot hole and work up to the the anchor hole diameter. For drywall, drill a test hole to find out if an anchor is required. If you're lucky and you hit a stud, you'll just need a screw to secure the mounting plate. If not, install a hollow-wall anchor.

**3** **INSTALL THE ANCHOR.** In tile, press a heavy-duty expansion anchor, such as the Toggler® Alligator®, into the hole by tapping it with the heel of a screwdriver or a small hammer (inset photo). In drywall, press firmly on your drill/driver to slowly twist in a self-

tapping, coarse-threaded anchor. Set the drill/driver clutch at its lowest setting to avoid overdriving the anchor. Safer still, drive in the anchor with a screwdriver.

**4** **SECURE THE ACCESSORY.** When all the anchors are installed, position the mounting plates and attach them with screws using a screwdriver or a drill/driver at the lowest clutch setting. Then attach your accessory. In this case, the towel bar attaches with screws. Other towel bars may be secured with small set screws using a hex key (also known as an Allen wrench).

**1** **2**

**3** **4**

**There are a multitude of useful items** that you can mount to your bathroom walls, all of which can be installed using the skills shown in this book. When buying bathroom accessories, keep in mind that they are offered in suites (such as the one shown in our project), as well as in unusual one-of-a-kind designs. The former is easier to coordinate, but there are rewards for being daring.

**Toothbrush and soap holders can be found in a style to match most bathroom fixtures. These models are fun to look at and functional, too.**

**A magnifying wall extension mirror is a good addition to any bathroom, but it is particularly useful if your vanity is installed without a large mirror over it.**

Double towel bars (right) and triple versions (below) add space for hanging lots of towels—a good solution for small bathrooms that see a lot of use.

Accessories, such as these robe hooks, are available in more finishes than ever, from traditional chrome and brass to brushed nickel and antique bronze.

A one-armed toilet paper holder makes changing rolls easy.

# Stronger than Dirt

Conquer laundry room clutter with **WIRE SHELVES & CABINETS** you can assemble and install yourself

**T**HIS CABINET AND SHELF SOLUTION to laundry room clutter just might change your attitude about getting your clothes clean. Check out the cabinet part of this project—it can be a great storage solution outside the laundry room, too. "Ready-to-assemble" cabinets cost a fraction of what you'd pay for fully assembled versions, and you'll find base and wall cabinet sizes to fit any space. Wire shelves take up where cabinets leave off, giving you a storage system that's clean looking, accessible, and easy to customize with loads of accessories. You'll save enough by tackling this project yourself to buy a compact stereo—a helpful accessory in any laundry room.

**WALL CABINETS**   **BASE CABINET BASICS**   **HANG WIRE SHELVES**   **ADD END SUPPORTS**

# Tools & Gear

**DRILL/DRIVER.** As it is for so many projects today, the drill/driver—and a few basic accessories such as a magnetic bit holder—is a key tool for both of these projects.

**HAMMER & SCREWDRIVER.** Some assembly still requires an old-fashioned hammer and screwdriver, in this case a 16-oz. nail hammer and #2 Phillips driver.

**QUICK CLAMP.** A padded clamp won't harm cabinet finishes.

**LEVELS.** To get cabinets and shelves installed correctly, you'll need a small "torpedo" level and a 2-ft. or 4-ft. level. A laser level can take the place of these larger levels.

**CIRCULAR SAW.** If you plan to include a counter-top, you'll need a circular saw to cut it.

**SAWHORSES & 2x4s.** To cut your countertop, you'll need to support it solidly with 2x4s laid across a pair of sawhorses.

**STUD FINDER.** You'll need a stud finder so you can find and mark studs before installation.

**TAPE MEASURE.** You'll use a tape measure to mark locations for the screws and drywall anchors.

## COOL TOOL

**T**his compact laser level can be attached to the wall and project a level line to position shelves or mounting hard-ware. It can also be used to project plumb lines and other straight layout lines.

# What to Buy

**1 | BASE & WALL CABINETS.** Your local home center will have a good selection of "ready-to-assemble" (RTA) cabinets available. Size your cabinets to fit the space in your laundry room. Cabinets will come with either a white melamine or wood-grain finish. Different door styles may also be available.

**2 | LAMINATE COUNTERTOP.** Pick a laminate finish from the countertops stocked at your home center, or order a special countertop. Buying a stock countertop will save you money, but you'll probably have to cut it to length. (See DO IT RIGHT, below.) Buy an end trim kit with a matching laminate finish.

**3 | SHIM PACK.** Since floor and wall surfaces aren't always flat, level, and plumb, it's good to have a pack of tapered shims handy to "true up" your cabinets when you install them.

**4 | WIRE SHELVING & HARDWARE.** Measure the space where you plan to install your wire shelves, and have the shelves cut to length where you buy them. You'll also need braces, end caps, mounting clips, and other hardware. Consult with your dealer or read the manufacturer's guidelines to determine what hardware to buy.

**5 | CAULK & GLUE.** You'll need wood glue for cabinet assembly and some latex caulk to fill gaps between the wall and the countertop or cabinet.

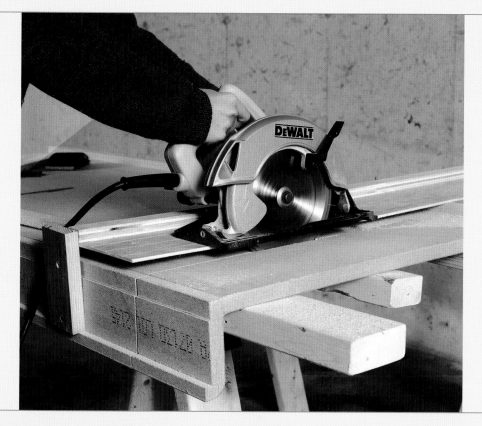

## DO IT RIGHT

**C**utting a laminate countertop to fit your base cabinet isn't as difficult as it seems. Get set by supporting the C-top upside-down on some 2x4s set across sawhorses. Put a finish-cutting blade in your circular saw, and set up a straightedge guide for your saw. Insert scrap-wood filler strips under the straightedge to create a flat cutting surface. Make the long cut first, across the bottom of the countertop. Then set up and cut the backsplash. Smooth the cut surface with some 120-grit sandpaper wrapped around a sanding block.

▶ **DO IT RIGHT**

**To square the cabinet:** Measure the diagonals from corner to corner and rack the case by pushing or tapping on the corner where the measurements need to shorten slightly. You're square when diagonal measurements are equal.

❖ **DO IT NOW**

**After you locate the studs** where your cabinet will be installed, attach a temporary cleat to support the cabinet along its bottom edge while you install it. Use your tape measure to transfer the stud locations to the mounting cleats inside of the cabinet, then drill clearance holes for your installation screws.

✚ **WHAT CAN GO WRONG**

**If you drill holes** for door handles without clamping on a backer board, the drill can splinter the face as it exits. This is particularly true for wood-veneered cabinets.

# Installing a Wall Cabinet

**1** **ASSEMBLE THE CASE.** Assemble the case with the provided fasteners. Square the case (see DO IT RIGHT, left) before attaching the back with glue and nails. Drill pilot holes for these nails to make them easier to drive.

**2** **HANG THE CABINET.** Attach a temporary cleat to the wall with drywall screws to support the cabinet weight and prepare the cabinet (see DO IT NOW, left). Using a stud finder, mark the studs. Position the cabinet and drive #10 x 2½-in. cabinet screws through the mounting cleats and into each stud. If you need to join two cabinets together, follow the manufacturer's instructions for doing so.

**3** **INSTALL THE DOORS.** Each hinge has two parts. One fastens to the door; the other fastens to the side of the cabinet. Install both halves of each hinge. To mount the door, slide the hinge parts together and tighten the mounting screw. Close both doors to check for proper alignment. Turn the adjusting screws as explained in the manufacturer's directions to get each door aligned correctly.

**4** **INSTALL THE SHELVES & KNOBS.** Clamp a block of wood to the face of the door and finish drilling the holes for door handles. Insert the mounting screws, then install the handles. Figure out what shelf heights will work best for you, then insert shelf supports into the holes in the cabinet sides. Install your shelves, and start making the most of your new storage space.

**To make your cabinet fit** against the wall, you'll probably need to notch the bottom of each side to fit over baseboard trim. Position the cabinet near the wall and use a compass as shown to transfer the profile of the base trim to the side of the cabinet. Make the cut with a jigsaw.

**When doing assembly** and installation work in your laundry room, it's easy to damage the floor or even the finishes on your washer and dryer. To avoid this, lay down a protective layer of cardboard. You'll have plenty from the cartons that contain your cabinets.

# Base Cabinet Basics

**5** **ASSEMBLE THE CASE.** Recruit a helper and you'll have an easier time handling heavy case pieces. Get set for assembly by placing one case side flat on the floor. Tap assembly hardware and wood dowels (use glue on the dowels) into the case sides and rails as shown on the manufacturer's directions. Insert the rails into one, slide in the back as shown, then attach the other side. Tighten all connecters using a screwdriver by hand; don't use a drill/driver.

**6** **SET THE CABINET.** Level the cabinet by inserting shims under and behind it as necessary. If there is base molding, notch the back of the cabinet to fit over it using a jigsaw (see DO IT NOW, left). Bore clearance holes through the mounting rail at two stud locations, and drive in #10 x 2½-in. screws to fasten the cabinet to the wall. Cut off excess shim material using a utility knife.

**7** **PREPARE THE COUNTERTOP.** Cut the countertop to the length you need (see DO IT RIGHT, p. 237). Then attach the filler pieces (in your end cap kit) with glue and ¾-in. brads. Use a household iron to adhere each iron-on end cap. Take the sharp edge off with a rubber sanding block.

**8** **ATTACH THE TOP.** The countertop is usually installed with plastic tabs that are included with other assembly hardware. Screw the tab to the top of the cabinet case first, following the manufacturer's directions. Then position the countertop, duck inside the case, and drive a screw up through each tab and into the underside of the top. It's smart to drill pilot holes for these screws.

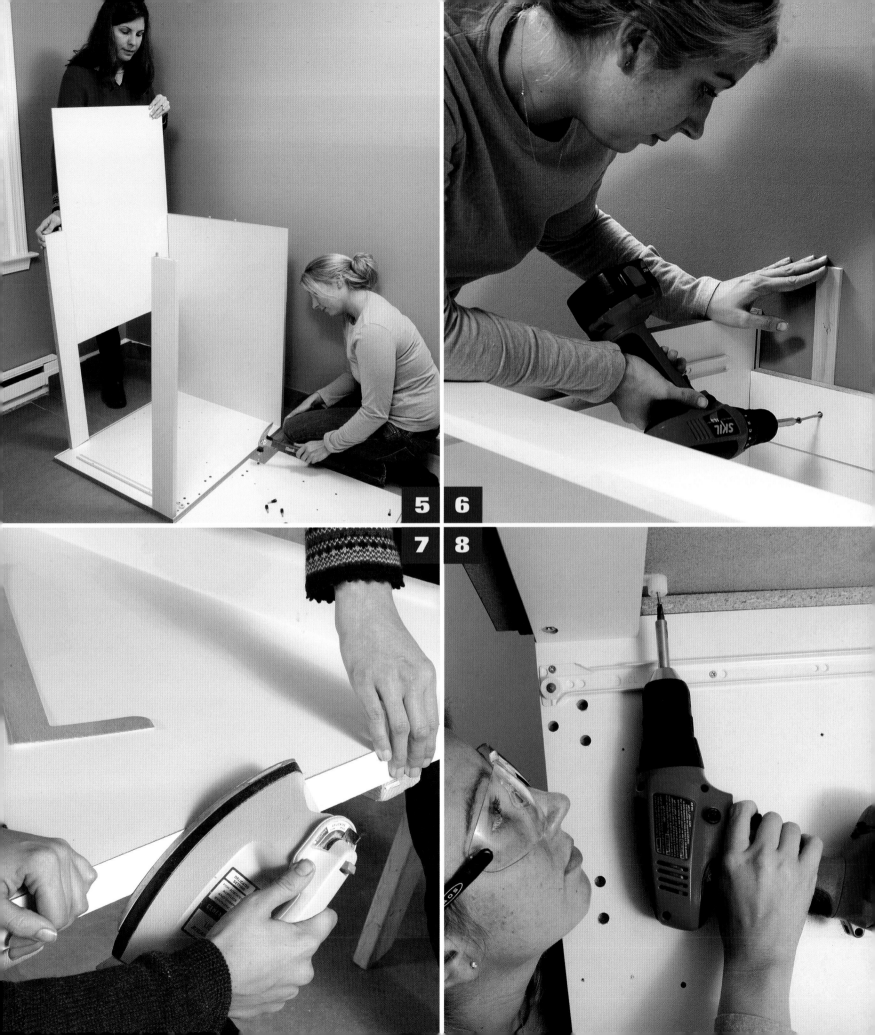

# Doors & Drawer

**9** **INSTALL THE DOORS.** Fasten the hinge halves to the door and cabinet, using the screws included in your cabinet's hardware package. Mount the door by sliding the hinge parts together and tightening the mounting screw. Close both doors to check for proper alignment. Turn the adjusting screws to fine-tune door alignment until both doors hang straight and evenly.

**10** **ASSEMBLE THE DRAWER.** Like the cabinet case, the drawer is assembled from precut parts. Join the front, bottom, and back to the sides, following the manufacturer's instructions. Finish assembling the drawer case by driving screws at designated locations. Then insert the drawer into the cabinet.

**11** **ATTACH THE DRAWER FRONTS.** This drawer has two fronts that need to be screwed to the front of the drawer case. Install knobs or pulls as shown in step 4 before you attach the drawer fronts, using predrilled holes and the provided screws. Tighten the screws fully after you check and adjust the alignment of both drawer fronts when the drawer is closed.

**12** **FILL GAPS WITH CAULK OR TRIM.** Don't worry if you find gaps between the cabinet and the wall or floor. Use latex caulk to fill gaps less than about ⅛ in. wide. For large gaps, simply cut and attach a small molding.

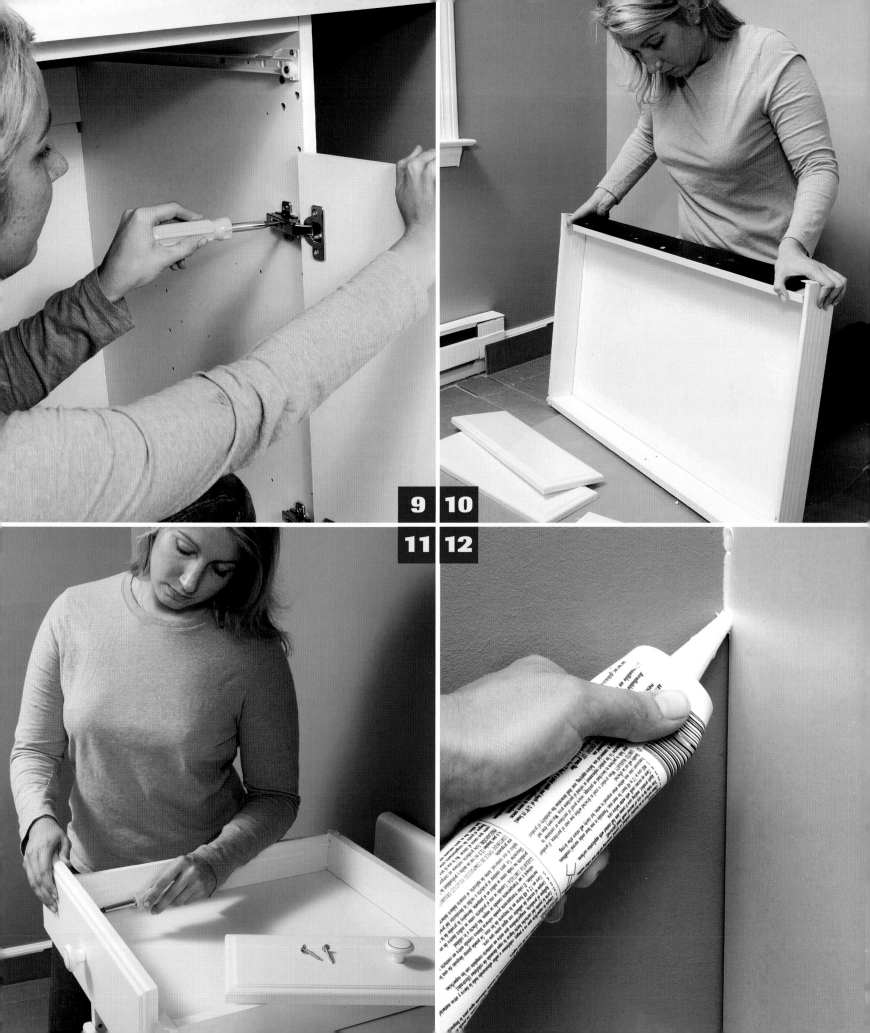

9 10
11 12

# Installing Wire Shelving

**13** **LOCATE YOUR SHELVES.** Mark a level line on the wall where each shelf will be installed. If you don't have a laser level, a regular 2-ft. or 4-ft. level will work fine. Mark an anchor location every 12 in. along each shelf line. Drill a ¼-in.-dia. hole through the drywall at each mark.

**14** **INSTALL A SHELF.** Tap a drywall anchor into each hole and tighten its screw with your drill/driver, being careful not to overdrive the screw. Hook the back rail of the shelf over the anchors, and press at each anchor to snap the back rail in place.

**15** **INSTALL AN END BRACKET.** Placing a torpedo level across the top of a shelf will enable you to keep it level. With the shelf held this way, position the end bracket to mark its mounting holes. Drill ¼-in.-dia. holes at your marks and install the bracket by tapping in the anchors and then driving the screws.

**16** **ADD DIAGONAL BRACES.** Add diagonal braces at every other wall-anchor location. Hook the bracket on the front of the shelf and press the other end against the wall to mark its mounting hole. Drill a ¼-in.-dia. hole and install a drywall anchor. Then reposition the bracket and screw it to the anchor. Use this same installation sequence for every shelf. Nice work. Now you're ready to load 'em up!

**13 14**

**15 16**

**Storage solutions abound** for laundry rooms. To find out what's right for you, start by thinking about what should be visible and accessible, and what you'd rather store in a cabinet. Give yourself space for laundry baskets, clothes poles, and other essential elements. Durable components are important in this hard-working room. Don't forget about bright colors and good lighting to keep the mood upbeat.

Chrome-plated standards and slotted steel shelves look sharp in a lavender laundry room with white appliances and baskets.

Perforated wall panels work like pegboard but come with a durable factory-applied finish. Shelf support brackets, hooks, plastic bins, and clothes-pole supports are easy to install and reposition.

A corner in a mudroom or bathroom is a perfect spot for fitting in a skinny laundry-storage system. Basket drawers let air circulate around towels and dirty laundry.

Make your washer and dryer feel like built-in kitchen appliances by surrounding them with cabinets. Laminate-covered cabinets are inexpensive, durable, and easy to keep clean.

Although these rugged-looking cabinets are most often used in garage and workshop spaces, their durable, no-nonsense design makes a style statement in this laundry room.

Tuck a storage system into a closet with a stacked washer-dryer unit and you have an instant laundry room that's easily concealed by handsome bifold doors.

For a storage strategy that's fast, flexible, and inexpensive, it's hard to beat this combination of medium-duty shelving standards and plastic-coated wire shelving.

Who would guess that behind these handsome sliding doors is a small but serviceable laundry space? Since the washer and dryer are both front-loading models, a large countertop could be installed, creating ample storage and folding space.

# Closet Makeover

**Put an end to messy, inefficient closets with MODULAR COMPONENTS you can customize to suit your needs**

**Y**ES, THERE ARE COMPANIES THAT SPECIALIZE in closet makeovers. But this is a project you can do on your own, thanks to the wide range of closet-organizer systems available. The wood-slat system we installed is just one of your options. Wire components and other systems even include drawers and cabinets. No matter what components you choose, you'll find that many of the installation details are the same. The work usually begins with a total closet cleanout; you'll have to remove the old cleats, shelves, and poles. When your makeover is complete, you can expect your closet's storage capacity to increase by 50% to 75%. That's a great incentive to get started.

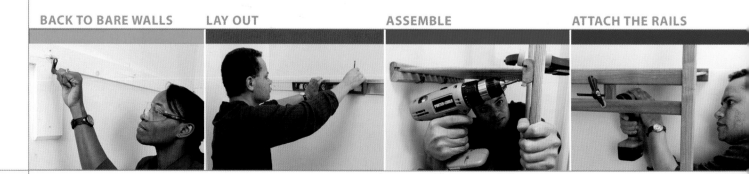

**BACK TO BARE WALLS**   **LAY OUT**                **ASSEMBLE**                **ATTACH THE RAILS**

**Cut down on your** stair time by putting your tools and gear in a tool bucket or toolbox and getting them upstairs in a single trip.

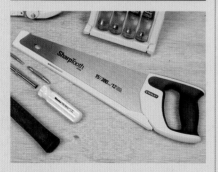

**A short, toolbox-size handsaw is** a very handy tool to have in your arsenal. It's much easier to carry around than a full-size saw, and it cuts just as well.

# Tools & Gear

**DROP CLOTH.** Protect carpets and simplify cleanup by laying down a canvas drop cloth before you start.

**HAMMER & PRYBARS.** You'll need these tools to remove the wood cleats that support the old shelf and clothes pole. A small "cat's paw" prybar designed for pulling nails is helpful; so is a larger prybar, sometimes called a "trim bar."

**TAPING KNIVES.** You can expect some damage to closet walls from removing the cleats and shelf. If you're careful, the only damage from removing your old closet system will be small nail holes that you can fill with spackling compound. Use the wide knife to hold a working quantity of compound and as an edge to clean the smaller blade that applies it.

**ROLLER, BRUSH & TRAY.** It's smart to repaint the closet before you begin to install the new components. Get a 3-in. synthetic brush to cut in and to paint any trim and a 9-in. roller (with $\frac{1}{2}$-in. nap cover) to paint the walls.

**CORDLESS DRILL/DRIVER.** Can you use a regular screwdriver? Sure. But a cordless drill will get the job done a lot faster.

**DRILL ACCESSORIES.** You'll need a quick-change bit holder, a #2 Phillips-head bit, a combination countersink/counterbore bit, and two small bits: $\frac{1}{32}$-in. and $\frac{5}{16}$-in.

**TAPE MEASURE.** A 16-ft. or 20-ft. model with a 1-in.-wide blade is stiff enough to extend several feet without support, making one-person measuring a breeze.

**SAW.** There's very little cutting, so a toolbox handsaw will do.

**RAFTER SQUARE.** Use this to mark square cuts and when cutting shelves.

**QUICK CLAMPS.** These lightweight bar clamps have padded jaws, so they won't damage your closet components; they're also easy to operate with one hand—a great advantage if you're working alone.

**LEVEL.** This will help you mark level lines throughout the closet to guide your installation.

# What to Buy

**1 | JOINT COMPOUND.** A gallon of "lightweight" joint compound or even a small container of spackling compound will do.

**2 | SANDING SPONGE.** You just need a fine-grit one for this project. It lasts a long time, it's washable, and it's stiff enough to smooth flat surfaces yet flexible enough to conform to irregular ones.

**3 | CLOSET SYSTEM & HARDWARE.** Systems are available in wire, melamine, and wood. Many systems offer drawers and easily adjustable shelves and rods. You can buy components separately or in kit form. Kits are often sold according to closet size and come in many configurations. Most kits come with hardware, but be sure to check the box.

**4 | WALL PAINT.** Measure the area to be covered. You might get by with a quart of interior latex paint.

## DESIGNING YOUR NEW CLOSET

**S**tart by determining your needs. Chances are you'll want hang-up space for long clothes, such as dresses, as well as shorter items, such as shirts. You'll also need to store shoes and boots. And you may want to include shelves or drawers for folded items and accessories. Next, measure your closet (be sure to remove anything in the closet that might hamper measuring). Choose a system that best suits your needs and budget. Manufacturers offer a range of design help, from simply stating the heights required for rods to elaborate online planning programs that give you a materials list, pricing, and detailed step-by-step instructions. The larger your space or the more varied your needs, the more help you may appreciate, but honestly, most planning can be easily done on graph paper. Just record your measurements and start playing with fitting the components you want. It's nice to have it all on paper during installation so you can remind yourself just where you thought everything would fit.

# Get a Fresh Start

**1** **REMOVE THE EXISTING ROD & SHELF.** Protect floors with a drop cloth. Lift out the rod and unscrew its brackets. If the shelf is attached to the cleat with screws, remove them. If it's nailed, tap up on the shelf with a hammer.

**2** **REMOVE THE SHELF CLEATS.** Look for dimples that indicate fastener locations. Drive the tip of a prybar into the wood and over the head of the nail to pry it out. If you can't find the nail heads, pry cleats loose using your hammer and a prybar.

**3** **SPACKLE & SAND.** Spread a thin coat of joint compound over damaged areas. Sand your patched areas smooth when the compound has dried completely—it turns bright white. Make a second application if necessary.

**4** **PAINT.** Apply a fresh coat of wall paint. (You might want to brighten up the ceiling now, too.) Use a paintbrush to cut in a 2-in.-wide border at the ceiling and along inside corners, door casing, and baseboard molding. Then use a paint roller to fill in the rest.

**1** **2**

**3** **4**

**You'll find it easier** to attach the wooden garment rail hangers to the shelves before installing the shelves.

**Bore a countersunk pilot hole** in the back of the shelf rail with a combination bit at an angle that lets you use a drill/driver to drive the screw.

# Install the Closet System

**5** **MARK THE HEIGHT.** Figure out how high you want the shelf, then lightly pencil a level line on the closet walls at the desired height. Use a level as a guide.

**6** **ATTACH THE HOOKS.** Mark shelf-hook locations along the line, evenly spaced and no more than 16 in. apart. (The manufacturer's directions may have specific information about spacing.) If attaching the hook into a stud, use a screw. If there is no stud, predrill a $\frac{5}{16}$-in.-dia. hole, then drive in a winged hollow wall anchor.

**7** **INSTALL AN END SUPPORT.** Put the shelf into the mounting hooks, and while holding it level, position an end bracket and mark its location on the side wall. Then remove the shelf and install the brackets, using mounting hooks as in the previous step.

**8** **INSTALL THE SHELVES.** After first attaching rail support cleats (see DO IT NOW, left), place the shelf in its supports, level it, and clamp the shelf's front rail to a freestanding vertical support. Use a level to make sure the vertical support is plumb. Then fasten the shelf front rail to the vertical support with supplied screws. Make sure to drill a pilot hole for each screw to avoid splitting the wood.

**5**

**6**

**7**

**8**

**If you drill the pilot holes** for the garment rail too deep, you may drill through the face of the garment rail. To avoid this, attach a depth stop to the bit as shown, or simply wrap masking tape around the bit at the point you want to stop drilling.

# More Shelves & a Rod

**9** **INSTALL THE CENTER SHELVES.** Assemble and position the second vertical support. Then install your first center shelf by first anchoring shelf hooks to the wall (steps 5 and 6), then clamping and screwing the shelf's front rail to the vertical supports. Repeat this procedure to install all remaining center shelves.

**10** **CUT THE LAST SHELF.** Cut the remaining shelf to fit between the vertical support and the other side wall. To make a smooth, accurate cut, set the shelf on a pair of 2x4s and guide the blade of your handsaw against a straightedged board held square across the shelf.

**11** **INSTALL THE LAST SHELF.** Fasten shelf hooks to the wall and mount the end support (steps 5, 6, and 7) to install the last shelf or shelves. Then, after all shelves are installed, drive a screw through each rear-support bracket and into the shelf it supports.

**12** **ATTACH THE GARMENT RAILS.** Measure and cut the garment rails with a handsaw. Clamp the garment rail to the hangers that you attached to the shelf before you installed it (step 8). Drive a screw through the predrilled hole in the cleat and into the rail. Vacuum up, and you're ready to hang clothes!

**9** **10**

**11** **12**

## Peaceful mornings at last. An

organized, accessible closet is more than a space-
and time-saver, it's a peacemaker, too. Imagine
calm mornings with everything at your fingertips
instead of the usual frantic search through too-
deep drawers or crammed closets. Such systems
are not only easy to build but also easy on the
eyes and accommodating to changes in size,
season, or owner. No space goes wasted—tuck in
another shelf or rearrange clothes poles to suit.

**Closet components can be a gadget-lover's dream. Every piece has a function; this slide-out rod can hold a stack of jackets or tomorrow morning's outfit.**

**A makeover can double the usefulness of a walk-in closet. This stacking basket system allows clothes to be instantly visible and also provides a countertop.**

**Don't shortsheet your linens when redoing closets. These wire components allow linens to breathe and can be adjusted to accommodate various stack sizes.**

A coated wire closet system is easy to install and far sturdier than its lightweight lines suggest. You can choose from many configurations and components.

There are three secrets to success in a kid's closet: lots of light, durable construction, and adjustable heights for shelves and clothes poles.

With its cherry veneer finish, this system is too handsome to cover up and provides enough space for two people.

Wood-veneered shelves and drawers add elegance to this modular system. All components are mounted on slotted vertical standards that are screwed to the wall. The photo at right shows another configuration that's possible in the same amount of space.

A sunny, open storage niche is painted a solid yellow to complement wallpaper. As the little girl grows, it's easy to change clothes rod heights as well as wall colors.

If you like to look at your clothes and favor "grab-and-go" convenience, try an open closet arrangement like this.

# Garage Makeover

## With a combination of **SHELVES, RACKS & CABINETS**, you can transform a garage from messy to magnificent

**S**OONER OR LATER, you have to deal with the jumble of odd but essential stuff that fills your garage. This makeover plan is sure to help out in three major ways. First, we'll install a sturdy cabinet, countertop, and pegboard combination that gives you storage space and a compact workshop setup. Second on the list is a heavy-duty shelf that will (finally!) get bulky items out of your way. The final clutter-control weapon is a storage rack made from 1x4 pine boards. This wooden grid is a great place to hang garden tools, extension cords, ladders, and anything else that you haven't already stowed. Let's dig in; the best-organized garage in your neighborhood begins here.

**INSTALL CABINETS**   **INSTALL HIGH SHELVES**   **FIGURE OUT THE LAYOUT**   **INSTALL A TOOL RACK**

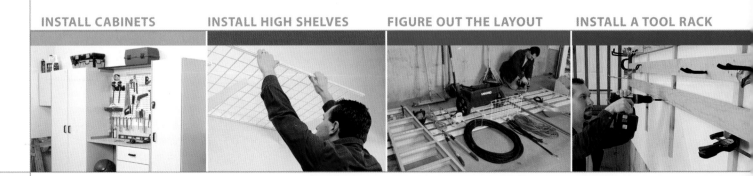

### ✛ WHAT CAN GO WRONG

**It can be difficult** to judge distance when parking your car in tight quarters. To make sure you don't hit your new cabinets when pulling your car into the garage, hang an old tennis ball from a string that contacts the windshield at the point you want to stop.

### ⊛ WHAT'S DIFFERENT?

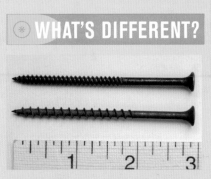

**"Drywall" screws are available** with fine and coarse threads. The fine ones work best on metal studs. Use coarse-thread screws in wood.

# Tools & Gear

*With a couple of exceptions in each case, the tools required for all three projects are the same.*

## FOR ALL PROJECTS...

**LEVELS.** To keep your installations level and plumb, you'll need a 2-ft. level and a torpedo level.

**STUD FINDER.** You need to find the studs before you put up your shelves and tool rack.

**TAPE MEASURE.** For this job, a 25-ft. tape will serve you best.

**CORDLESS DRILL/DRIVER.** To avoid unnecessary delays, make sure that you've got two fully charged batteries before you begin.

**DRILL ACCESSORIES.** A quick-change "drill-and-drive" kit will help you to work faster. Your kit should include a #2 Phillips bit, a selection of small-diameter drill bits ($1/16$ in. to $1/4$ in.), a $7/16$-in. hex-head diver, and a #6 combination countersink/counterbore bit.

**STEP LADDER.** A 4-ft. to 6-ft. ladder will help you with installation work that needs to happen at overhead heights.

**RUBBER MALLET.** Since it delivers a cushioned blow, this mallet is helpful when assembling cabinets. If you don't have one, it's OK to cushion the blow from a regular hammer with a block of wood.

**BAR CLAMPS.** Thirty-in.-long ones will work for clamping the trays during assembly.

**SAW.** You'll need a circular saw or a crosscut handsaw to build the storage rack.

**RAFTER SQUARE.** This triangular "speedsquare" also does a good job of guiding your circular saw when cutting boards to length.

## COOL TOOL

**E**lectronic sensors (aka stud finders) do a quick and foolproof job of finding studs, ceiling joists, and other framing members. Simple models flash or beep when the device is over the center of a stud. This model shines a light line at the edge of the stud. More expensive versions can even detect hidden wiring and plumbing pipes.

# What to Buy

*Since there are three different storage projects featured in this chapter, your shopping list depends on which project(s) you're doing. That's why the list is divided below.*

## CABINET/WORKBENCH/PEGBOARD COMBINATION

Different cabinet combinations are available to fit your budget and the space available in your garage. If you can't find garage-style cabinets like those discussed here, you can use ready-to-assemble cabinets like those featured in our laundry room makeover (p. 234). Either way, cabinets include all assembly hardware.

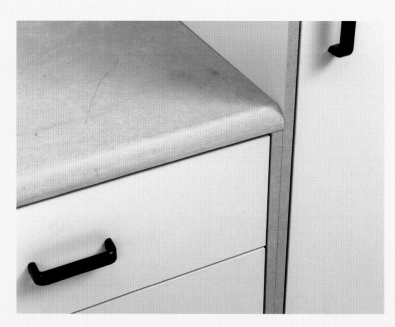

## HEAVY-DUTY SHELF

The shelf system discussed here comes in kit form, with a pair of 48-in.-long shelves, four support brackets, and mounting screws. Other heavy-duty shelving options are also available, including steel brackets that can support wood shelves that you purchase and cut separately.

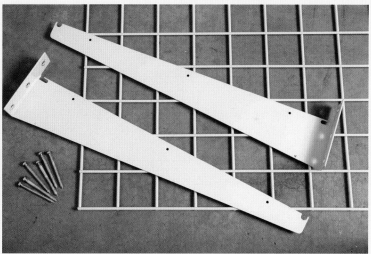

## GARDEN TOOL RACK

To build and install a 12-ft. rack like the one discussed here, use the following shopping list:

**LUMBER.** Get 14 ft. of 1x2 pine or spruce for the vertical battens. For the horizontal boards, you'll need five 12-ft. 1x4s.

**FASTENERS.** Buy a 1-lb. box of 2½-in. deck screws.

**HOOKS & HANGERS.** You can have some fun here. Make a list of all the tools and items you'd like to hang on your rack, and note what kind of hardware you need to support this gear. Make sure to get installation screws as necessary, so you can mount your hangers on the rack.

**Make sure that the legs** on all base cabinets are fully screwed in before you lift each cabinet up and into position. This helps prevent the legs from breaking and also gives you plenty of length for leveling.

◆ **COOL TOOL**

**The torpedo level** works comfortably where a standard 2-ft. level won't. It's small enough to fit in a small toolbox or in your pocket. To get accurate readings over longer runs, pair a torpedo level with a straightedge.

# Assembling Cabinets

**1** **ASSEMBLE THE CABINETS.** The cabinet parts and the assembly hardware will come in the box. Attach the top, bottom, and (on tall cabinets) fixed center shelf to the side panels. Then attach the cleats, inserting screws into factory-drilled holes. Fasten the mounting plates for the legs to the bottom front edge of the cabinet, then screw the legs in all the way.

**2** **ASSEMBLE THE DRAWERS.** For units with drawers, assemble each drawer case by fitting all four case sides around the drawer bottom. Secure corner joints with glued wooden dowels inserted in predrilled holes. Attach the handle to the drawer front, then loosely attach the front to the drawer case with screws.

**3** **INSTALL THE DRAWER SLIDES.** Attach a drawer slide to the bottom edge of a drawer, flush with the front edge. Secure the mating slide to the side of the cabinet. This should be quick and easy, since holes for installation screws have been predrilled at the factory. Repeat this step for all drawer-slide hardware.

**4** **POSITION & LEVEL THE CABINETS.** The smartest strategy here is to position and level the tallest cabinet first, then level the others to it. When the cabinet is roughly in position, mark stud locations on the wall, just below the bottom edge of the installation cleat. Position the cabinets against the wall and screw the legs up or down to get the cabinets level and plumb.

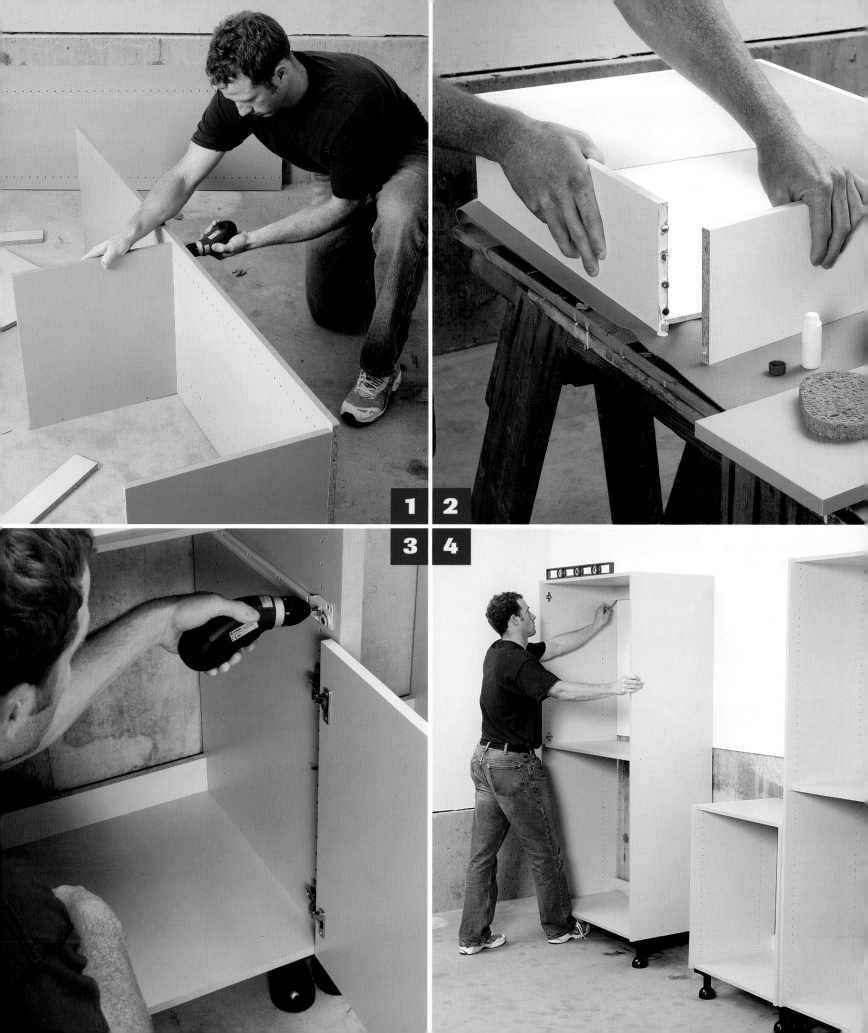

**The fastest way to install** cabinets against a concrete or concrete-block wall is to use 2-in. Tapcon screws. Bore a ¼-in.-dia. clearance hole through the cleat on the back of the cabinet. Then use the special masonry bit that comes with your Tapcon screws to bore installation holes in the concrete. You can drive these screws using a nut driver or a socket wrench, as shown here.

**To align the drawer** front with the benchtop and cabinet sides, close the drawer, make adjustments, and, while holding the pieces together, slide the drawer open while a helper applies clamps. Tighten the screws. Check the alignment, and drive two 1-in. screws through the drawer case and into the false front.

# Installing Everything

**5** **INSTALL THE FLOOR CABINETS.** Use a ³⁄₁₆-in.-dia. bit to drill two installation holes in the top cleat and two in the bottom cleat. To fasten the bottom cleat against a concrete wall, drive Tapcon screws as we did here, or use a heavy-duty masonry anchor. Use

heavy-duty drywall anchors to fasten the top cleat against drywall. Insert wood shims behind cleats if necessary to keep cabinets plumb.

**6** **INSTALL THE BENCHTOP.** Place the benchtop on the base cabinet and rest any unsupported end on a clamp. Using a #6 combination bit, bore three countersunk pilot holes through the cabinet side and into the edge of the top. Then drive in 2-in. screws. Similarly, connect the adjoining cabinets, but with 1¼-in. screws.

**7** **INSTALL WALL CABINETS.** The wall cabinets used here are designed to be supported by a rail screwed to the wall. Install the rail following the manufacturer's instructions, making sure to keep it level and at the proper height. Hang the cabinet on the rail, and drive extra installation screws through the top and bottom rails and into studs or drywall anchors, as in step 5.

**8** **INSTALL DOORS.** Attach the hinges to the door and the mounting plates to the cabinet with screws. Engage the hinges on the mounting plates and tighten the mounting screws. Make side, height, and depth adjustments to fit the door squarely over its opening. Nice work so far; your cabinet-workbench combination is looking good.

**Chuck a ⁷⁄₁₆-in. hex driver** in your drill/driver for speedy installation of the 4-in. lag screws. If your cordless drill/driver is overpowered by this task, you may need to use a corded drill. It also helps to spray the lags with silicone lubricant before driving.

**Large plastic tubs** are great for storing smaller items and anything that needs protection from dust and moisture. Look for clear plastic boxes if you need to see what's inside. Or simply stick on a label.

# Installing Heavy-Duty Shelves

**9** **LOCATE THE SHELF.** With this type of shelving, your best bet is to set shelf height high on the wall, but within reach. Mark a level line on the wall at the planned height of your shelf. You can use a regular level or a laser model. Extend the line about 2 ft. longer than the planned length of the shelf being installed.

**10** **MARK STUD LOCATIONS.** Using a stud finder, locate your first stud. Then measure 16 in. from the stud's approximate center and test for a neighboring stud. Keep marking stud locations along your shelf line.

**11** **INSTALL SHELF BRACKETS.** Hold each shelf bracket in place on the line and centered over a stud location. Trace the bracket's mounting holes onto the wall in pencil. Remove the bracket to drill pilot holes for installation screws. Reposition the bracket and secure it with the lag screws that come in the kit (see also DO IT FAST, left).

**12** **INSTALL SHELF SECTIONS.** Place shelves atop the brackets following the manufacturer's instructions. Secure each shelf section to holes in the brackets and to neighboring shelf sections with plastic tie-straps. That's it. Now you can load 'em up.

**9**  **10**

**11**  **12**

**It's a lot easier to determine** accessory placement if you make a temporary version of the rack on the floor, perhaps tacking on two or three battens. Then position the tools, etc. and pre-install the accessories. Tip: Make a quick sketch or take a digital photo so you remember what goes where later!

# Rack 'Em Up!

**13** **CUT & SAND THE PARTS.** Cut your long 1x4s to a uniform final length using a circular saw or cutting by hand with a cross-cut saw. Using sandpaper wrapped around a sanding block, smooth rough edges and round over sharp corners. Stain or varnish the boards for a more finished appearance, if you wish. Hey, with a garage, every little bit helps!

**14** **HOOK UP!** Space your boards evenly apart on the garage floor, just as they'll be installed on the wall. You can temporarily tack a couple of battens across the boards to hold them in place, if necessary. Next, position the tools and other stuff you want to store on the rack. Select and install the best hooks and other hang-up hardware, drilling pilot holes and driving screws as necessary.

**15** **INSTALL THE BATTENS.** Mark stud locations on the wall, and establish a level line to determine where the top or bottom of each batten will be. Locate the studs just as you did in step 10. Then use your drill/driver to screw battens to the wall at these locations. Install each batten with three 2½-in. deck screws.

**16** **ATTACH THE BOARDS.** Use your drill/driver to screw each board in place across the battens. Keep a uniform space (we used 1 in.) between boards, and use a pair of screws at each batten connection. To avoid splitting the batten, it's best to drill pilot holes for your screws. When your last board is in place, load up your rack and listen carefully: Your car is saying "thanks."

**Slat wall systems are based on slotted wall panels designed to hold a variety of specially made hangers and storage fixtures.**

**Versatility is usually important when you're shopping for a sport storage rack.**

**The key to** organizing a garage is to move stuff from the floor to the walls by making use of every vertical inch of space. The challenge is to find the right combination of hooks, hangers, and specialized hardware for all your gear. Keep tools and toys accessible, but do the opposite for solvents and other dangerous materials. Once you get your garage organized, it's much easier to keep it that way.

Individual hooks and a wire grid system combine to get this garage wall organized.

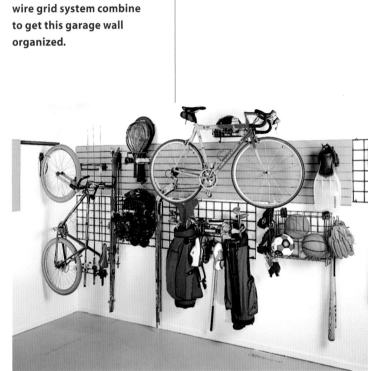

Bikes used to be awkward to store for easy retrieval, but two workable ways are shown here.

A heavy-duty standard-and-bracket system gives you shelf space that's adjustable. A folding step stool provides easy access to high shelves.

These heavy-duty adjustable shelves are easy to install, thanks to a horizontal mounting track that you screw to the wall as a support for the vertical standards.

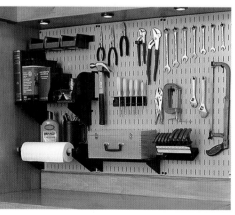

A combination of shelves and cabinets is often the best storage strategy in garage and utility-room areas.

Pegboard paved the way for this slotted wall panel designed to hold different hooks, hangers, and shelf supports.

Closed storage is ideal for chemicals, paints, and other items that should stay clear of kids. A garage can get pretty dirty, too, so doors cut down on dust.

Not all cabinets are meant for the kitchen. This rugged cabinet system is designed to provide storage and workshop space—a great storage solution in a garage, basement, shed, or utility room.

# Overhead Organizer

Get ahead of your clutter with **OVERHEAD SHELVES** that take advantage of out-of-the-way space in the garage

I F YOUR GARAGE IS OVERWHELMED WITH CLUTTER, from bikes to boxes of holiday decorations, things are looking up…literally. The ceiling of your garage—including the area above your open garage doors—is the perfect spot for things you use only occasionally. In just an afternoon using a basic set of tools and prefabricated components, you can install these overhead shelves, stow away your stuff, and enjoy a garage that looks and feels more organized. Made from industrial metal and hung from the structural frame of the garage ceiling, these tough, good-looking racks can hold up to 250 lbs. of items you want to park in long-term storage.

| LOCATE THE FRAMING | MOUNT THE BRACKETS | INSTALL THE SUPPORTS | FASTEN THE SHELVES |

Your ceiling's structural frame has many names—joist, beam, chord, and rafter—but they all mean the same thing. These generally synonymous terms identify the wooden framing members to which you'll fasten your organizer's mounting brackets and struts.

### ◆ DO IT NOW

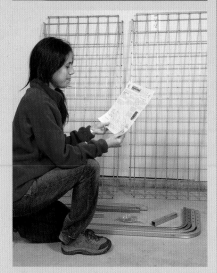

**With any ready-to-assemble shelf,** make sure you've got all the parts and fasteners before you start the installation. The instructions should include a complete parts list. Set aside each piece (or groups of pieces) and check their size and number against the instructions. By taking inventory, you will also get familiar with the manufacturer's lingo.

# Tools & Gear

*Dig through your basic tool set to find what you'll need to drill holes, assemble the organizer, and fasten it into the ceiling, including these tools:*

**DRILL.** Use a corded or cordless drill to make pilot holes into the ceiling frame. It also will tighten the bolts and screws that hold the shelves to their supports and the brackets to the beams.

**TAPE MEASURE.** A retractable-steel tape measure determines the amount of clearance between the garage doors and your vehicles and measures the proper distance between the mounting brackets.

**STUD FINDER.** Find the location of your roofing frame's joists with this handy tool.

**RUBBER MALLET.** Nudge the supports into place without marring the organizer's finish.

**SOCKET SET.** A manual set will work fine, or get socket bits that will slip into your drill for more torque and tightening power.

**STEP LADDER.** Put your tools and yourself up close to the ceiling on a 6-ft. or 8-ft. stepladder.

**CARPENTER'S PENCIL.** Keep the tip sharp for accurate marks, especially when you locate the garage's ceiling beams.

## COOL TOOL

**Tape measures are all the same, right?** No. It's true that they all perform the same function, but today's retractable steel tapes offer some cool features, including ergonomic molds for comfort and better grip, and they're equipped with locks that keep the extended tape in position while you mark your measurements. A tough, brightly colored housing makes the tape measure easy to find. Go for a 25-ft.-long tape to handle almost any household task or project.

# What to Buy

**1| READY-TO-ASSEMBLE ORGANIZERS.** These self-contained, ceiling-mounted shelves come with everything you need, including support posts of different lengths that can be screwed together to accommodate different depths or telescoping supports to fit the shelves into your allowable clearances. You'll find fasteners inside the package—often even a wrench, drill bit, or a socket bit—to speed the installation. The components are all lightweight industrial metal with a bright steel or shiny white, powder-coated finish for a clean look. Assembled, the system supports up to a maximum of 250 lbs. of evenly distributed weight across standard ceiling frame designs or beam spacing.

## OVERHEAD ORGANIZER DIAGRAM

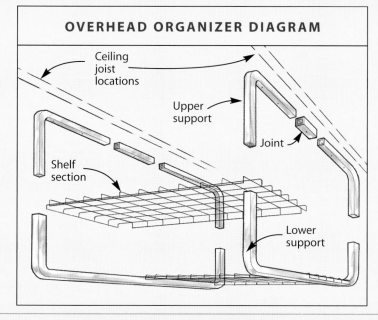

Ceiling joist locations

Upper support

Joint

Shelf section

Lower support

## CHECK YOUR FRAME

**If your house was built before 1984,** chances are good that its ceiling joists or beams are at least 2×6 lumber spaced 16 in. apart—on center—and capable of carrying quite a bit of weight; houses built after that tend to rely on 2×4 components or prefabricated, engineered trusses spaced 24 in. on center, which reduces their load-carrying ability. Check with the shelving manufacturer to make sure your garage's roof frame can handle the load, especially if you install multiple organizers or plan to store heavy items. When in doubt, restrict the load to lightweight objects, or span several joists with two 8-ft.-long, 2×4 ledger boards to spread out and share the weight across several joists.

**If you plan to add a shelf** in the void between the top of your open overhead garage door and the ceiling, you'll need at least 19 in. of clear open space to permit usable storage without intruding on the door's operation. Also, try to avoid placing the shelves adjacent to or too close to the garage door tracks, which can limit usable storage apace.

**If you install your overhead shelf** in a location near the garage door, test the clearance between the top of the open garage door and the ceiling before you install the shelf supports. Loosely mount a post to the first bracket you install, open the garage door, and check to make sure the door doesn't hit the post. If the clearance is okay, install the remaining mounting brackets; if not, choose another location.

# Install the Shelving Unit

**1** **FIND THE FRAMING.** This is easy in an open-ceiling garage. If the garage ceiling is finished with wallboard, however, use your stud finder to pinpoint the location of the ceiling's structural beams. Use a pencil to mark the outside edges of each ceiling beam every 12 in. along its length to ensure that both mounting bolts for each bracket can be fastened to the structural frame. If you have access to the attic space above the garage's ceiling, you can also climb into the space and find its beam locations.

**2** **MOUNT THE BRACKETS.** With your pencil, mark the location of the overhead shelf's brackets and mounting screws, and drill pilot holes for the screws; depending on the dimensions of the shelving unit, there will be one or more mounting brackets to install on each ceiling beam. Use your socket set or a socket bit in a cordless drill to drive the screws, tightening them against the brackets.

**3** **INSTALL THE SUPPORTS.** Determine the maximum length of the mounting posts to which you'll fasten the supports. If the unit uses telescoping supports, fit the pieces together, adjust their length, and insert their pins and retainer clips. For screw-together support designs, screw the supports tightly into the threaded opening in the center of each mounting bracket, then fit the shelf support  into the sleeves between two posts; if necessary, tap the sleeves with a rubber mallet. Use a tape measure to confirm that all of the supports are set at the same depth. Repeat with the second support on the other side.

**4** **FASTEN THE SHELVES.** Place the shelves on top of the shelf supports, with the raised edge or lip facing down to fit snugly on the shelf supports and add structural strength. Connect the shelves to the supports using the hardware provided, following the manufacturer's directions. Load the shelves, taking care to distribute the weight of each object and the total load as evenly as possible. Check the mounting bolts at each bracket every six months and tighten them, if necessary—vibration from operating the garage door could loosen the nuts.

Some overhead racks designed for use with garage-wall panel systems are enclosed on their tops, bottoms, and sides and have an overhead door. They help keep stored goods from becoming dusty and can protect valuable items from theft.

Install two rows of overhead shelves along the perimeter sides and the end wall of your garage (left) to store heavy items that are supported by the wall's frame members rather than the ceiling joists. Compact overhead storage units (right) pull down for filling and unloading, then fold back up against the ceiling.

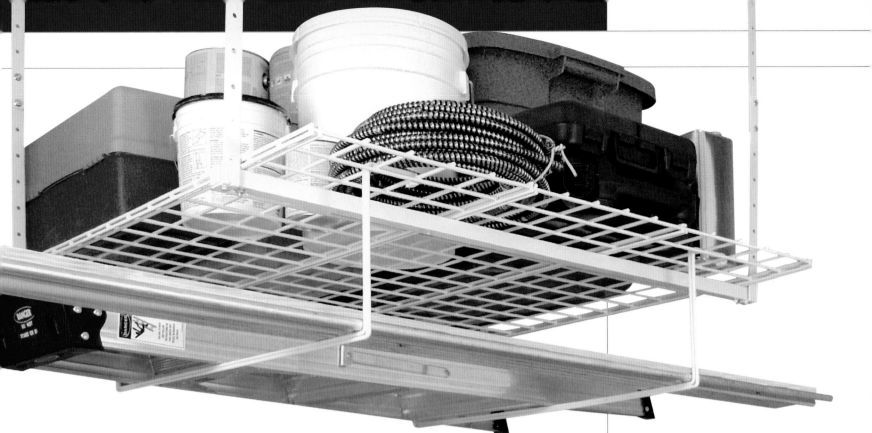

**Your garage ceiling and walls** can help solve your storage woes. The sky's the limit in terms of the options and accessories you can use to make your storage fit your lifestyle—and all your gear! Start by taking stock of what you have, separate it into groups by how often you need access to it—as well as by sizes and weights—and then look for storage systems and accessories that accommodate the items and your needs.

Lift bikes off the floor and out of your way—but keep them easily accessible by every member of the family. A ceiling-mounted pulley system evenly distributes the load to both wheels or the bike's frame.

If you have installed high shelves made of welded wire, use hooks to suspend items under them. It's also a great way to raise long-handled tools and sports equipment off of your garage floor.

287

# Workshop Solution

**Transform a bare garage wall into a multipurpose WORKSHOP AREA featuring cabinets, work surface & electrical outlets**

FOR MANY FOLKS, A GARAGE OFTEN DOUBLES AS A WORK AREA for hobbies and light-duty home improvement projects. This multipurpose workshop area will create a space where everything is organized and within easy reach—and it's easy to build on a base of ready-to-assemble cabinets. The cabinets are lockable, so they can keep sharp tools, paints, and solvents child-safe. Add a generous work surface and a handy pegboard to the setup and you'll enjoy even more utility and convenience. All it takes is a little carpentry skill and a spare Saturday to transform a blank wall or corner into a useful workshop.

**ASSEMBLE THE CABINETS    HANG THE CABINETS        SET THE COUNTERTOP        ADD ELECTRICAL OUTLETS**

▶ **LINGO**

MDF is an acronym for medium-density fiberboard, a composite wood made from wood fibers glued under heat and pressure that is denser and stiffer than solid woods such as oak and pine. RTA is shorthand used by cabinet parts manufacturers; it means ready to assemble.

◆ **DO IT NOW**

**Before you purchase cabinets,** make sure you've got the space and the clearances to accommodate them. Be sure vehicles will still fit in the garage once the workshop is finished, and that the doors of the upper cabinets can swing under or are clear of the garage door and its track or springs.

# Tools & Gear

*The ready-to-assemble (RTA) cabinets are built quickly and installed easily with a basic set of tools, including these items:*

**DRILL.** You'll need one of these to drive in the lag screws that secure the cabinets to the wall. In addition to a set of drill and screwdriver bits, consider a socket set (see COOL TOOL, below).

**CARPENTRY TOOLS.** Keep on hand a 12-oz. hammer, rubber mallet, hand saw, combination square, measuring tape, carpenter's pencil, and 4-ft.-long carpenter's level.

**STUD FINDER.** This electronic tool makes it easy to find the wall studs behind wallboard for attaching the cabinets.

**ELECTRICAL TOOLS.** Use a voltage tester, both lineman's and needle-nose pliers, electrical tape, and wire nuts to extend a circuit in the garage to the workshop area.

**STEPLADDER.** You'll need this to safely hold the upper cabinets in place as you attach them to the wall.

## COOL TOOL

A **set of sockets** for your drill makes it easier and faster to drive lag screws and other hexagonal-headed fasteners than you could with a manual socket wrench. Each socket features a stem similar to a drill or screw bit that fits and tightens in the drill's chuck. Sockets are sold in metric or standard fractional measurements (e.g., 3/4 in.), so choose a set the same size as the dimensions of the lag screws that come in the cabinet package you purchase.

# What to Buy

**1| READY-TO-ASSEMBLE (RTA) CABINETS.** For lasting durability, look for solid wood or medium-density fiberboard (MDF) construction—as opposed to pressed wood or particleboard—on the box panels, frames, doors, and drawers.

**2| FASTENERS.** Unless supplied with the cabinets, get a small box of 2-in. lag screws to attach them to the wall. For the 1×2 frame, use 3-in. lag screws to fasten the frame to the studs. Use wood glue and ¾-in. wood screws to attach the pegboard to its frame.

**3| PEGBOARD AND HOOKS.** You'll need a 24-in. by 48-in. piece of pegboard and a set of hooks to hang your small tools.

**4| 1×2 LUMBER AND SHIMS.** You'll use a pair of 8-ft. lengths to frame the pegboard and a bundle of wood or composite shims to level the base cabinets, if necessary.

**5| COUNTERTOP.** Go with a premade laminate countertop over a composite wood substrate, sold in standard dimensions and easily attached to RTA cabinets.

**6| WIRE MOLD AND OUTLET STRIP.** You may need a wire mold—a flexible, prewired plastic channel—to extend wires from the nearest junction box to a 6-ft.-long strip of electrical outlets mounted across the back of the countertop.

## A READY-IN-MINUTES WORKSHOP

**P**airs of premade wall and base cabinets, a laminate countertop, and a pegboard panel combine to make a tidy workbench with convenient tool and material storage that fits neatly against a garage sidewall. Kits that contain complete RTA cabinets you can assemble in minutes means that your workshop will be finished and ready for your use in record time. Always check the parts list; inventory the components, fasteners, and supplied tools; and follow the manufacturer's directions for the best result when you assemble factory cabinets.

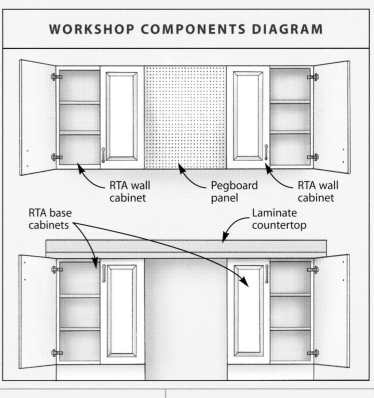

**WORKSHOP COMPONENTS DIAGRAM**

RTA wall cabinet — Pegboard panel — RTA wall cabinet

RTA base cabinets — Laminate countertop

## ✚ WHAT CAN GO WRONG

**If your garage walls** have a concrete foundation curb, you'll have to cut out the back and sides of the cabinet box to fit over it. This extra step requires some precision and perhaps refinishing. If possible, choose a wall for your workshop without a curb.

## ✦ DO IT NOW

**If you plan to refinish** your garage floor with epoxy paint, finish that project before you add a workshop. If you wait until the workshop is in place, you'll have to refinish around the base cabinets, which might mar their surfaces or make for a less-than-ideal floor finish. Use sheets of cardboard or butcher paper to protect the new floor finish as you assemble this workshop.

# Assemble the Cabinets

**1** **LOCATE AN AREA.** Look for a blank wall with one or two existing electrical outlets and, if possible, no foundation curb (see WHAT CAN GO WRONG, left). The space should be 78 in. across, 30 in. deep, and 72 in. tall. Use a stud finder to locate each wall-frame member behind the wallboard; with a 4-ft. carpenter's level and a pencil, mark along the length of each stud within the project area.

**2** **BUILD THE CABINET BOXES.** Working one cabinet at a time, remove all the components of the RTA cabinet from their shipping box and check them against the list provided with the assembly instructions, along with any hardware, fasteners, and tools. Read  and follow the manufacturer's instructions exactly to assemble the four cabinets, repeating this process with each unit.

 **3** **READY THE DOORS.** Add door hinges and drawer hardware, as directed by the manufacturer. Attach the hardware first to the door, then to the cabinet's walls. Mount and test the operation of the doors and drawers, and adjust them, if necessary, so they swing or slide open, close smoothly, and are flush to the cabinet frames with their latches secure.

**4** **PROTECT THE FINISHES.** Once you are satisfied with the doors' and drawers' operation, remove them, as well as any adjustable shelving inside the cabinets, and set them aside in a safe place, where they will be protected from damage as you move and install the units on the wall. This makes the cabinet boxes lighter and easier to transport and shim, ensuring a good result. Most concealed hingesets have release clips that facilitate easy removal and reattachment of the doors without unscrewing the hinges from the cabinets or doors.

**Even without its doors or drawers,** a storage cabinet can become heavy or awkward to hold in place as you level and plumb it, back it up to a wall stud, and set it squarely over a base cabinet—much less fasten it. Have a helper hold it in place, and adjust it as you position and install it, saving time and preventing mistakes.

**If the back of a cabinet** covers an existing electrical outlet, use your measuring tape and pencil to transfer its location to the inside back panel of the cabinet. Then cut out a hole to fit the outlet box, using a drill bit on your drill to make starter holes at two of the marked corners, followed by a small hand or power jig saw to cut the hole's straight lines.

# Build the Workshop

**5** **HANG THE BASE CABINETS.** Place the base cabinets 24 in. apart, with at least one wall stud running behind each cabinet. Adjust the first cabinet for level, checking with a carpenter's level and adding shims under the frame, if necessary. Drill three pilot holes through the back of the cabinet box and wallboard into the stud, then drive in 2-in. lag screws or the supplied fasteners to secure the cabinet to the wall. Do not over-tighten the fasteners. Measure 24 in. across, position the other base cabinet, then install it the same way; use your level across both cabinets as you shim to ensure a level surface for the countertop (see Step 9, p. 296).

**6** **HANG THE WALL CABINETS.** With a helper, lift and place a wall cabinet directly over a base cabinet. Use your carpenter's level to check that it is plumb—vertically straight—and level. Make pencil marks at the top, bottom, and sides of the cabinet for reference. Measure from the nearest corner to the stud and use your pencil to transfer the stud's location to the inside back panel of the cabinet. Drill three pilot holes through the back of the cabinet box and wallboard into the stud, then drive in 2-in. lag screws or the supplied fasteners to attach the cabinet to the wall; avoid overtightening the fasteners. Repeat for the second cabinet, checking for level and spacing to the other cabinets.

**7** **FRAME AND INSTALL THE PEGBOARD.** Measure the area between the two wall cabinets; it should be 24 in. wide by 30 in. tall. Cut the pegboard on a table saw or with a circular saw to fit the space. Measure and cut 1×2 lumber to frame the perimeter of the pegboard's back. Attach the frame flush with the pegboard's outside edges, using wood glue and wood screws every 6 in. around its perimeter. Position the assembly on the wall and drive lag screws through the pegboard, its frame, and the wallboard into the wall studs.

**8** **FINISH WITH HOOKS.** Attach removable hooks, shelves, fittings, and other small tool hangers to the pegboard.

**5**

**6**

**7**

**8**

A backsplash is a 3-in.- to 4-in.-high vertical piece along the back edge of many premade counter-tops. It helps contain any spills, debris, tools, or fasteners from falling behind the countertop.

◆ **DO IT NOW**

**Check the available amperage** of the circuit you intend to extend before connecting a new outlet strip at an outlet or junction box. You'll find the amperage of the circuit on the circuit breaker or fuse in the main service panel. If there's not enough amps to power a full strip, consider a shorter strip or simply mount one or two new outlets on the wall above the counter-top and extend service to them.

# Finish the Job

**9** **ATTACH THE COUNTERTOP.** The base cabinets either allow for fastening the countertop through the cabinets' tops or feature preinstalled cleats at each corner for this purpose. Position and shim the laminate countertop over the base cabinets and against the wall, then loosely fasten it to the cabinets from the underside with lag screws. Set each screw once all of them have been started, tightening them flush with the wood's surface.

**10** **FIND THE SOURCE.** Locate the nearest electrical outlet or junction box and turn off power to its circuit at the service panel, then remove its cover, expose the wires, and extend electrical service. Mount clamps for the outlet strip. It's best either to fit the outlet strip flush to one end or to center it, then fasten it to the wall with screws at each stud location; you should have stud locations marked every 16 in. or 24 in. along the strip's 6-ft. length.

**11** **ATTACH THE OUTLET STRIP.** Fit the outlet strip along the back edge of the countertop or backsplash. If the garage walls are covered with wallboard or made of concrete blocks, install a wire mold as a bridge from the nearest outlet or junction box to the outlet strip; it will protect and hide the wires.

**12** **CONNECT THE CIRCUIT.** Connect the outlet strip's wires, following the instructions in the outlet strip's package. Turn on the circuit and test the outlet with a voltage tester before pushing the wires back into the junction box and attaching its cover. Finally, reattach the cabinet doors, drawers, and shelving to complete the project, making sure they still swing or slide open, close smoothly, and rest flush and flat with the cabinet boxes. Adjust the shelves inside the cabinets as necessary to accommodate your storage needs. Mount and plug in accessory lighting.

**Your own garage workshop** has never been easier. A quick web search or trip to your nearest home improvement store will reveal a variety of RTA cabinets and countertops in a range of sizes to suit any taste, special need, or available space. You also have a choice of small tool hangers if a pegboard isn't your style, including magnetic strips and slotted racks that fit a number of tools and gear, and which fasten easily and quickly to the wall. Don't forget to incorporate other benchtop organizers, such as bins, baskets, shelves, and book and magazine holders.

**Specialty hanging racks (above) are the right choice to give easy access to frequently needed tools. Another choice worth considering is a magnetic bar rack (below) that holds steel and iron tools.**

**Use a ready-made leg assembly to support one end of a counter-top and a cabinet for the other. An adjustable stool on rollers makes working at close range a snap.**

This complete auto shop setup has drawer cabinets to hold an assortment of large and small shop tools, a large work surface, a pegboard rack for hand tools, and wall storage for large equipment, such as an under-car creeper and an airtight receptacle for the safe disposal of oily rags.

Organize your wrenches, pliers, screwdrivers, saws, and hammers by size to make finding them easy. Outline each tool with a marking pen to make it easy to spot its place on the pegboard.

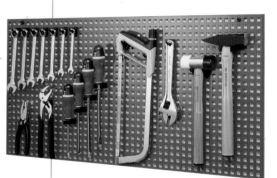

Use a cabinet with both large bins and smaller cubbyholes to hold tools, materials, and partially finished projects. Look for a unit with deep bins and a raised lip, or choose one that has slanted openings to hold objects inside.

Heavy-gauge legs and strong braces mean an unshakeable workbench. Choose one that bolts together if storing the bench flat between uses is a necessity.

# Main Entry Makeover

Give your home **A GRAND ENTRANCE** with a new walkway fashioned from precast-concrete pavers

DMIT IT: THE PATH LEADING TO YOUR FRONT DOOR isn't exactly what you'd call inviting, much less a design element. Even if it's still in pretty good shape, you may just be tired of looking at it and wish it were different. With precast concrete pavers, you can take action and create a quick, easy, and beautiful makeover of that main entry walk. You'll enjoy ripping out the old concrete and preparing the base for your new path, then find out how simple it is to lay a new path of pavers and secure them in place. At that point you can step back and take pride in your handiwork—and wait for guests to beat a path to your door.

EXCAVATE AND COMPACT    PREPARE THE BASE        LAY PAVERS              COMPACT

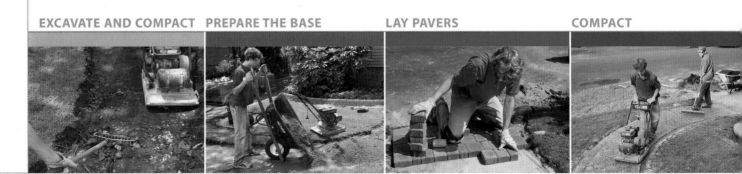

**A gas-powered diamond blade cutoff saw** is great for cutting the walk edge in place and saves hours of time compared to a table-mounted masonry wet saw, but it has drawbacks. It produces enormous clouds of hazardous dust (wear a dust mask and warn neighbors to close windows); it's also loud and not as easy to control safely. Saws of both types are available for rent.

**The minimum recommended slope** for drainage—along the length or, when that's not possible, side-to-side— is 3/16 in. for every foot of pavement. The maximum slope along the length for comfortable walking is 1½ in. per foot.

# Tools & Gear

*Complete instructions, including a tools and materials list, are available from your paver supplier. What's needed will vary according to the scope of your project and the existing site conditions, but this project requires relatively few tools.*

**LEVEL.** A 4-ft. level will do unless your walk is narrow, which may necessitate a 2-ft. version.

**TAPE MEASURE.** You can get by with a 25-ft. retractable tape.

**SHOVEL(S).** You'll find good use for both square and spade types for excavating.

**PICKAX OR MATTOCK, PRY BAR & 12-LB. SLEDGEHAMMER.** Three tools essential for removing an existing concrete walk.

**CONTRACTOR'S WHEELBARROW.** There's lots of heavy stuff to move around.

**STEEL GARDEN RAKE.** Use this for spreading and leveling.

**TIN SNIPS.** You'll need a sharp pair of these to cut the plastic tubing.

**TURF EDGER.** This handy tool makes it easy to cut and remove turf along the walk's edges.

**MASONRY TOOLS.** You'll need a pointed trowel and a steel float to create a subsurface edge.

**RUBBER HAMMER OR MALLET.** This is the tool used to set the pavers tight to each other.

**PUSH BROOM.** The easiest way to fill the joints between installed pavers is to brush dry sand diagonally across the surface of the walk.

**SAFETY GEAR.** Don't work without eye protection, earplugs, a disposable dust mask, work gloves, and knee pads.

**PLATE COMPACTOR.** Rent a vibrating plate compactor to properly compact the base, sand, and pavers. Although it is heavy and might appear difficult to control, the vibration is managed with the throttle, and the machine moves along by itself. It's easy to steer.

**HAND TAMPER.** Use this where the machine can't go. Pad the plate to avoid chipping or damaging pavers, and tamp straight down to make sure the pavers remain flat and even.

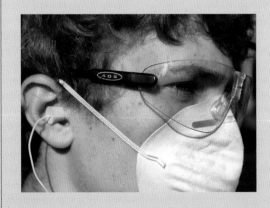

## BE PREPARED

**This is hard work**; drink plenty of water and take frequent breaks. In addition to knee pads, which you will want when you install pavers, and work gloves, which you may never take off, you will need eye protection when breaking up a concrete walk along with earplugs and tight-fitting disposable dust masks when cutting the pavers.

# What to Buy

**1| CONCRETE PAVERS.** Pavers used for walkways and residential driveways are 2⅜ in. thick and come in a variety of sizes; this walk required three different sizes to achieve the desired pattern.

**2| CRUSHED STONE.** Whatever it is called in your area—process screenings, Item 4, or simply crushed stone—make sure the mix varies in size from dust to ¾-in. pieces. It will eventually compact rock-hard over time, which is why it is such a good base material.

**3| SAND.** Order "washed concrete sand" for the setting bed that lies directly below the pavers and for filling joints. (Do not use stone dust or screenings such as Item 4 or mason's sand.)

**4| PLASTIC TUBING.** Use a length of flexible, ½-in.-diameter tubing or garden hose to define the edges of a curved walk.

**5| CARPENTER'S PENCIL.** Use a carpenter's pencil to mark the curve you'll cut along the edge pavers; maintain a sharp point with a carpenter's-pencil sharpener.

**6| PREMIXED CONCRETE.** A half-dozen 50-lb. bags should suffice for the subsurface edging and any handrail posts.

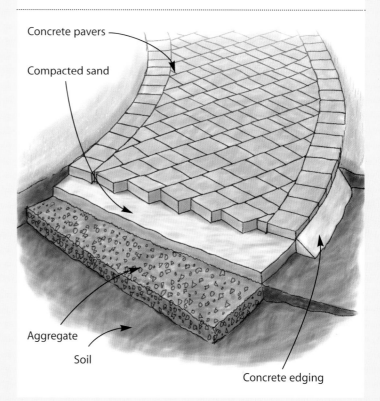

PAVERS ON SAND

Concrete pavers

Compacted sand

Aggregate

Soil

Concrete edging

## ESTIMATING MATERIALS

**For the 4-in.-thick base of crushed stone,** first calculate cubic feet: Multiply the walk length by its width, both in feet, and then multiply by 0.33. Divide that result by 27 to get cubic yards. Multiply the number of cubic yards by 1.6 to get the results in tons. Order about 1,200 lb. of sand per 100 sq. ft. of walk. Order enough pavers to cover the walk area (in sq. ft.) plus 5% for breakage and later repair. If the edges are to be cut, allow an extra 30 sq. ft. for every 100 linear ft. of cut edge. For the hidden concrete border, order a 90-lb. bag of Portland cement. Have all these materials delivered.

**Wedge a stone under** a large piece of concrete before taking a whack at it with a 12-lb. sledgehammer. It breaks easier that way. Wear eye protection!

**The cutoff saw** was invaluable here when we needed to cut the concrete landing pad for the front steps and the paver edging stones. Wear eye protection, earplugs, and a disposable dust mask.

# Preparing for Pavers

**1** **REMOVE THE EXISTING WALK.** Use the cutoff saw to divide the existing walk into sections and to cut it away from the front steps, ideally along the control (or expansion) joints, if any exist. Starting at one end of the walk, use a sledgehammer and a pickax or a mattock (which has a point on one side and a wide flat part on the other) to break up the concrete and pry up the pieces. Carefully load the broken pieces of concrete into a cart for transfer to a vehicle for disposal or recycling.

**2** **EXCAVATE.** Dig out to a minimum depth of about 8 in., removing all remaining pieces of concrete (careful, they're sharp!) and loose soil in the area of the walk, plus about 8 in. on each side, cutting turf as needed. Drive a stake to help gauge the extra width needed. Rake the soil level with a steel garden rake and tamp it firm with a vibrating-plate compactor.

**3** **PREPARE THE BASE.** Using a wheelbarrow or garden cart, haul the crushed stone and distribute it in piles along the excavated walk area. Spread it with the steel garden rake to a 4-in. depth, or until the top of the base is about 3½ in. below the desired finished walk surface. Tamp the base using a rented plate compactor to provide a firm foundation that won't later settle or shift under the weight of the sand and pavers.

**4** **PREPARE THE SAND BED.** As with the crushed stone in step 3, distribute the sand along the path and rake it level and smooth to a 1-in. depth. With a helper, use a straight-edged board as a screeding tool to level the bed and remove excess sand. Check for proper slope using your level. The end far-

thest from the house should be at least ¾ in. above the sand bed when the bubble reads level. Or, if a walk is level along its length, the sand bed should slope ¾ in. side to side (or "crown" in the center) so that water runs off to either edge.

# Setting the Pavers

**5** **PLACE THE PAVERS.** Position the pavers tightly against each other, using a rubber mallet when a little persuasion is required. Shift the courses as necessary to follow a curve or other changes in the shape of the walk. Leave an irregular edge on both sides, as you will cut those pavers to make a smooth edge in the next step.

**6** **MARK AND CUT THE EDGES.** Use plastic tubing to define the curve along the edges of the pavers. Hold it in place with spare pavers while you mark the cut line with a carpenter's pencil along the tubing's inside length. Remove the tubing and cut along your line with a cutoff saw equipped with a diamond grit blade. Make a shallow (¼-in.-deep) guide cut first along the pencil line, followed by another pass that cuts through the pavers.

**7** **INSTALL THE EDGING.** Place the edging stones next to the cut edges of the path, marking, removing, and cutting them to fit. Cut a 2-in.-deep trench along the outside of the edging stones for a banked-concrete edge, 3 in. wide and deep, that will contain the pavers. Mix concrete according to the bag's instructions, and shovel it into the trenches. Form a long wedge with a pointed trowel, and keep it damp with a sprinkler or a garden hose set on mist for at least 3 hrs., allowing it to cure properly and not crack.

**8** **FINISHING TOUCHES.** Sweep *dry* sand into the joints and have a helper follow with the compactor, going over the walk again and shaking the sand into the joints. Repeat this a few times and again in a couple of weeks until the joints are full of  sand. Repair the soil along the walk with topsoil and grass seed, covering the subsurface concrete edge.

**Concrete pavers offer a wide range** of design options to create a front walk that adds interest, value, and style. You can vary the look of the walk to fit your personal taste or your yard's existing design by using a mosaic of colors, sizes, and shapes; or, for a more formal look, stick to one size paver, but use a herringbone or crosshatch pattern, perhaps with square edges instead of a curve. Install matching veneer (or half) pavers on the steps leading up to the front door to tie the design together.

**Change levels in a concrete-paver walk by placing a cut stone at the point where the surface rises. You can also stand pavers on edge or end to make steps.**

Concrete pavers can follow curves. Use edging rows (top), random patterns made with pavers of different sizes (center), and cut pavers (bottom) to emphasize the curved sections.

Pavers come in all colors and shapes, so look over the selection carefully before choosing your materials. Choose colors that blend or contrast with your home's hue.

Common bricks have a pleasing appearance and are placed in a manner similar to pavers set on sand. A grouted joint makes the surface weatherproof, adding to its longevity. Bricks can also be mortared atop an existing concrete sidewalk.

# BBQ Headquarters

Give yourself (and your grill) a stage worthy of a backyard gourmet with a **PERFECT PATIO** of precast pavers

**S**AY GOODBYE TO THAT RUSTED, RICKETY BARBEQUE KETTLE sitting precariously on a patch of grass in the backyard. Today's tricked-out grills, and the cooks who use them, deserve a stable platform suitable for full-fledged outdoor cooking and entertaining. Here's an idea: install a backyard patio using precast concrete paving stones. Today's pavers come in a variety of shapes, colors, and sizes to suit your outdoor decorating tastes. And they install quickly on a bed of sand over gravel aggregate, making it simple to create a beautiful and durable patio you'll enjoy during cookouts for years to come.

EXCAVATE THE AREA          PREPARE THE SITE          PLACE THE PAVERS          INSTALL THE EDGE

● **NEED A HAND?**

**A mini-backhoe** makes backyard excavating a bit easier, especially when you have a large area to dig and wide-open access. Also called a "loader" because of its ability to lift and carry loads of soil and other material, a backhoe fits and turns in tight spaces and is easy to control, even for a novice. Rent one to save time—and your back.

✳ **WHAT'S DIFFERENT?**

**Concrete pavers** are a lightweight aggregate of cement and sand mixed with water and cast in many shapes and sizes. When put together they create many different designs. By contrast, bricks are kiln-fired clay and minerals, typically in rectangular shapes; brick pavers are simply thin bricks for non-structural uses, including patios and walks.

# Tools & Gear

*Beyond your basic gardening tools used to help with the excavation, gather extra gear to prep and pave the patio, including:*

**MASONRY TOOLS.** To cut the pavers to fit the diagonal design, make sure you have a brickset, chisel, and masonry hammer handy.

**TAMPERS.** Rent a mechanical tamper to compact the sand base and a padded hand tamper to set the pavers in tight spots.

**LINE AND CARPENTER'S LEVELS.** The former will help set your string line level, while the latter confirms if your patio is level across several pavers.

**PUSH BROOM.** You'll need a high-quality, densely woven push broom to make sure your topdressing of sand gets into the joints between the pavers.

**STRING LINE.** A handheld spool of heavy-duty string will help keep your pavers aligned and level.

**HAMMER.** You'll need a 20-oz. hammer to install the U-shaped landscape fabric stakes and the permanent edging spikes.

**WET TILE SAW.** Rent a saw with a diamond-grit blade suitable for cutting concrete pavers.

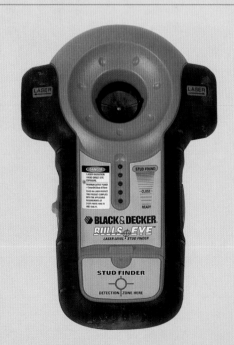

— STRING LINE

— WOOD STAKES

## COOL TOOL

**W**hen you're working alone** and want the job to go quickly and be accurate, a laser sighting device is the tool you need. Replacing manual tools, this battery-powered high-tech treasure delivers a dot or line of light to determine plumb, level, and square across longer distances than a tape measure or chalk line and with greater accuracy than a 4-ft. level or a framer's square. Use a self-leveling handheld model to establish a particular spot or mount the device on a tripod for a steady, precise measurement or mark. Some models also are equipped with a stud finder for multifunctional value.

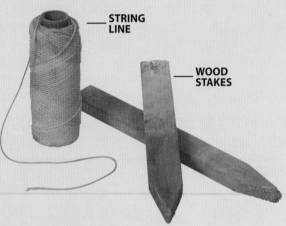

# What to Buy

**1| PRECAST PAVERS.** For this project, we selected rectangular concrete pavers measuring 7 in. wide by 9 in. long by 2 in. thick. The design of the pavers in your patio might require some of them to be cut, so order an extra 5% to 7% to account for waste.

**2| WASHED AGGREGATE.** For the 10-ft. by 15-ft. dimensions of this project, a 2-cu.-yd. load of washed, ¾-in. aggregate or pea gravel provides a solid foundation.

**3| SAND.** Purchase 2 cu. yds. of sand to cover the gravel as a stable, level base for the pavers, as well as more sand to broom into the paver joints to lock them in place.

**4| LANDSCAPE FABRIC.** Also called a weed screen, landscape fabric helps keep weeds from growing through the blocks. Secure it with 6-in.-long, U-shaped stakes spaced every 8 in. and tacked in with a hammer.

**5| EDGE RESTRAINTS.** Replace the temporary edge boards you use to align the pavers with a permanent plastic border set in place with 8-in. galvanized spikes.

**6| PVC PIPE.** Two 10-ft.-long sections of 1-in. PVC pipe will serve as a homemade guide for screeding the sand base to level before you install the pavers.

**7| 1× AND 2× LUMBER AND STAKES.** You'll need straight, 10-ft.-long pieces of lumber and wood stakes to support your screed pipe and scrap lumber for batter boards, screeds, and temporary edge boards.

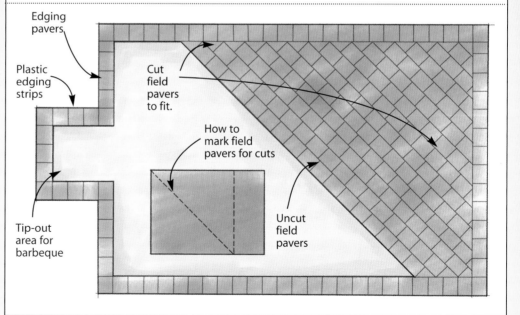

**PLAN FOR A PRECAST-PAVER PATIO**

Edging pavers

Plastic edging strips

Cut field pavers to fit.

How to mark field pavers for cuts

Tip-out area for barbeque

Uncut field pavers

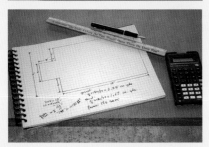
# Preparing the Bed

**1** **OUTLINE AND EXCAVATE THE AREA.** Transfer your plan on paper to its eventual location using a tape measure and batter boards at each outside corner. Pound nails into the batter boards and attach level strings as guides to the desired finished grade and outline of the patio's shape. Use

a line level to determine a slight slope for drainage away from the house (about 1½ in. every 6 ft.). Measure all diagonals to confirm 90 degree corners (they should all be of equal length), then excavate the area to 6 in. to 8 in. below the finished grade, following the slope.

**2** **LEVEL THE PAD.** Use a rake to smooth the excavated area along your slight slope (as set by your string lines) and remove roots and other debris as necessary. Install a porous weed screen or landscape fabric, tacking it in place with U-shaped stakes every 8 in.; overlap the edges of the landscape fabric at least 12 in., and install the stakes along the edge of the top layer.

**3** **INSTALL THE GRAVEL.** Use a wheelbarrow or garden cart to transfer and dump gravel into the excavated area, piling each load in a different section to make spreading it easier. Spread the aggregate out across the patio bed to a thickness of 3 in. to 4 in., but no more than 4 in. from the top of the finished grade established by measuring down from your string line. Make sure the grade follows the slight slope of the string line.

**4** **TAMP IT DOWN.** Use a mechanical tamper to compact the gravel. Add more gravel or remove some, so that the bed is 3 in. below the finished grade. Use a carpenter's level to check the slope of the gravel bed across its breadth, width, and edges. As in step 1, set a string line across the area at a few points to confirm proper depth.

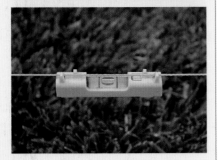
# Work the Angles

**5** **SPREAD THE SAND.** Use a wheelbarrow or garden cart to transfer sand into the gravel bed. Dump the sand in several piles to make it easier and faster to spread across the area. Roughly level the sand with a rake to at least 2 in. below the finished grade set by your string lines. Install and level temporary support boards 2 in. below grade across the patio for your PVC screed pipes to rest on, following the slope of your string line.

**6** **SCREED THE BASE.** Attach pairs of 1-in. PVC pipes to the temporary support boards with pipe clamps (cut the pipe 8 in. longer than the boards). Beginning at one end of the patio, slowly but forcefully drag a screed board across the pipes toward the centerline, removing excess sand as needed. Lift the pipes and supports out, and repeat the process across the site.

**7** **CUT THE ANGLES.** Pencil a 45 degree angle on each field paver requiring cutting, and cut it with a wet tile saw. For jobs requiring only a few cuts, score the pavers with a brickset or chisel, and tap the scored line with a masonry hammer to break them.

**8** **INSTALL THE PAVERS.** Before you set your first paver, install temporary edge boards using 1×4s and wood stakes to form a straight, stable edge. Lay all the outer pavers first, snug to the edge boards, then start the diagonal pattern inside. Stagger joints between the pavers, using a rubber-headed mallet to set them in the sand base and to narrow the joints between them. Check for a level surface with your carpenter's level.

**5**

**6**

**7**

**8**

**Take care when you tamp down** the paver bed. The hard edges of a steel-headed hand tamper can easily chip or crack a paver's surface. Make sure the tamper has an adequate and soft pad that covers the sides—foam carpet pad wrapped around the head and secured with duct tape is a good choice—and be sure to tamp straight down when compacting the pavers.

### ✴️ WHAT'S DIFFERENT?

**Edge treatments are available** in a variety of styles, including those in the same color and texture as the pavers. A plastic edge restraint provides an effective, stable edge for pavers, often disappearing into the grass for an almost seamless transition. It is more subtle than brick or concrete edge treatments.

# Ready, Set, Grill

**9** **WORK TO A CORNER.** Continue to install pavers one course at a time across the width of the patio's base, cutting the field pavers to fit against the edge pavers as you go. Make sure that each paver is firmly set (but not buried) in the sand and level to the slight slope you've established. Periodically check and tighten your string lines, as necessary to ensure the pavers follow your desired finished grade.

**10** **REPLACE THE EDGING.** Once you've installed all of the pavers, gently remove the temporary edge boards by rocking them upwards, and replace them with sections of permanent plastic edge restraints. Secure each section of the edge restraints in place by pounding 8-in. galvanized spikes into their mounting holes. Galvanized spikes resist corrosion in soil or wet weather.

**11** **TAMP IT DOWN.** Use the mechanical tamper that previously set the gravel base to lock the pavers firmly in their sand bed without risk of chipping or cracking their surfaces (see step 4, p. 314). Start at one corner and work your way back and forth across the patio, tamping each paver and joint to ensure that all the pavers sit evenly in the sand. Test the patio by walking on each paver and tamp any that "rock" back and forth on the sand until each one sits flush to all the adjacent pavers. Use a padded hand tamper in tight spots.

**12** **BROOM IT OUT.** Sand acts as the grout between the paver joints. Carry and dump small piles of sand on the patio in several spots. Use a stiff-bristled push broom to spread the sand across the pavers. Work the sand into the joints, sweeping it several times in different directions until you fill all the gaps. Sweep any excess into a corner and scoop it up off the surface, then sweep the entire patio one more time. Finish the patio's edges with turf or flower plantings, or by applying mulch.

**9**

**10**

**11**

**12**

The same techniques used in the project were used to make this pool deck, patio, and steps. Where the steps rise, pavers were set on edge and capped with overlapping pavers.

For informal planting beds, remove groups of pavers, sand, and aggregate and fill the area with potting soil and your favorite plants.

# The variety of available concrete

pavers allows your imagination to run wild with colors, shapes, sizes, and edge treatments. The shapes afforded by precast pavers enable you to design square or curved patios or mix and match shapes and colors— all the while creating a flat, stable, and durable base for your outdoor cooking center, patio furniture, and potted plants. Of course, you can also go "old school" with cobbled pavers and wide-set paver joints (try it with a durable ground cover planted between the stones) to create an informal country patio that quickly looks decades old.

Opposite: Define a seating area by laying a circular pattern of concrete pavers. The courtyard shown here is 12 ft. in diameter, large enough to hold chairs, benches, and end tables.

Change the pavers' pattern to define areas and outdoor rooms with different purposes. Here, a circular pad used for dining is adjacent to a passageway and deck suited for lounging.

Water drains easily through pavers set on sand. Plan to grade areas where patio furniture will be placed, so that table surfaces will be level.

Many precast concrete paver patios are set with tight joints. By opening space between the pavers and using coarse sand as a filler, the patio has a more whole feeling because the pavers and joints blend together.

Choose darker colors for paving you want to blend into plants. Here, multi-toned pavers help soften the look of the patio.

Designs with random patterns have a casual feel and are pleasing to the eye.

# Stepping Stones

Build your version of the **PERFECT PATHWAY** using random-sized paving stones

THE RANDOM COLORS, SHAPES, AND TEXTURES OF FIELDSTONES softened by a traffic-tough ground cover create a durable and natural-looking path that adds a timeless element to any home. This informal trail gently guides you through the garden as if it were a meandering stream. It may seem to have been formed over time, but it took just a weekend to complete. With a variety of ground covers to choose from, as well as patterns to suit your garden's overall design scheme, you can easily create a bordered fieldstone path that will suit your lifestyle, climate, and decor, as well as to make a beautiful landscape statement.

**EXCAVATE THE AREA**    **LAY THE STONES**    **FILL AROUND THE STONES**    **PLANT THE PATH**

### ▶ DO IT RIGHT

**Have your fieldstone** delivered as close as possible to the location of the path; unload and stack or place the stones off the path so you can excavate the area without having to move them again.

### ❖ COOL TOOL

**Garden gloves** should be made of lightweight, flexible, washable, and durable stretch nylon and feature a padded palm and reinforced fingers for added protection. Look for gloves with adjustable cuffs to keep out dirt and debris and with convenient cloth brow wipes on the back side.

### ▪ LINGO

**Steppers are smaller and lighter fieldstone pieces, generally measuring less than 15 in. across and 1¹/₂ in. thick. They're ideal for smaller pathways and light foot traffic. Set them farther apart to achieve an informal, almost random design.**

# Tools & Gear

— NARROW TROWEL

**KNEE PADS.** Save your knees from the strain and pain of kneeling on fieldstones with soft, contoured, and adjustable knee pads.

**NARROW TROWEL.** Measuring about 9 in. long and less than 3 in. across with a pointed, concave blade, a narrow garden trowel helps carve out the location of your ground cover plantings.

**HAND TAMPER.** Use a 3-ft.-long hand tamper with a wood handle and a padded metal base plate to gently secure the fieldstones in their bed before you plant your ground cover.

**LEVEL.** A wood or metal level 2 ft. to 4 ft. long is used to create a level path spanning wide distances. It should feature bubbles in the center and near each end so you can level your sand-and-topsoil bed before installing your stones.

**RAKE.** Use a metal-toothed garden rake to spread and level your sand-and-topsoil bed.

**BRICKSET OR CHISEL.** Use a brickset or a stonemason's chisel to score and cut fieldstones.

**SOFTHEADED MALLET.** You'll need one of these to gently tap fieldstones into the sand-and-topsoil bed and for cutting stones to fit (used with a brickset or stonemason's chisel).

**SAFETY GOGGLES.** They're a good idea no matter what you're doing in the yard but are especially helpful when you cut or chisel a stone and want to protect your eyes from debris.

**TAPE MEASURE.** You'll need at least a 25-ft. retractable tape measure to determine dimensions, so you can calculate square footage (length × width) and purchase the right amount of materials.

**GARDEN HOSE OR ROPE.** Use a length of hose or rope to simulate your path on a flat surface near the path's actual site, designing the layout pattern before setting the fieldstones in the bed.

**MISTER OR GENTLE-SPRAY NOZZLE.** Plants need a gentle touch. Attach one of these to your garden hose to avoid exposing the roots of your ground cover and the edges of your fieldstones during watering.

## COOL TOOL

**A** **garden cart is essential for safely** transporting fieldstones, each piece of which can weigh 50 lbs. or more. Axled wheels provide strength and proper balance for heavy loads, while a removable side panel allows you to easily slide the stones in and out. Make sure to check the weight-load restrictions for the cart, as they can vary by size and construction.

# What to Buy

*This project has a short shopping list, though it's important to properly estimate the quantities you'll need.*

**1| TOPSOIL.** A yard of topsoil typically covers about 108 sq. ft. at a 4-in. depth; you'll be mixing it with an equal amount of sand. Calculate the amount you'll need based on the surface area of your path, then divide it by two to arrive at the amount of topsoil to order. Have it delivered or drop it as close to the location of the path as possible, ideally on a concrete surface or on a lawn or garden tarp.

**2| SAND.** Like topsoil, a yard of builder's sand covers about 108 sq. ft. at a 4-in. depth (a single 60-lb. bag generally covers only 3 sq. ft.). Order the same amount of sand as you do topsoil. If you can get a supplier to premix the topsoil and sand, you can have it delivered in one load; otherwise, make sure the loads are dropped as close to the path location as possible and next to each other to make on-site mixing easier.

**3| 2×4.** Find a straight, 6-ft. to 10-ft. length to screed and level out your sand-and-topsoil bed and to use with a level to check that the bed is flat and even across longer distances.

**4| FERTILIZER.** Liquid fertilizer helps the ground cover develop roots quickly.

**5| FIELDSTONES.** You have a lot of choices here in terms of size, color, texture, and cut. For informal, high-traffic paths, select stones that are at least 2 ft. across and 1½ in. to 2 in. thick (steppers can be used for smaller and low-traffic paths). A ton of fieldstone at these dimensions covers about 90 sq. ft., but you'll want to buy 10% to 20% more than what you calculate to give yourself plenty of flexibility as you lay out the stones; you can use any leftover materials as a border in your yard or store them to use later for repairs. Fieldstone is available in lava, limestone, granite, sandstone, and slate—each with a distinctive color and surface texture, but all timelessly durable.

**6| GROUND COVER.** As with fieldstones, you have several choices of ground covers that can withstand light foot traffic, from tough woolly thyme to colorful creeping speedwell varieties and tiny, bright green rupturewort—even true mosses or mosslike leafy plants. Ground covers vary in terms of sunlight needs, eventual height, and ideal spacing; they should spread within a season so you can buy fewer to start and should be appropriate for the climate in your planting zone.

## ✳ **DO IT FAST**

**Use a digital camera** to take photos of your mocked-up path pattern for reference, especially if it's far away from the eventual path location, before transferring the stones to their places on the path.

## ▶ **DO IT RIGHT**

**Lay out all your fieldstone** near the project location—on a driveway or lawn—and create a pattern the same size as your project using a length of hose or rope for reference. Lay the stones about 1 in. to 2 in. apart to accommodate the ground cover plants between them. Match contours, shapes, sizes, and colors to create a random design. Then transfer each stone to its location on the path bed, crossing the width of the path and working from one end to the other.

## ✛ **WHAT CAN GO WRONG**

**If you have to cut a fieldstone,** lay it under the adjacent stone and use that stone's edge as a pencil guide to mark the shape of the cut on the stone to be cut, then score the pencil line with a brickset. Lay the cut edge over a scrap piece of wood and strike along the scored edge using a brickset and soft-headed hammer to break off the unsupported section. Chisel off any sharp edges or to refine the form you want.

# Laying the Paving Stones

**1** **EXCAVATE THE PATH.** Once you've determined the general course and size of your path, dig out the area (including turf and other material) to its desired width and length and to a depth of at least 6 in. (or to 8 in. in freezing climates). Check level with your 2×4 and level and add or spread soil as necessary to take out any high or low spots. Pile or haul excavated soil and turf to an out-of-the-way location, compost pile, or elsewhere in the yard where it can be reused.

**2** **MIX AND INSTALL THE SAND AND TOPSOIL BED.** Mix equal parts of sand and topsoil in a garden cart or wheelbarrow. Spread and level the mix with a shovel and rake, and screed with a 2×4 to a flat, level surface no deeper than your thickest fieldstone to ensure that your finished path will be level with the existing grade. Check level at several places on the path across its width and length, using the 2×4 and level together to span and check the longest distances possible.

**3** **SET THE STONES.** Lay out all of the stones on a nearby site. Choose each stone by comparing its size and shape to the space you will fill. Lift stones carefully to prevent injury; they are heavy. Set, check, and gently tap each stone into the sand-and-topsoil bed, and then check that the stones are level to each other and to your finished or desired grade. Make sure each stone is set solidly (doesn't rock) in its bed to avoid breaking or chipping under foot traffic. You may have to lift a stone, refill beneath it, and reset it.

**4** **BACKFILL THE EDGES AND JOINTS.** Use remaining topsoil without sand to fill in around the edges and between the fieldstones in preparation for planting the ground cover. Broom the topsoil over the path and stones, then use a padded hand tamper to secure the stones and firm the soil. Water the area to encourage settling, and fill any gaps with more soil until the entire path is level.

### ✳ LINGO

The term stepables refers to ground covers that are tough enough to withstand foot traffic and thrive between fieldstones, quickly softening the edges of your steps and borders. Stepable ground covers are available in several textures and colors for every hardiness zone.

### ◆ COOL TOOL

Use knee pads to take the stress off your joints, especially when you're planting several packs of ground cover, without hindering your flexibility. Look for soft, durable, and contoured pads that can be easily adjusted to fit snugly and are waterproof to keep moisture away from your knees.

# Planting between Stones

**5** **REMOVE AND INSPECT THE PLANTS.** Ground cover should appear and feel healthy, carpeting each pack with firm and colorful foliage. Once you select the variety you want, remove a plant from its cell and inspect the roots; they should be firm and plump, somewhat molded to the shape of the pack, and with a healthy amount of soil exposed between the roots. A tight cluster of roots along the bottom inch or more of the plant indicates a root-bound plant. Make sure your ground cover meets your aesthetic and climate needs. Choose a stepable variety according to the amount of direct sun the path will receive; most ground covers thrive in full sun.

**6** **DIG THE HOLES.** Use a narrow trowel to carve out holes for the ground cover along the edges of the path and between the fieldstones. Pay attention to the recommended spacing between plants indicated on their tags.

**7** **BACKFILL THE ROOTS.** Use the topsoil you removed for each plant's hole to cover and firmly hold the roots in place in the soil. Use more soil to top dress around the base of each plant. Mix liquid fertilizer with twice as much water as recommended on the package directions, and apply it to the plantings with a hand sprayer.

**8** **WATER THE PLANTS.** Use a light spray or mister attachment on your garden hose to deliver the proper volume without the force that could expose the roots or the edges of your fieldstones before they have time to settle in and take hold. Follow the instructions on the ground cover's tag for proper watering frequency. Keep a close eye on its condition for the first few weeks, until new growth appears, then water regularly as the grower directs.

Mosslike but broadleaved Scot's moss, baby's tears, or one of the true mosses makes a very low filler for a fieldstone walk. Protect plants from being crushed by grading the soil between the joints 1 in. to 2 in. below the level of the tops of the stones.

Fieldstone path joints can be filled with crushed gravel or fine bark, both of which contrast nicely with a mixed planting border.

## Combining varieties of fieldstones and ground covers according to your own personal style and tastes means you'll create a truly unique fieldstone path in your garden. Consider mixing colors and shapes of stones, using a taller ground cover along the edges or even cut stones set more closely together for a more formal look and feel. Fieldstone paths can also connect patios of the same materials and design for a cohesive theme or be used to guide visitors to your front door or lead them to a pond or vegetable garden elsewhere on your property—all with the timeless beauty and certain durability of fieldstone.

Use fieldstones set into the lawn to make casual, low-use paths to connect areas where cut-across is inevitable. The stones will bear the weight of frequent footsteps and help keep the soil under the turf from compacting.

Use groups of four cut-stone blocks instead of irregular fieldstone to make geometric stepping-stone paths.

Connect low-use areas with narrow paths suitable for foot traffic but too small for garden wheelbarrows and carts. Small steppers are best for paving such walks.

# Lighting the Way

Bring safety and style to your new walks, paths and patios with **LOW-VOLTAGE LIGHTS**

DDING PATHS AND PATIOS increases the value of your home— even more so when they're easy to see and use after the sun goes down. Low-voltage lighting allows you to showcase your handiwork after dark, highlighting your favorite features, casting dramatic shadows, and illuminating walks and patios for better safety and stunning beauty. Not only that, but low-voltage light fixtures are simple and inexpensive to install and maintain, requiring only your existing electrical service and a few components to create a lighting scheme that adds interest to your home and leads visitors to your door.

**PROVIDE POWER**   **LAY CABLE**   **ATTACH THE FIXTURES**   **SET THE TIMER**

# Tools & Gear

**A piercing electrical connector** easily connects one low-voltage line to another without the need to strip and splice wires or cables. Simply align the ends of the wires in the terminal's slots and clamp them down with a screwdriver. Sharp conductor prongs driven into the cables and make a path to transfer power from one cable to the other. It's infinitely easier than splicing the cables.

**▪ LINGO**

**Footcandles measure brightness; one footcandle equals a 1-sq.-ft. area illuminated by a lamp that is equivalent to the light of a candle held 1 ft. away. Check the foot-candle rating on your lamps to figure out how far apart you should place them.**

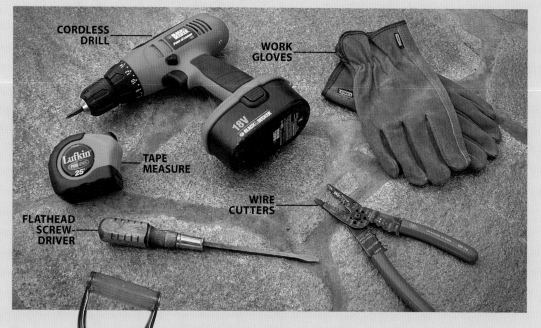

CORDLESS DRILL

WORK GLOVES

TAPE MEASURE

WIRE CUTTERS

FLATHEAD SCREW-DRIVER

**CORDLESS DRILL.** Make quick changes from a drill bit to a screwdriver bit. Choose a model with at least 12 volts of power and 350 ft. lbs. of torque.

**TAPE MEASURE.** A 30-ft. retractable tape measure or a reel model follows the contours of your trench and gives precise placement for the light fixtures.

**WIRE CUTTERS.** You'll need these to cut and strip cable wires at the transformer and to make splices between cables that extend power to each fixture.

**WORK GLOVES.** Save your skin by slipping on a pair of these when you dig your trench and posthole.

**FLATHEAD SCREWDRIVER.** When you need a little more control over a screw, use a long-handled flathead screwdriver.

## COOL TOOL

A narrow trenching shovel comes in handy for digging a deep, narrow ditch for the low-voltage cable and utility posthole when you're butting up against paths and patios. The long, thin, round-ended blade cuts cleanly through turf to the desired depth, enabling you to save and reuse the same section of grass to conceal your underground work. Look for a shovel with a comfortable handle and a steel blade for safety and ease of use.

# What to Buy

**1| STEP-DOWN TRANSFORMER.** This is the brains of the operation, converting (or stepping down) a 120-volt AC line to 12-volt direct current and serving as the hub of your cable run. Get one rated to handle the number of fixtures you plan to use and with a timer so you can program your lights for automatic operation.

**2| THREADED SUPPORT STAKES.** Attach these 8-in.-long, barbed stakes to the threaded base of your light fixtures as a secure anchor.

**3| CABLE.** For this project, you'll need a 100-ft. coil of 12-2 UF-rated 12-amp cable (a sheathed pair of #12 wires suitable for underground use). Most UF-rated cable can be buried directly without a conduit.

**4| LIGHT FIXTURES.** These low-voltage lamps are rated for 24 footcandles. Calculate how many fixtures you need and how far apart they'll be by their footcandle rating (see LINGO, opposite). For this project, the lamps are placed 6 ft. apart.

**5| ACCESSORIES.** Make sure you have T-splices, piercing connectors, survey marker tape, and a nearby GFCI-protected outlet (see WHAT CAN GO WRONG, p. 338) in a weather-proof housing to prevent shock hazard during wet weather.

**6| UTILITY POST.** You'll need a 3-ft.-long, 4×4 pressure-treated post with a beveled (or chamfered) top end to hold the transformer. A 40-lb. bag of fast-setting posthole concrete will anchor it in place.

**STEP-DOWN TRANSFORMER**

**12-2 UF CABLE**

**LIGHT FIXTURES**

**THREADED SUPPORT STAKES**

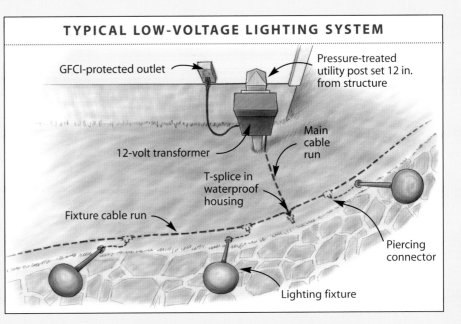

### TYPICAL LOW-VOLTAGE LIGHTING SYSTEM

GFCI-protected outlet

Pressure-treated utility post set 12 in. from structure

12-volt transformer

Main cable run

T-splice in waterproof housing

Fixture cable run

Piercing connector

Lighting fixture

## + WHAT CAN GO WRONG

**A single outdoor outlet** can serve all of your low-voltage lighting needs for this project, but code requires it to have a built-in ground-fault circuit intrerruptor (GFCI), which grounds the wires and cuts off the current in case of a short circuit to eliminate electrical shocks and surges.

# Install the Transformer & Cable

**1** **SET YOUR POST.** Using your narrow trench shovel, dig an 18-in.-deep, 12-in.-diameter hole within 12 in. of an exterior GFCI-rated outlet. Set a 3-ft.-long, pressure-treated 4×4 chamfered post into the hole, and fill the hole halfway with water. Use your level to keep the post plumb—perfectly upright—as you pour in the quick-setting concrete. Add water as the package directs, holding the post steady and plumb as the concretes sets.

**2** **HOOK UP YOUR CABLE.** Use your wire cutters to divide the two strands of wire and allow 6 in. to 8 in. of slack. Strip back the plastic sheathing to expose about 1 in. of raw wire on each strand, then connect and tighten each to their respective hot and ground

terminals on the transformer. Connect all of your cable and fixtures before you plug the transformer into the GFCI-rated wall outlet to avoid blowing the fuse or tripping the circuit breaker at the service panel.

**3** **MOUNT THE TRANSFORMER ON THE UTILITY POST.** Measure the location of the mounting screws on the transformer and attach scrap 2×2 lumber to the utility post as brackets for the box. Mark and preset the mounting screws on the brackets so that the transformer's mounting holes slip onto the screws, then tighten the screws to secure the box to the post.

**4** **EXCAVATE YOUR TRENCH AND LAY THE CABLE.** Before you do any digging, use a length of rope or garden hose to determine the contour of your trench, which will serve as a guide for its excavation. Using

your narrow trench shovel, remove the turf layer in as few pieces as possible and set it aside, then dig a trench for your cable, 18 in. deep and 3 in. wide. Lay the cable in the trench, uncoiling it as you go; make a 1-ft. loop at the location of each fixture, every 6 ft. along the trench. Coil any unused cable at the end of the trench as you place and hook up the light fixtures.

**Protect the exposed ends** of stripped and spliced wires with waterproof, gel-filled splice protectors. Buried with the cable, it keeps your splices dry while enabling a reliable and steady connection between the two wires.

**Make sure your 12-volt cable** has 12-amp wires to reduce resistance in long runs and ensure that every lamp burns at the same brightness. Cables with 14-amp or 18-amp wires can cause lights at the end of a long strand to dim from electrical resistance as the current travels from the transformer to the light fixtures.

# Attach the Lights

**5** **SPACE OUT YOUR LIGHTS.** Use a retractable or reel tape measure to place your light fixtures 6 ft. apart along the trench. Backfill the trench and bury the main cable 4 in. deep, then place survey marker tape over the backfill to mark the location of your cable—a warning to anyone excavating near the trench in the future.

**6** **MAKE THE TURN.** For this project, the trench took a right-angle turn so that the lights could follow a path. Always connect the transformer lead cable to the center of the lighting run, and use a T-splice to extend the fixture cable each way along the sidewalk. Remember to backfill and place survey marking tape over that section of cable as well.

**7** **CONNECT YOUR FIXTURES.** For each light fixture, thread and attach the support stake, run the lead wire out of the hole provided, use the loop slack to position the fixture exactly, and connect the wire to the main cable using a piercing connector (see COOL TOOL, p. 336). This quickly and easily connects the lead and main wires at each light fixture. Stake the fixture in the space between the trench and the path or sidewalk.

**8** **TEST YOUR LIGHTS AND REPLACE THE TURF.** Before you completely bury the cable, plug the transformer into the GFCI outlet and make sure every light comes on. Repair any that don't illuminate (typically from a bad bulb, faulty socket, or loose piercing connector). Backfill the trench, compact the dirt, and replace the turf so it lays flat and flush on the surface.

Set the timer on the transformer to automatically activate the lights, making sure the switch that controls the outlet, if any, is in the "on" position. Plug the transformer into the outlet and enjoy your yard day and night.

Illuminate the central path and the plants around the margin of your yard. Leave unlit areas of turf between the lights to make your yard appear to be larger.

Safety first is the watchword when it comes to steps and slopes in a path. Center-mounted light fixtures help you see the steps in the dark.

## Low-voltage lighting offers a wide range of options to illuminate the features and functions of your yard. You can create dramatic shadows or highlight the rugged bark of a tree. You can also use lighting to direct attention to a focal point or destination—a gazebo or pond, for instance—by creating a line of sight with low-voltage lamps. Such perspective lighting schemes also make a small yard feel bigger.

Add artistic lighting fixtures of textured metal, blown glass, brass, and wrought iron.

Define different areas of your yard for maximum appeal. Spotlights on trees make them into night-time accents, and uplights on a stone wall or house draw attention to their textures.

Choose lights that are shielded when viewed from normal eye height. They cast their light downward, illuminating the ground beneath the fixture.

Avoid light fixtures that shine directly upward near paths and patios. The lights also should be tall enough to clear any flowers or shrubs beneath them.

# Photo Credits

p. i: © Randy O'Rourke

p. ii: (top left) Carl Weese, © The Taunton Press, Inc.; (top right) John M. Rickard, © The Taunton Press, Inc.; (bottom left) Christopher Vendetta, © The Taunton Press Inc.; (bottom right) © Randy O'Rourke

p. iii: Christopher Vendetta, © The Taunton Press Inc.

p. v: (top left) Christopher Vendetta, © The Taunton Press, Inc.; (top right) © David Bravo; (middle left) John M. Rickard, © The Taunton Press, Inc.; (bottom right) Joseph Kugielsky, © The Taunton Press Inc.; (bottom middle) © Randy O'Rourke; (bottom left) © Stephen Carver.

p. vi: (top) © Randy O'Rourke; (second row from left to right) © Randy O'Rourke; © David Bravo; © Grey Crawford; © Randy O'Rourke; (third and fourth rows) © Randy O'Rourke

p. 1: (top) © David Bravo; (second and third rows) © Randy O'Rourke; (fourth row) Christopher Vendetta, © The Taunton Press Inc.

p. 2: (top) Christopher Vendetta, © The Taunton Press Inc.; (second from top) Carl Weese, © The Taunton Press, Inc.; (third from top) Carl Weese, © The Taunton Press, Inc.; (bottom) John M. Rickard, © The Taunton Press, Inc.

p. 3: (top) Christopher Vendetta, © The Taunton Press Inc.; (second from top) Carl Weese, © The Taunton Press, Inc.; (third row from left to right) © Randy O'Rourke; © Randy O'Rourke; © Randy O'Rourke; John M. Rickard, © The Taunton Press, Inc.; (fourth row) John M. Rickard, © The Taunton Press, Inc.

p. 4: (left) © David Bravo; (right) © Stephen Carver

p. 5: © Randy O'Rourke

p. 6: (left and right) John M. Rickard, © The Taunton Press, Inc.

p. 7: (top and bottom) Carl Weese, © The Taunton Press, Inc.

p. 8: Christopher Vendetta, © The Taunton Press Inc.

p. 9: © Randy O'Rourke

p. 10: Christopher Vendetta, © The Taunton Press Inc.

p. 11: John M. Rickard, © The Taunton Press, Inc.

pp. 12-13: © David Bravo

p. 14: Stephen Carver, © The Taunton Press Inc.

p. 16: (top left) Carl Weese, © The Taunton Press, Inc.; (bottom left) Christopher Vendetta, © The Taunton Press Inc.; (top right) Carl Weese, © The Taunton Press, Inc.

p. 17: Carl Weese, © The Taunton Press, Inc.

pp. 19-22: © David Bravo

p. 23: © Randy O'Rourke

pp. 24-25: © David Bravo

pp. 26-29: Stephen Carver, © The Taunton Press, Inc.

pp. 30-43: John M. Rickard, © The Taunton Press, Inc.

p. 44: © David Bravo

p. 45: © Randy O'Rourke

pp. 46–52: © David Bravo

p. 53: (left) Charles Bickford, courtesy *Fine Homebuilding*, © The Taunton Press, Inc.; (right) © Randy O'Rourke

p. 54: (left) Charles Bickford, courtesy *Fine Homebuilding*, © The Taunton Press, Inc.; (right) © Dutch Boy

p. 55: (left) © Randy O'Rourke; (right) © davidduncanlivingston.com; (bottom) © Dutch Boy

p. 56: © David Bravo

p. 57: © Randy O'Rourke

pp. 58–61: © David Bravo

pp. 62–63: © Randy O'Rourke

p. 64: © David Bravo

p. 65: © Grey Crawford

pp. 66–73: © David Bravo

p. 74: (left) © Pete Hecht/Mark Lisk Studio; (right) © Kerry Hayes

p. 75: (left) Charles Miller, courtesy *Fine Homebuilding*, © The Taunton Press, Inc.; (right) Andy Engel, courtesy *Fine Homebuilding*, © The Taunton Press, Inc.

p. 76: © Stephen Carver

p. 77: © Randy O'Rourke

pp. 78–83: © Stephen Carver

p. 84: (right) © Christian Korab; (left) Stephen Carver

p. 85: (left) © Randy O'Rourke; (right) Stephen Carver

p. 86: © Stephen Carver

p. 87: © Randy O'Rourke

pp. 88–93: © Stephen Carver

p. 94: (left) Andy Engel, courtesy *Fine Homebuilding*, © The Taunton Press, Inc.; (right) Scott Gibson, courtesy *Fine Homebuilding*, © The Taunton Press, Inc.

p. 95 (left) Charles Miller, courtesy *Fine Homebuilding*, © The Taunton Press, Inc.; (right) © Stephen Carver

p. 96: © Stephen Carver

p. 97: © Randy O'Rourke

pp. 98–103: © Stephen Carver

p. 104: (top) © Randy O'Rourke; (bottom left) © Style Solutions

p. 105: (left) © Randy O'Rourke; (right) © Style Solutions

p. 106: © Stephen Carver

p. 107: © Randy O'Rourke

pp. 108–113: © Stephen Carver

p. 114: © davidduncanlivingston.com

p. 115: (left) © Style Solutions; (top right) Tom O'Brien, courtesy *Fine Homebuilding*, © The Taunton Press, Inc.; (bottom right) © davidduncanlivingston.com

p. 116: © Randy O'Rourke

pp. 117–123: © Stephen Carver

p. 124: (top) © Randy O'Rourke; (bottom left) Roe A. Osborn, courtesy *Fine Homebuilding*, © The Taunton Press, Inc.

p. 125: © Randy O'Rourke